D1601099

◇

NUCLEAR ANNIHILATION AND CONTEMPORARY AMERICAN POETRY

**UNIVERSITY
PRESS
OF
FLORIDA**

GAINESVILLE
TALLAHASSEE
TAMPA
BOCA RATON
PENSACOLA
ORLANDO
MIAMI
JACKSONVILLE

**JOHN
GERY**

Nuclear Annihilation and Contemporary American Poetry

**WAYS
OF
NOTH
ING
NESS**

01 00 99 98 97 96 6 5 4 3 2 1

Library of Congress Cataloging-in-Publication Data
Gery, John.
Nuclear annihilation and contemporary American poetry / John Gery.
p. cm.
Includes bibliographical references and index.
ISBN 0–8130–1417–4 (alk. paper)
1. American poetry—20th century—History and criticism. 2. Nuclear
warfare in literature. 3. Literature and history—United States—
History—20th century. 4. Apocalyptic literature—History and criticism.
5. End of the world in literature. 6. Nothingness in literature. 7. Atomic
bomb in literature. I. Title.
PS310.N83G47   1995
811′.509358—dc20   95-11052

The University Press of Florida is the scholarly publishing agency for the
State University System of Florida, comprised of Florida A & M Univer-
sity, Florida Atlantic University, Florida International University, Florida
State University, University of Central Florida, University of Florida,
University of North Florida, University of South Florida, and University
of West Florida.

University Press of Florida
15 Northwest 15th Street
Gainesville, FL 32611

for Barbara
hers in kind

**CON
TENTS**

AC KNOWL EDG MENTS

I want to thank a few of those who helped to bring this book to fruition. Among my helpful colleagues at the University of New Orleans I am especially grateful to Mackie J. V. Blanton and John Cooke for their sound advice and to Rick Barton, Linda Blanton, Anne Charles, Jeanne Cunningham, Cynthia Hogue, James Knudsen, Srimati Mukherjee, and Elizabeth Penfield for their sustaining support. I also appreciate the UNO College of Liberal Arts and the Graduate School Office of Research for providing two summer fellowships and allowing me time away from teaching. During my time in Iowa City, Kathleen Diffley, Ed Folsom, David Hamilton, Brooks Landon, Teresa Mangum, Alan Nagel, John

Raeburn, and Jon Wilcox of the University of Iowa each provided valuable assistance. I also want to thank Paul Zimmer for referring me to poems I would otherwise have missed, for reading my manuscript with care, and for believing in its value. The large number of students who, to my good fortune, have challenged my thoughts on most of the poems I discuss here makes it impossible to name each of them, but I could not have written this book without their enthusiasm for poetry.

For editorial responses to sections of the manuscript, I am grateful to Donald Anderson, Jacqueline Brogan, Dana Gioia, Alan Golding, Thomas P. Joswick, Lynn Keller, Carol MacCurdy, Robert McPhillips, Kathy Rugoff, Adam J. Sorkin, and Leonard Trawick. I am especially indebted to William J. Scheick for scrutinizing the whole text and steering me to essential sources. I am thankful as well to the International Society for the Study of Nuclear Texts and Contexts for compiling so much useful material on nuclearism in one place. For their letters, suggestions, and engagement in my work over the years of its making, I want to thank Dick Allen, Darrell Bourque, John Bradley, Courtney Cooper, Joel Dailey, Mary de Rachewiltz, Douglas Duany, John Engels, Skip Fox, Anne Giovingo, Marilyn Hacker, Hank Lazer, Denise Levertov, Mike Mahoney, David Maloney, David Racker, Chris Semansky, Stuart Sherman, Larry Sicular, Frederick Turner, Tom Whalen, Laurie Williams, Ivan Zaknic, and Robert Zackowski, as well as my family, especially my mother, Gunesh.

Among those with whom I have worked on nuclear and other issues, I must acknowledge Wayne Barbee, Stewart Butler, Russ Henderson, Darrell Malek-Wiley, Rebecca Malek-Wiley, Suzanne Poulton, David Schwam-Baird, Monte Thornburg, Sandy Thornburg, and the late Jack Gillespie for their inspiring commitment to peace through action and education, as well as the Educators for Social Responsibility whose work nationwide convinced me that a study of nuclearism and poetry could be useful.

My thanks, too, to Walda Metcalf, Judy Goffman, and the staff at the University Press of Florida for their efficiency and indispensable attention to details in getting this work into print.

Finally, this book could not exist without the wisdom and worldly compassion of Barbara Eckstein, who helped to shape it, who coaxed me to keep at it, and whose mark is evident on every page.

Sections and passages of this book appeared in different versions under these titles in the following publications: "How Nothing Has Changed: From Steven's 'The Snow Man' to Gunn's 'The Annihilation of Nothing,' " *Poesis* 7.1 (1986): 23–34; "En Route to Annihilation: John Ashbery's *Shadow Train*," *Concerning Poetry* 20 (1987): 99–116; "The 'Sensible Emptiness' in Three Poems by Richard Wilbur," *Essays in Literature* 16.1 (1989): 113–26; "The Sigh of Our Present: Nuclear Annihilation and Contemporary Poetry," *Self, World, Poem: Essays on Contemporary Poetry*, ed. Leonard Trawick (Kent, Ohio: Kent State University Press, 1990); and "The Atomic Test Poems of Paul Zimmer," *War, Literature, and the Arts* 6.1 (1994): 1–19. I thank the editors of these publications for permission to reprint them here.

The Way of Nothingness

With the advent and proliferation of atomic weapons in the second half of the twentieth century, we entered an era in danger of initiating its own annihilation. Even before the technology of atom bombs and missile delivery systems developed to the point of making annihilation possible, we had already begun to adjust to our newly precarious physical situation, and although most of us conduct our lives as though the continuum of the past through the present and into the future will proceed indefinitely—beyond our individual deaths—slowly we have come to accept, if only subconsciously, that in the few hours it might take to complete a global nuclear war everything we know and take for granted could be eradicated.

Psychiatrist Robert Jay Lifton has characterized this "post-modern" condition as an existential absurdity, or "the absurdity of our double life," which he argues can have "far-reaching psychological consequences," including "individual-psychological responses to a sense of futurelessness, as well as certain forms of collective behavior such as widespread fundamentalism on the one hand and psychic numbing on the other" (Lifton and Falk 4).[1] What has evolved in the course of the nuclear age, according to Lifton and political scientist Richard Falk, is a social and psychic "deformation of *attitude*" which they call "nuclearism": the "psychological, political, and military dependence on nuclear weapons [and] the embrace of the weapons as a solution to a wide variety of human dilemmas, most ironically that of 'security' " (ix).[2] Whether the weapons actually exist or not, Lifton and Falk suggest, we have come to accept them as having the power to define time, the boundaries of life as we experience it, and human continuity. As the crowning achievement of modern technology, they have attained both material and symbolic prominence in contemporary Western culture.

Lifton's psychosocial diagnosis of nuclearism developed from his extensive investigation in the 1960s of the *hibakusha*, or survivors of the atomic bomb dropped on Hiroshima on 6 August 1945. In the course of analyzing the long-term psychological consequences of the attack on the *hibakusha*, he began to distinguish different ways in which individuals cope with and respond to mass annihilation. Among those he interviewed, for example, was a history professor, a man more reflective than some of the other survivors. At one point during his interview, this man suggested that "we should figure out the exact hypocenter—and possibly put some small artistic monument on it—or better still, leave it devoid of anything at all . . . in order to symbolize nothingness at the hypocenter—because that is what there was. . . . Such a weapon has the power to make everything into nothing, and I think this should be symbolized" (*Death* 278). Having gazed at the devastated plain where the city of Hiroshima once stood, the history professor recognized nothingness as both a material absence and a spiritual void. Later when discussing his sense of the future, he again invoked this idea of "nothingness at the hypocenter." "The story of Noah's ark is more than a myth to me," he said. "Except for a few humans and animals, it is a story of everything becoming nothing. Maybe this will happen again—everything disappearing and becoming nothing." Then he confessed, "As for myself, I go the way of nothingness. I don't have a strong desire to go about telling people about these things, or to talk in a loud voice about my A-bomb experience. But if I am able to be useful, I like to do what I can" (*Death* 392–93). For one who has survived atomic war, nothingness is not only an absence and a void; it has also become a way of life.

For Lifton, the history professor's paradoxical attitude toward his own existence expresses a double consciousness: first, what the Japanese call *akirame*, an "adaptive resignation" to the fact that one is alive rather than dead, and second, an even more deeply ingrained awareness of the impending annihilation of the world. On the one hand, one may carry on one's life "psychologically 'taking in' an experience, however extreme, and simultaneously reasserting one's sense of connection with the vast human and natural forces which extend beyond that experience" (*Death* 186), but at the same time one lives with an abiding consciousness that, in the case of the nuclear threat, *all* life and civilization is threatened with extinction. Although going "the way of nothingness," as the history professor depicts it and Lifton diagnoses it, may seem a contradictory, even self-deceptive rationale for conducting life, it has arguably become the central premise of the nuclear age, an age of self-inflicted uncertainty about its own destiny.

I shall explore here how "the way of nothingness"—that individual sense of continuity coupled with a global sense of impending annihilation—has been manifested in the work of American poets over the last generation. Despite the apparent gap between the production of nuclear weapons and the art of poetry, there is, I believe, a unique and intricate link between the two that has existed from the time the first weaponry was conceived. To the degree that most Americans have had little or no actual interaction with nuclear weaponry, nor much more than incidental experience with nuclear power, their existence remains primarily an abstraction to the individual mind—much discussed, roundly feared or respected, yet mostly repugnant when imagined as a physical presence, whether as bombs, fallout, or waste matter. However, because of the overwhelming power they wield over *material* existence, they loom large in American culture in the same way that other technological phenomena do—automobiles, communication mechanisms, medical equipment. Unlike our experience of these technological devices, though (with rare exceptions, such as DNA experiments), whose material manifestation we encounter every day, our basic understanding of nuclear weapons and power is almost entirely a symbolic, not a material, one. The danger of understanding them empirically, of course, is that we might destroy ourselves in the doing. Consequently, even though culturally speaking they are commonplace

material artifacts, they function almost exclusively within the imagination. And as though they were immaterial gods, their mostly abstract
presence makes them fodder for wide-ranging creative interpretations.
As Ira Chernus has aptly described them, as "a powerful symbol of both
omnipotence and omniscience," nuclear weapons represent "the power
and wisdom and mystery at the source of creation"; and given that the
secrets concerning their whereabouts also suggest their omnipresence,
they have taken on "those attributes that have traditionally been ascribed to the God of Western religions. . . . Their effect is everywhere
and inescapable" (17).

Indeed, because of the weapons' prominent place in the public eye, it
is easy to find evidence of a nuclear awareness manifested in contemporary poetry of all schools. Nearly every poet of the last fifty years has
written at least one poem in reference to nuclear weapons or power.
More significantly, though, the very multiplicity of these poets' responses to the nuclear presence indicates what role poetry has begun to
play in the nuclear age—first, as a chorus of diverse voices joining in
protest against the end of the world, but secondly, as the embodiment
of "the way of nothingness" in contemporary experience. No matter
how annihilatory, eclectic, or paradoxical its form, as with all art, poetry expresses the right of the human spirit to exist, and in so doing it
protests against whatever threatens that spirit. But besides that protest,
by virtue of its ability to conjure images, its literal specificity, and its
exploitation of the limits of language, poetry can also renew or at least
expand our means of articulating what we feel, how we think, or why
we act in our own uncertain era. It expresses not only who we have been
and are but also who we might become. Despite poetry's relative ob-
scurity, especially in the United States, by its shaping of language, its
inventive use of metaphor and imagery, and its taking free reign with
ideological concepts, it can, I believe, imagine not just one but multiple
"ways of nothingness" and therefore offer alternatives for getting
through this age and into another. We may, of course, reject those alternatives and annihilate ourselves instead. But in the meantime poetry
is a pertinent voice in the discourse of survival.

To link nuclear annihilation and poetry, then, first requires accepting
that humans have developed nuclear technology to the extent that it
can eradicate all life and civilization. Regardless of the number of
weapons currently in existence, regardless of any further developments
in the type or quality of offensive or defensive weaponry, and regardless
of who possesses those weapons or what the state of relations may be

among potential antagonists, the world now contains the human-made capacity to annihilate not only peoples or continents but the planet. At the same time, despite this knowledge which (short of our annihilation) we cannot expect to forget, the technical, political, and social realities of our predicament mean that we can only speculate on what such annihilation would be like because any experience of it we may have will be one that none will survive and for which no history will be written (Zuckerman, *Nuclear Illusion*, 40). Herein lies a central paradox of the nuclear age: What we have come to know has forced us to acknowledge that what we do *not* know we now cannot afford to know.

Concerning what we *do* know about the destructive power of splitting the atom, few believe anymore that it would be possible to scratch nuclear technology altogether in order to spare the world from its dangers. To be sure, with the ever-changing relations among world powers, recent agreements and resolutions have initiated a process of substantial reductions in the number of stockpiled weapons and missiles by the start of the next century. Nevertheless, recent assessments of the number of nuclear warheads in the world estimate that in the mid-1990s there still exist 26,700 weapons, not including the approximately 20,000 additional warheads waiting to be dismantled and disposed of. If current agreements between the United States and the former Soviet Union are honored, by 2003 each of those nations will retain 3,500 "accountable" nuclear warheads (any one of which has up to 300 times the explosive force of "Little Boy," the bomb that was dropped on Hiroshima). This will be the fewest number of warheads the United States will have had in fifty years but a number "still far greater than most nuclear specialists regard as necessary for deterrence" (Sivard 12). In addition, China, France, Great Britain, and (as of this writing) the Ukraine also possess nuclear weapons, while India, Israel, and Pakistan remain "clandestine nuclear powers" (Sivard 11).[3] Furthermore, although Argentina, Brazil, and South Africa have recently opened their nuclear-related activities to international monitoring, Iraq and North Korea resist outside inspections or have concealed their weapons projects. Beyond them, another twenty-five nations, at least, have the technology to develop nuclear capability, though they are not presently known to be doing so, and nuclear weapons and nuclear-armed ships are currently stationed or docked at over a dozen additional sites around the world, ranging from Turkey to Diego Garcia, with a total of approximately fifty-five countries and five territories housing nuclear weapons and nuclear power plants.[4]

With such a wide distribution of nuclear technology, even the safe elimination of all present warheads could only be considered a form of limiting the chance of nuclear warfare, not erasing it.[5] While antipathies between the former Cold War powers have diminished, other venues of potential danger remain not only among smaller nations, ethnic groups, and terrorist organizations, but also among larger states, including the United States—the only nation so far to have employed nuclear weapons in wartime and one that still spends $35 billion a year to maintain its nuclear strike force (Wood A-12). As Martin van Creveld points out, the argument that nuclear weapons pose little threat so long as they are kept out of the hands of Third World nations is "distorted, ethnocentric, and self-serving," since its "real objective is to perpetuate the oligopoly of the 'old' nuclear powers"; by characterizing Third World governments as "unstable, cuturally biased, irresponsible," nuclear policymakers contradict themselves whenever "weapons and technologies that used to be presented as stabilizing" in the stand-off between East and West are "suddenly described as destabilizing when they spread to other countries" (123–24). The case made by state leaders that they are developing nuclear capabilities solely for purposes of defense and deterrence should come as no surprise to the major powers, who have not only been using the same reasoning themselves for decades but who have been the central source of information and education for those leaders. In fact, a nuclear war could be provoked or initiated by virtually anyone in possession of the basic technology.[6] Beyond the delicate negotiations of nuclear build-up and international diplomacy, however, the "real race," as Peter Schwenger puts it, "is not between superpowers but between proliferation of a mechanistic, supremely paradoxical system of armament and the consciousness of its creators" (xvii).

As critics of nuclear strategy often point out,[7] nuclear history has removed the primary responsibility for conducting warfare (on all but a small scale) from military leaders and turned it over more and more to scientists, technicians, economists, and, by extension, other "experts" at one time thought to be outside the realm of war. As World War II strategist Solly Zuckerman argued for decades, for instance, since nuclear weapons have only been used on civilian populations (in Hiroshima and Nagasaki), they have not yet been proven to serve any useful military function whatsoever, so that in the nuclear age "military chiefs, who by convention are a country's official advisers on national security, as a rule merely serve as the channel through which the men in the laboratories transmit their views" (*Nuclear* 105). This co-opting of command has diminished the attention given to the strategic value, if any, of the weapons produced, because the drive for technical knowledge, while it has led to enhanced nuclear machinery and greater power over the environment, has also diverted technologists from considering the practical implications of their work—that is, from recognizing that what they have uncovered obligates them to speculate on the extent of the unprecedented destructive power they have unleashed.

One case study that bears out Zuckerman's observations about the narrowness of technologists, not only at the level of scientific research but among ordinary citizens, is Paul Loeb's *Nuclear Culture*, a detailed account of the social organization of the Hanford (Washington) Nuclear Reservation in the early 1980s. Loeb's book portrays the Hanford reservation, the largest complex in the world to have produced weapons-grade plutonium for nuclear warheads, as a microcosm of postwar America in which, despite differences in class, age, sex, race, and education, a universal repression of moral vision prevails, to the degree that it begins to infect the author himself (244–49). By becoming accustomed to the everyday nature of their work at the facility, those whose work sustains the nuclear threat learn to excuse themselves from any responsibility for their labor. Like Zuckerman's technologists, "merely doing what they saw to be their job" (*Nuclear* 108), Loeb's ordinary citizens take on the responsibility for the nuclear system once belonging to others (such as military and political leaders), yet they refuse to acknowledge their own place within that system:

Just as America is in general a culture in which most of us . . . leave control of our world to others, the Hanford workers possess a range of vastly different sensibilities whose common thread is acquiescence to authority. The old hands who desire only to invent and to see their atomic mission bear fruit, have a far different attitude from that of the young cynics who log their hours, doing as little as possible, then come home to "real life," their own private time—and certainly a different outlook from those who, like the Germans termed "inner immigrants" by Hannah Arendt because they always privately abhorred the Nazis, mistrust the potential consequences of what they produce. Yet these inner immigrants go in each morning to participate halfheartedly, just as they do in other industrial enterprises across the country. And . . . neither the old nor the young ever refuse their assignments on moral grounds.

Even as Hanford's routine inures people to the possibility that the technology they work with might somehow run out of control and create some catastrophic accident, so the daily repetition and tedium remove responsibility for another possibility: that the systems might all work, that the switches and circuits might all connect, and that weapons whose plutonium was produced here might bring atomic holocaust to people the Hanford workers have never laid eyes on. (200–201)

Given the intricate involvement of so many specialists, each performing his or her duty with certainty and confidence, Loeb wonders, "Can anyone claim specific responsibility for dropping the nuclear bombs?"

The answer, of course, is "Everyone can," for anyone who does his or her part to sustain the nuclear industry contributes to the eventual use of the weapons, while any refusal to participate obstructs (if not corrodes) the culture of nuclearism. Nevertheless, aggressively to take responsibility for the social or moral consequences of one's actions requires acknowledging the second half of the assertion about our paradoxical situation as well—that we cannot know for a fact what the consequences of our actions will be, nor do we dare experiment, unless we are willing to risk the very annihilation we hope to avert. Moral authority, in this sense, can only be approached using the imagination in ways usually associated not with empirical or technical research but with political, social, or psychological speculation of the sort we associate with alternative endeavors, such as scientific hypothesizing, game-playing, story-telling, philosophical inquiry, and, as I hope to demonstrate, poetry. It is here—at the point where the technology of nuclearism reaches its limits and where its potential impact takes on a largely speculative nature, that is, at the point where the *image* of a nuclear catastrophe joins with the more abstract *concept* of annihilation—where the critical link between nuclearism and poetry can be found.

Taking as his subject the political history of nuclear diplomacy, Lawrence Freedman addresses the essential role of speculative thinking in the development of deterrence strategies in U.S. and Soviet nuclear politics between 1945 and 1980. After noting in his introduction the unique nature of the nuclear threat, which, unlike other threats to the "eco-structure" of the world, could be carried out quickly, Freedman describes the limits that threat has imposed on the "evolution" of strategic debates about it: "The use of the word 'evolution'. . . is somewhat misleading for it suggests progress along a learning curve, implying a higher level of present understanding than thirty, twenty or even ten years ago." What impresses Freedman instead "is the cyclical character of the debates. Much of what is offered today as a profound and new insight was said yesterday; and usually in a more concise and literate manner" (xv). The unprecedented conditions of the nuclear age have generated a plethora of literature offering widely diverse views on nuclear strategy, yet Freedman writes, "To help order and explain such a novel situation, new and arcane concepts have been developed, which sometimes serve to clarify but often obfuscate" (xv). Again, the problem becomes one of authority: With so much unreality surrounding the weapons themselves, what must one be able to prove he or she knows in order to speculate authoritatively on what cannot be known?

Many replies have been offered to this question. One example of applying *technical* methods to speculate on the course of nuclear war, Freedman points out, is the RAND Corporation's introduction of "systems analysis" as an approach to strategic thinking in the 1950s. In this approach the word "system" indicated "a capacity to view problems as a whole, rather than in fragmented components, and to master complexity" (179), thereby providing a logical means of overcoming the divisive tendency of technical labor. But despite multiple attempts "to make the best of the available information and even to work out how to generate some more, . . . it was not possible to compensate fully for the lack of hard information," so that, for example, analysts tended to place sophisticated technical analyses within insufficiently complex political frameworks. "Little could be known about the likely responses of human beings to any of the situations that they were liable to find themselves in during a nuclear war—either in deciding whether to launch a nuclear attack, or in implementing this decision, or in anticipating and suffering the results," and since nuclear war necessarily entails "unavoidable uncertainties" that make it unlike any previous wars, systems analysis proved to have limited value (179–80). Elsewhere, when reviewing the application of Game Theory (a mathematical analysis that gauges the varying degrees of gain and loss when conflicting interests compete, as in an economic or military confrontation) in the development of deterrent strategy, Freedman reaches a similar conclusion: Game Theory "could not predict or explain actual behaviour"; in fact, "there was no valid, empirically founded theory available. Men fighting nuclear wars had not been observed in action. There were no analogous situations to draw upon. Human imagination or intuition was inadequate to cope. The abstractions of Game Theory and similar devices were useful as much because of the lack of suitable alternatives than anything else" (185).

The theme of uncertainty in any speculations of how humans would act during a nuclear war or in its aftermath eventually becomes the focus of Freedman's discussion of deterrence policy itself. Yet what most disturbs him is not this lack of certainty but its effect on policy makers, an effect contrary to reason: While the "legion of uncertainties" surrounding the nuclear condition ought to have created among political strategists and others "a common humility—to be so much in the dark with so much at stake," instead, he laments, "the frustration with this predicament led many strategists to show astonishing confidence in their own nostrums, combined with vindictiveness against those who differed" (395). Such posturing among nuclear "experts" is frightening to contemplate.

Meanwhile, as ordinary citizens disturbed by the uncertainty of the effects of nuclear war, as Joseph Dewey puts it, "We cast suspicions on politicos, for they deal in the irrational jargon of nukespeak; we withhold faith from scientists, for they fashioned the Frankenstein that pounds at the door; we cast troubled eyes on the military, for it too often seems hungry; and we cannot move into the simple vernal embrace of a natural world, for that itself seems dwindling and threatened" (238). For those, then, who hesitate to leave the reins of the nuclear future entirely in the hands of technologists, strategists, and politicians, ideas from outside those arenas might also provide alternatives for survival, not *because* they are outside those arenas of power, but because they are founded on alternative conceptions of paradox itself.

◇ To examine how potential nuclear annihilation has contributed to a redefinition of the present, and to point to the parameters of possible ways of nothingness, I shall begin, in my first chapter, by turning to the work of Lifton, Theodor Adorno, and Edith Wyschogrod and, through them, shall attempt to critique the late twentieth-century phenomenon of the threat of nuclear annihilation, with a focus on the precedent of mass death in the Nazi concentration camps. To be sure, sharp distinctions must be maintained between the horrific methods used in the systematic genocide of the Jews and the indiscriminate species suicide that would occur in a nuclear catastrophe. Still, in their diverse yet compatible analyses of the former, Lifton, Adorno, and Wyschogrod link the technological realities of human-made mass death to the psychosocial and ontological premises of postmodern or postnuclear thought, particularly in relation to the less logocentric, more symbolic methods of art and poetry. Once that link is made, I shall assess the broader critical debate over the function of art in Western culture after the horrors of Auschwitz and the siege of nuclearism—a debate ranging from Jonathan Schell's controversial remark that art in the nuclear age can only tell lies to Martin Heidegger's claim for poetry's unique ability "to speak about nothing" (26), and finally, to Jacques Derrida's insinuation that in our time nothing less than "the remainderless and a-symbolic destruction of literature" is "the ultimate referent" (28) of writing.

What I want to emphasize by scrutinizing these various arguments in a book about poetry—arguments that have rarely been juxtaposed and never been applied to a criticism of American poetry—is the fundamental challenge that the concept of annihilation poses to poets in the nuclear era. Nothing less than how poetry functions in or for life itself is at issue. And once we start to distinguish how different poets have approached and imaginatively attempted to meet this challenge, the range and ingenuity of their art present a convincing case for how survival depends on more than technological research and political negotiation. By exposing how we have come to picture ourselves in the nuclear age, the best poets express what is needed to outlive it—an articulation and critique of our current paradoxical situation. So although it is not wrong to say that nuclear-age poetry unites in resistance against annihilation, it also serves the more reconstructive function of portraying "ways of nothingness" by which, like Lifton's history professor, we can carry on a meaningful existence.

In the second part of chapter 1, I briefly consider the historical context of the poetry of annihilation and then examine the precedents of two modernist poets who open themselves to annihilation, rather than resort to the reductive tropes of most public debates. Reading them chiefly for their assumptions about annihilation, I contrast two early poems after Hiroshima—Gertrude Stein's "Reflection on the Atomic Bomb" and Williams Carlos Williams's "Asphodel, That Greeny Flower"—which use opposite but finally reconcilable tactics in countering the seductive power of nuclearism while implying means for living with it.

In the four chapters that follow this theoretical look at the dynamic relationship of poetry to nuclear annihilation, I distinguish four of the ways of nothingness I have discovered among American poems. Several alternative approaches to these poems might also work. One method, for instance, would be to write a history of American poetry written af-

ter 1945, from Stein's "Reflection on the Atomic Bomb" to James Merrill's *The Changing Light at Sandover*, in order to see not only how poets react to developments in nuclear technology, but how they reflect
(or influence) cultural change in the nuclear age. But I have decided
against this method for two reasons: Though poems written about the
nuclear threat have often reflected the historical moment of their composition, unlike works of science fiction they have had little direct historical or literary impact on each other, since poets are apt to find their
poetic influences outside of nuclearism itself; therefore, a history of the
poetry would largely reiterate the history of nuclear politics and culture
itself, a history more thoroughly and impressively handled elsewhere
than I could hope to do here.[8] Second, a criticism of nuclear age poetry
that relied on identifying poems written explicitly in reaction to historical events would deter me from ranging into a discussion of images,
metaphors, and tropes in poems not overtly about nuclear issues at all,
a restriction I want to avoid.

Alternatively, I might choose to identify certain paradigms of subject
matter or theme, in order to group poets and poems according to particular concerns.[9] Such a method would contrast how different poets look
at the same subject—for example, how Denise Levertov, William Stafford, Paul Zimmer, John Engels, and Toi Derricote differ in their imagery
of atomic bomb tests, or how William Carlos Williams, Alan Dugan,
Adrienne Rich, C. K. Williams, and others confront nuclearism's degra-
dation of interpersonal love. However, rather than arrange the poems I
discuss by theme or subject, I prefer to classify them by the formal technique and stylistic devices each uses when encountering annihilation.
Because I believe that the unique contribution poetry makes to resisting
as well as engaging nuclearism is found in its speculative use of language
and form more than in its explicit subject matter, I want to underscore
how poets have imagined the nuclear world more than what they explicitly say about it. In addition, classifying poems by technique and
style (while admittedly subject to some overlap between categories) allows in particular cases a more thorough investigation of the oeuvre of a
poet's nuclear poems, rather than restricting me to specific poems on
this or that subject. By employing this principle, I am able within each
chapter not only to examine individual poems that use a comparable approach but also to concentrate on one poet whose body of work demonstrates that approach. After all, it is in the characteristic styles of strong
poets across time, more than in single examples of their work, where we
can better discern an expansive vision of the nuclear age.

A third reason for my method of organization, despite the serious nature of my subject and despite its resulting sometimes in unorthodox pairings of poems or poets, concerns their imaginative scope. In stressing that, besides a unified voice of resistance, what these poets offer are multiple "ways of nothingness" by which we can reconcile living in the shadow of extinction, I want to do more than criticize the degree of success with which poets treat issues of survival. I also want to inscribe the parameters of those "ways" as suggested paradigms of contemporary existence itself. What recommends the poetry of nuclear annihilation, what will contribute to its survival beyond its own era—if there is to be a future reconciled with the human-made power to commit global suicide—lies not solely in its oppositional posture, nor in its historical moment, but in its unique imaginative ability to connect the material threat and symbolic presence of nuclearism with the deepest confines of the human spirit.

To simplify, then, I want to distinguish four ways of nothingness in American poetry, as manifested in poems that speak *against, through, around,* and *from within* potential nuclear annihilation. In chapter 2, I first examine poems that speak *against* annihilation, usually by protesting government, industry, and business practices that foster nuclear arms and power. Because they publicly exert moral pressure to change those practices, these poems are generally the most well-known for their "political" content. Among these protest poets, Denise Levertov has emerged as a leading voice in opposition to nuclear weapons, and many of her poems inspire that cause; often, however, statements of political protest in her poems are composed in a less telegraphic, more subtle voice, as they search for a spiritual center to her political convictions. In her profession of faith despite the vulnerability of the world underpinning it, Levertov embodies the first way of nothingness. In the second part of the chapter, therefore, I discuss how Levertov's nuclear protest poems attempt to reconcile the threat of annihilation with her religious faith.

Less overtly oppositional, the poets I discuss in chapter 3 have expressed themselves in more "private" or apolitical works than most protest poems. Approaching potential nothingness by thinking *through* its figurative impact on the individual, these poets tend to create images of holocaust in order to convey the *subjective,* individual experience of nuclearism. Conversely, these poets also incorporate nuclear imagery into metaphors for personal experience, in the way that Sylvia Plath used the imagery of the Nazi concentration camps in poems de-

picting her own psychic traumas. Rather than blatantly oppose nuclear
technology, these "apocalyptic lyrics" weave together the public and
the personal, therein reflecting the ubiquitous nature of nuclearism. In
the second part of this chapter, through a reading of three poems that
span three decades in the accomplished work of one of these poets,
Richard Wilbur, I want to illustrate how, in the course of the nuclear
age, even a poet's basic assumptions about the natural world in relation
to nothingness have been subtly yet dramatically altered. Wilbur's sublime expression of selfhood in a threatened world represents a second
way of nothingness.

Chapter 4 focuses on my third category, poets who write *around* nuclearism, often by experimenting with alternative forms to the meditative lyric, in order to open themselves to broader discussions of the scientific, historical, cultural, and mythic conditions of the nuclear age.
Fewer in number than the others, the works of these poets are often
larger in scope, pairing the issue of annihilation with other contemporary ideas and issues, because they mean to speak less for individuals
than for communities. A major work of this type, which I call "psychohistorical poetry," is James Merrill's epic trilogy, *The Changing
Light at Sandover*, a poem I explore especially for its staging of ambiguity in a serious yet oddly playful vision of annihilation. By dexter-
ously courting uncertainty without abandoning humor and erudition,
Merrill's epic illustrates a third way of nothingness.

Finally, in chapter 5, I consider poems composed *from within* the idea
of annihilation. These poems often, though not always, forego explicit
nuclear concerns and instead approach annihilation from the more
metaphysical perspective of nothingness itself, as we experience it in
the nuclear age. In contrasting their methods for and speculations on
nothingness, whether in relation to nuclear technology or not, and then
in considering, specifically, John Ashbery's vision of nothingness, I
want to argue how in form these "poems of destinerrance" embrace the
uncertainty at the heart of most thinking about nuclear annihilation.
Because Ashbery and others delve stylistically into uncertainty itself in
order to explore its bond to the continuity of life, I therefore feel justi-
fied in including the poems in this fourth way of nothingness with the
other three groups.

Following this general outline, a reader may suspect a bias in my order of categories, with the implication that the fourth one contains poems of the greatest literary significance for the nuclear age. In fact, I
have arranged the categories with the intention of progressing from the

most direct encounters with nuclearism to the most oblique. What I want to contend is that the cultural paradigms for thinking about annihilation are expansive—from specific models of overt resistance to broader models of adaption to the knowledge of our capacity for species suicide. Furthermore, because of my interest in the far reaches of the poetry of annihilation, I do not always choose the most famous or most obvious nuclear-related poems to illustrate each category but instead focus on those that display the most distinct features. Nevertheless, I maintain the conviction that no single response to potential annihilation is sufficient to secure survival or to gain precedence over others. Rather, only by combining efforts to think through the uncertainty of nuclearism can we begin to construct harmonious ways of nothingness to bear us, as a complex community, through this age. So I prefer to think of these categories as components in a cooperation of poets, a chorus of voices, who despite their vivid differences in style, attitude, and music finally share a commitment to life.

At the end of *Negative Dialectics*, Adorno writes, "Represented in the inmost cell of thought is that which is unlike thought" (408). The implicit power of the best poetry, whether widely read or not, whether able to survive annihilation or not, is its ability to imagine what is found in that cell and express it in words we can recognize as speaking for us. Therein lies a definition of poetic beauty. Like the history professor from Hiroshima, poets need not go about boasting of these things nor speaking in loud voices, but if they can be helpful—and they certainly can—it is essential to discover, engage, and celebrate their vision.

ONE

Poetry and Annihilation

The Crisis for Poetry in the Nuclear Age

To the extent that they participate by vocation in neither military, technological, scientific, nor governmental affairs, poets seem to have little role to play in the world of nuclear technology. As makers of metaphor, lovers of beauty, or even unacknowledged legislators of the world, they appear as far removed from the highly technical, politically sensitive business of weapons production, management, containment, and control as any ordinary citizen could be. Yet the very developments since 1945 that have made nuclear weapons fixtures in the lives of other citizens have created a crisis for poets as well: Given the danger posed to a world threatened by its own eradication, and given further how little direct impact poetry can hope to have in relieving that danger, poets might ask themselves, "What is the point of writing?"

Of course, poets have always asked themselves this question, yet because of the unique constraints of the nuclear age, we need to rephrase the question more appropriately to our historical context. Before we can look at how American poets have responded to impending extinction, we need to define, if only in part, what it means to be alive in an age of annihilation. By correlating the ideas of various thinkers, I want to begin to sketch out not only the nature of the crisis for poetry in the nuclear age, but the special task for poets who choose to address that crisis—for the sake of their art as much as for the sake of the world. Once the crisis is characterized, and despite what poetry's detractors might believe about its failure to respond effectively to the contemporary world, we can begin to see how poets have reacted to their (and our) endangered condition and, as first exemplified in contrasting poems by Gertrude Stein and William Carlos Williams, how their imaginative language can speak for our era with power, insight, and beauty.

◇ What does it mean to live in an age of technological annihilation? Unlike the etymological trace of meaning in the words "eschatology" (which derives from the Greek word for the study of last things—as in the *Oxford English Dictionary* definition, "the four last things: death, judgement, heaven and hell") or "apocalypse" (which as a Biblical term pertains to the "uncovering" or "disclosure" of the unknown to St. John at Patmos), "annihilation" derives from the Latin roots *ad* and *nihil* (meaning "to, towards, or at nothing"), suggesting a more secular sense of nothingness or of things being reduced to nothing.[1] Of course, images of and ideas about annihilation are not unique to the post-Hiroshima era, and useful precedents exist in eschatological and apocalyptic texts from before the Greeks, including, for instance, the myths of Noah's Ark and the Apocalypse, or the predictions of extinction that spread throughout Europe during the Black Plague. But what distinguishes our contemporary sense of annihilation, whether it come about by nuclear, ecological, biomedical, or other technological forces, is that we imagine it will occur not *in spite of* human efforts but *because* of them. As the philosopher Edith Wyschogrod stipulates, the time we live in is not just the nuclear age but the age of "man-made mass death," in which annihilation has taken on the form of species suicide.

Given this profound difference, twentieth-century precedents of the experience of technological annihilation are at least as helpful and appropriate to understanding the nature of nuclear culture as are more traditional apocalyptic tales. In this vein, writers as diverse as Hannah Arendt, Primo Levi, Terrence Des Pres, Theodor Adorno, Lifton, Wyschogrod, and others have reflected on the impact derived from the verifiable, and chilling, accounts of attempted annihilation in Auschwitz, Dachau, Belsen, and Buchenwald. However, most such efforts to compare the genocide of the Jews with nuclearism have been fairly recent. Spencer Weart, in his discussion of popular culture and nuclear imagery, remarks on the widespread resistance in the generation after World War II to comparing the events of the Nazi Holocaust to nuclear warfare. While acknowledging that the Holocaust was a historical massacre of unprecedented and unparalleled proportions—with the number of those slaughtered at Auschwitz alone surpassing Hiroshima by over ten times—Weart still considers the popular tendency to see the Nazis "as cardboard villains rather than as the ordinary humans that most of them in fact were" a failure to acknowledge how easily, "in a wrongly organized society, a person's normal will to dominate and harm could be entangled even with a crusade for rebirth" (410–11). He observes that, surprisingly, not until the 1980s did artists and others display much willingness "to connect nuclear war with the sort of internal forces, from which none of us is exempt, that built Auschwitz" (412). After a long hiatus, exploring that connection has now become a central method in shaping discussions of the ramifications of nuclearism.

Lifton, for example, who in addition to his research on the *hibakusha* has also conducted a massive psychosocial study of the doctors in the German concentration camps, has made the prescriptive argument that, as much as we may attempt to dismiss the imagery of both Auschwitz and Hiroshima, it is futile and self-destructive to try; rather than work to forget the horrors of genocide, which continue to plague the modern world, he believes we should accept that "we need Hiroshima and Auschwitz, as we need Vietnam and our everyday lives, in all their horror," to help our imaginations grasp the import of "the vision of total annihilation" and its "curse" on our lives (*Life* 132–33). Furthermore, in "Beyond the Nuclear End," Lifton reiterates the critical distinction between "older religious images of Armageddon," in which the end is inflicted by a higher power, and the contemporary sense of a "self-extermination" inflicted by human-made technology; however, despite our not sharing our ancestors' faith in the power of an eschatological event to cleanse humanity of guilt, so that it might be re-created in a purer form, we still must confront the threat of our own annihilation: "Given the temptation of despair," he writes, it is urgent that we "confront the image that haunts us, making use of whatever models we can," because "only then can we achieve those changes in consciousness that must accompany (if not precede) changes in public policy on behalf of a human future" (*Future* 149–50).

Without denying the particular facts of Nazi Germany—indeed, because of the systematic inhumanity it perpetrated—one of the most vivid models of modern annihilation (other than the "text" of Hiroshima) is Auschwitz, about which Lifton provides his own graphic details:

> When I visited Auschwitz recently, in connection with research on Nazi doctors, I saw many exhibits there that spared little in revealing what human beings can do to other human beings. But the two exhibits that had the strongest impact on me were two rooms: one that was simply full of shoes, many of them baby shoes; and another full of suitcases of the rectangular old-fashioned kind with the addresses of people on them. Such exhibits require the viewer to do the psychological work of imagining missing people. It is their absence—the element of nothingness—that captures the imagination. This form of nothingness, then, can serve to mobilize us to reject the elimination of human beings and to maintain the flow of life. Nothingness is thus part of our imaginative wisdom, helping us toward the only honorable path: prevention. (*Future* 157)

Not only does Lifton consider the horrors of Auschwitz an important reminder never to allow such barbarous acts to occur again (one justification for the Atomic Dome in Hirsohima as well, for instance, despite its additional ironic function as a tourist attraction), but he also sees in the imagery of absence at Auschwitz an agent to help human consciousness adapt to the threat of global annihilation. As Albert Einstein is often quoted, "The unleashed power of the atom has changed everything save our modes of thinking, and thus we drift toward unparalleled catastrophe" (Nathan 376). In the latter part of the twentieth century, as Lifton suggests, the material we need to change "our modes of thinking" is now before us; what we must do is symbolically come to understand that material, to "imagine the real" rather than resign in despair (Lifton and Falk 5).[2] Until we come to terms with how the potential for annihilation has already changed our sense of the world, we may unwittingly help realize that potential.

In his major work *Negative Dialectics*, in which he reflects on the impact of the Nazi holocaust more metaphysically than Lifton pretends to, Adorno examines this concept of changed "modes of thinking." Toward the end of his book, where he provides "models [that] are to make plain what negative dialectics is and to bring it into the realm of reality" (xx), Adorno asserts how the undeniable fact of Auschwitz has profoundly altered Western consciousness: "We cannot say any more that the immutable is truth, and that the mobile, transitory is appearance. The mutual indifference of temporality and eternal ideas is no longer tenable even with the bold Hegelian explanation that temporal existence, by virtue of the destruction inherent in its concept, serves the eternal represented by the eternity of destruction" (361). Given the appalling example of banal evil and pointless inhumanity exercised in the concentration camps, Adorno argues, we can no longer accept "one of the mystical impulses secularized in dialectics," namely, that history ultimately has a transcendent end. "After Auschwitz," he explains, "our feelings resist any claim of the positivity of existence as sanctimonious, as wronging the victims; they balk at squeezing any kind of sense, however bleached, out of the victims' fate. And these feelings do have an objective side after events that make a mockery of the construction of immanence as endowed with a meaning radiated by an affirmatively posited transcendence" (361). In other words, even the notion of our gaining wisdom about annihilation from the tragedy of Auschwitz repels any feelings we have for its victims, yet to accept that their deaths were meaningless makes "a mockery of the construction of immanence" and renders any further postulation about reality's purpose both inadequate and patently absurd.

Adorno argues that the hideousness of Auschwitz has thrown consciousness itself into crisis "because actual events have shattered the basis on which speculative metaphysical thought could be reconciled with experience." This rupture has created a whole new region of fear for the individual conscience—"that in the concentration camps it was no longer an individual who died, but a specimen—this is a fact bound to affect the dying of those who escaped the administrative measure" (362). The very existence of death through such an impersonal, technological means (where the only object is mass extermination) effectively eradicates the metaphysical dichotomy of identity and nonidentity altogether. "Absolute negativity is in plain sight," writes Adorno, "and has ceased to surprise anyone." But another fear, he argues, is that *any* justification for fear one might make based on one's self-preservation has been undermined as well: "Even in his formal freedom, the individual is as fungible and replaceable as he will be under the liquidators' boots" (362), thereby throwing into suspension all purpose to the lives of those outside the camps who are, in truth, equally vulnerable to annihilation. By removing any rational basis by which one individual might be distinguished from another, annihilation on this massive scale limits post-Auschwitz consciousness, not only by impressing upon us that merely by accident have we escaped being eliminated, but also by stirring our guilt as survivors, the ones who just happen to be left behind for no redeeming reason; our "mere survival calls for the coldness, the basic principle of bourgeois subjectivity, without which there could have been no Auschwitz; this is the drastic guilt of him who was spared" (363).[3]

In opposition to the existential (and Marxist) mandate that authentic living consists only in *praxis* or taking action in the world, Adorno argues that, given our post-Auschwitz consciousness of annihilation, to experience "a sense of being not quite there," of living not as oneself but as "a kind of spectator," may be closer to the truth of living than we have heretofore acknowledged. Paradoxically, the apathetic question "What does it really matter?" which "we like to associate with bourgeois callousness" may in fact be "the line most likely to make the individual aware, without dread, of the insignificance of his existence. The inhuman part of it, the ability to keep one's distance as a spectator and to rise above things, is in the final analysis the human part, the very part resisted by its ideologists" (363). This passage insinuates that for the thinking person in the aftermath of the horrors of Auschwitz to be alive means to encounter an emptiness or nothingness within the self. This is the paradox of post-Auschwitz consciousness.

It is important here to qualify Adorno's identification of this change wreaked on consciousness after the genocide at Auschwitz, a change that has left those who chance to be alive "spellbound . . . between involuntary ataraxy—an esthetic life due to weakness—and the bestiality of the involved" (364).[4] "Both," he says, "are wrong ways of living" and it is our guilt at being unable to reconcile the unacceptability of either "that compels us to philosophize" (364). But in granting this profound impact of annihilation on post-Auschwitz consciousness, Adorno does not suggest a nihilistic premise. Rather, the concept of "nothingness" itself as totalizing or absolute is as subject to negation as any other: "That men might want nothingness," writes Adorno, "would be ridiculous hubris for each definite individual will . . . even if organized society managed to make the earth uninhabitable or to blow it up" (379). That the technological reality of annihilation has imposed on us the sense of being spectators to our own extinction does not permit us to believe in nothingness as a kind of new faith, despite the widespread evidence of such a faith (what Lifton calls "nuclear fundamentalism" [Lifton and Falk 80–99]).[5] Embracing that belief is but a deeper manifestation of the same kind of arrogance Lawrence Freedman finds in the insistent arguments of nuclear strategists. To the contrary, rather than taking refuge in the cynicism or despair that such a belief ultimately rests on, it forces us to suspend (or negate) certainty and to search elsewhere for meaning. We may define ours as the age of uncertainty, but we cannot rest on that label more than on any other.

In her more recent philosophical analysis of modern consciousness and "man-made mass death," Edith Wyschogrod carefully investigates but then swerves from the notion of transcendence, rather than negate it as Adorno does. Unlike Lifton who constructs his theory on psychoanalysis and individual case studies, and even unlike Adorno who as a critical theorist grounds much of his thinking in material history, Wyschogrod concedes that her account of the crisis of the self in a world potentially annihilated derives neither from empirical observation of concentration camps nor from the words of survivors. "Rather," she says, "I appeal to the structures of existence opened up in a world of radically new, efficient technological forms of extinction powered by new social and political means" (201). Positing first that "the meaning of self, time, and language are all affected by mass death: from now on the development of these themes and the meaning of man-made mass death wax and wane together" (ix), Wyschogrod nonetheless resists constructing a "transcendental framework" for our "situation" under the threat of annihilation, "if we mean by it something eternal and immutable." Instead she attempts "to locate a new historically conditioned a priori by considering the logical and ontological structures exhibited by man-made mass death in our century . . . to bring into view a form of life, a region of being, whose manner of being is to exist as the obliteration of cultures and as the possible extinction of human life" (xi). Then, yoking together the "characteristic expressions" of both Nazi extermination camps and genocidal warfare under the categorical term "death event,"[6] she proceeds to argue that in the contemporary world, this annihilating condition "can be thought of as a 'stable' backdrop for the self's transactions with the world" (201).

Like Adorno, Wyschogrod grants that a distinctive aspect of mass death is how it throws into crisis what she calls the *"authenticity paradigm"* of the individual, or the "reciprocal relation between the manner in which death is appropriated and a person's moral situation" (3). Though we may continue to try to measure the value of life by the character of death, technological culture has changed the limits imposed on our thinking: "[I]f the appropriation of death is to be true to twentieth-century experience, if 'being full of life' we are also 'full of death' as it is present in our time, the authenticity paradigm is reduced to self-parody. If instead we choose to renounce the experience peculiar to the present age—that of mass death—and assess authenticity by integrating only one's own death into one's life, then life is lived in monadic isolation in which the deaths of others have lost significance" (13). As Adorno might add, both ways of living (and dying) are inauthentic, and Wyschogrod concedes that, given this dilemma, those who die "a simple death which occurs fortuitously through disease or accident" are the fortunate ones, since, "according to this new counter-poetry of survivors, it would no longer seem heroic to accept personal death in one of its expected forms given the possible terms on which we might be forced to encounter it" (13).

If we accept this incongruous challenge to the "authenticity paradigm" (that mass death undermines any "heroic" way of dying), our entire sense of the finitude of life is impaired by technological society. At all levels—the level of inanimate objects, the level of vital being, and the level of social interaction—the "life-world" has become the "larger whole" or "matrix" from which technological society has been alienated. Yet considering the pre-eminence and driving power of technological society (a fact of modern life acknowledged by Wyschogrod and others, as I note in my introduction), the result is that the "life-world" "now lies in concealment" while the "death-world" (or sense of annihilation) is everywhere present (23–25).

However, it is essential to Wyschogrod that we distinguish the "death-world" from technological society itself; although they may seem to share characteristics, they do not. In a crucial way, technological society is more closely related to the *life-world* than to the *death-world* because it depends on the indefinite continuity of the life-world:[7] At whatever point it might utterly "conceal" or use up the life-world it will itself cease to have meaning. But conversely, the primary feature of the death-world (that is, death) finally has nothing to do with technology, because, as Wyschogrod reasons, "If the death-world were the only world, the resulting monolith would spell the end of all life and so the end of technological society as well" (25).

Once categorically separated from the death-world in this manner, one apparently promising prospect of technological society is the familiar suggestion that the answer to a technological problem may well lie within technology itself.[8] But Wyschogrod labels this idea a " 'category mistake' which permits people to be fed into the maw of an efficient and impersonal productive process" (25). Rather, because unlike either the life-world or the death-world technological society has no mythic or meaningful foundation of its own other than "the increase of technique," it cannot by itself serve as a construction for any philosophical or symbolic a priori (26).

For Wyschogrod, the best evidence for the lack of a mythic foundation for technological society (already having alienated itself from the life-world) is in how that society expresses meaning, namely in the "ways in which language signifies" for it (26). Although only a part of what concerns her about the impact of man-made mass death on consciousness in general,[9] this turn to language bears pointedly on the meaning of annihilation in relation to poetry: In her alignment with Martin Heidegger, calling for the reassessment of the relationship between language and "*techne*," Wyschogrod draws attention to the role of literature, especially poetry, in the nuclear age. She writes:

> What is unique to the language of technological society is its non-teleological character. Nothing in the scheme tells why a given technique is desirable other than that it promotes some aspect of technique itself. Thus we may designate a stick as a lever, but in the framework of technique, *why* we should want to lift anything can only be answered in terms of further utility. Similarly, we may improve the efficiency of an organization, but the large context never transcends the sphere of means (it is cheaper or production is faster, and so on). The language of technological society cannot "refer" beyond utility because it can provide no encompassing structure of meaning to organize its disparate processes. What is more, such a meaning system cannot be derived from techniques themselves because techniques are devised to be self-contained. (27)

Indirectly addressing the same problem Paul Loeb describes, concerning the inability of the individual in technological society to justify his or her own actions, even after having removed responsibility for them from others, Wyschogrod locates the source of the problem in the shortcomings of the language of technology. That language is, in fact, devoid of any "mythical thought" that "could provide the relational structure for the unification of these diverse functions," and as a result, a "unique and paradoxical situation" has evolved: "A movement toward a single homogeneous culture, global in scale, whose functions are transparent to everyone has emerged along with technique, but no overarching system of meaning has accompanied it, because such meaning cannot derive from the language of utility and quantification" (27–28). Though responsible for perpetuating the death-world, technological society simply cannot justify itself mythically or morally in relation to that world.

The danger, of course, is that the gap in meaning (or "demythologized ground") opened by technological society will be filled by the totalizing and "annihilatory" power of the death-world, in "an attempt to make whole the broken cosmos by an imaginative act of radical negation" (28). But as it is for Adorno and Lifton, such a monolithic force is untenable; the "self-affirmation" of such a myth "requires accelerating the pace of annihilation since [its] power depends upon resistances to be overcome and preserves itself only by an increase in its exercise," and as Wyschogrod argues, any "present-day myths which organize existence in terms of annihilation lack fixity" (29). In effect, what Lifton calls "nuclear fundamentalism" can only be held as bad or false faith. We cannot build meaning on a belief in annihilation.

This lack of mythic power, however, does not necessarily keep us from reflecting on the way history has altered our sense of a priori knowledge. Thinking of Ludwig Wittgenstein's claim that "there are propositions which lie halfway between empirical and logical propositions," propositions that cannot be contradicted and consequently in a unique way "stand fast for us" (61–62), Wyschogrod contends that we *can* accept the a priori of annihilation without having experienced it and without assigning it absolute power; such a statement as "Nuclear weapons can destroy all living things," while it may have "profoundly unsettling" implications and may preclude "the possibility of any secure framework for experience," is nevertheless "more than an empirical generalization" because "it establishes a frame of reference: the possible destruction of the world" (62). As an idea, though, it cannot be so much the foundation of myth as "the actual contextual grid shaping our experiences" and, as a grid, therefore "itself subject to change if historical forces radically undermine it" (62). In other words, though paradoxically so, the fact of nuclear annihilation is an a priori which cannot be denied, but it is not a transcendent truth.

At this juncture—in positing what J. Fisher Solomon has called "the nuclear referent" (28)[10]—Wyschogrod swerves from Adorno's negation of any positivist overcoming of nihilism (Adorno 380–81).[11] Instead, she turns to Heidegger's definition of poetry in order to argue for an alternative response to our being merely spectators to our own annihilation at the hands of a rampant technology: "Either affirming or attacking technique would be beside the point," she argues, "man can, however, open himself to the essence of technology" (184). An encounter with the essence of technology, though, first requires a direct encounter with language itself, and herein lies the critical function of poetry in the age of man-made mass death—to cut to "the essence of technology," rather than submit to the demythologized, potentially annihilating power of technological society.

In a lecture first delivered in 1935, Heidegger himself makes the following case for poetry's special abilities in the context of annihilation:

> It is perfectly true that we cannot talk about nothing, as though it were a thing like the rain outside or a mountain or any object whatsoever. In principle, nothingness remains inaccessible to science. The man who wishes truly to speak about nothing must of necessity become unscientific. But this is a misfortune only so long as one supposes that scientific thinking is the only authentic rigorous thought, and that it alone can and must be made into the standard of philosophical thinking. But the reverse is true. . . . To speak of nothing will always remain a horror and an absurdity for science. But aside from the philosopher, the poet can do so—and not because, as common sense supposes, poetry is without strict rules, but because the spirit of poetry (only authentic and great poetry is meant) is essentially superior to the spirit that prevails in all mere science. By virtue of this superiority the poet always speaks as though the essent [sic] were being expressed and invoked for the first time. (25–26)

In criticizing scientific thought, Heidegger attributes only to philosophy and poetry the power "to speak about nothing" in anything like a meaningful manner. Whether his polemic against science is valid or not, it is this shared distinction of "thinking and poetry" that Wyschogrod also emphasizes when confronted with a demythologized, technological society. Citing Heidegger's bringing together the roots of the words *technē* and *poesis*, in that both imply the making of something and the "bring[ing] forth truth into the splendor of radiant appearing," Wyschogrod condones the fundamental power of poetry: "In the Greek world, art was not a cultural activity but a revealing-permitting of the true to shine forth. Since the essence of art is akin to the essence of technology but also different from it, art may be the power that will reveal the essence of technology in the age of technology" (189–90). For her, because of its unique predisposition to express ambiguity and paradox, art (especially poetry) can speak of and even to the "essent" of the nuclear age.

Wyschogrod further abides by Heidegger's conception of poetry when she adds that in speaking to "the destitution of our time," the poet "must speak not only of the visible devastation but of what is lacking, in order to highlight nonbeing" (190). However, she distinguishes her view from Heidegger's, in part by criticizing his emphasis on "things" instead of the social interaction of people, especially as embodied in love:[12] While it may be true that "poetry opens a discursive space for remembering the lost or dead other," poetry in this sense need not concern itself exclusively with "the death event" to achieve meaning: "To the contrary, such poetry may be didactic and trivializing, thus distorting what it tries to sustain. But, poetry is as primordially an invocation of the beloved other or others as it is of things" (196). For the socially concerned Wyschogrod, what is missing in Heidegger's pronouncement about poetry's unique ability to speak of nothing is its further ability to express love (as well as the loss of love) among people. In an age in which "expressive language itself has now been replaced by the language of calculation" (214), whether it be through "the silent renunciation of violence" (206) or through some other means, only poetry through its imaginative reconfigurations of love and life can mediate the self-affirming course of technological society. "How to do so," admits Wyschogrod, "is for poets to discover and not for philosophers to legislate" (196).

◇ To be sure, not everyone agrees with Heidegger's somewhat arcane endorsement of the transcendent power of poetry—nor by implication with Wyschogrod's of the fundamental role of love in poetic language—to steer us through the dangerous path toward annihilation. In order to arrive, then, at a more cogent, if less grandiose, definition of the postnuclear function of poetry, it is important to address the case against art and poetry's value in an age of annihilation. To begin with, in a dramatic statement in *The Fate of the Earth,* Jonathan Schell depicts the quandary for the artist in the nuclear age. "Art," he writes, "attempts both to reflect the period in which it was produced and to be timeless. But today, if it wishes to truthfully reflect the reality of its period, whose leading feature is the jeopardy of the human future, art will have to go out of existence, while if it insists on trying to be timeless it has to ignore this reality—which is nothing other than the jeopardy of human time—and so, in a sense, tell a lie" (165). By removing the opportunity for poetry to transcend time, annihilation, in Schell's view, removes even the possibility for transcendence of the sort Wyschogrod believes is necessary for a mythologically based truth. For American poets, whose homeland has been the chief breeding ground for the technology that has made nuclear annihilation a possibility, Schell's paradox may seem particularly apt, as the "jeopardy of the human future" casts its doubt on the survival of their art, let alone on its impact. Yet because of the uncertainty of their role in relation to nuclearism, contemporary poets often deliberately avoid the political, technological, and social realities of the nuclear age, as though to treat them in their work would endow them with a significance poets should instinctively resist.

Terence Des Pres has explained this argument for the implicitly political message of much contemporary poetry (and the fallacy in such an argument) this way: "By celebrating modest moments of the human spectacle—little snaps of wonder, bliss or pain—poetry implicitly takes its stand against nuclear negation. To say Yes to life, this argument goes, automatically says No to the Bomb. And yes, a grain of truth sprouts here. I expect many among us read poetry that way in any case. The upshot, however, is that poets can go on producing their vignettes of self, pleased to be fighting the good fight without undue costs—except *the* cost, which is the enforced superficiality, the required avoidance of our deeper dismay" (449). As Des Pres suggests, poetry unwilling or unable to confront nuclearism as both an external potential and an internal psychic crisis may inadvertently suffer from Lifton's "psychic numbing" or "desensitization," roughly analogous to that state of mind found among Auschwitz and Hiroshima survivors and "characterized by various degrees of inability to feel and by gaps between knowledge and feeling" (*Life* 79). While it is true that for an artist to refuse to confront potential extinction may constitute a healthy attempt to suppress an idea that might otherwise elicit only despair, it is also an assured means of desensitizing himself or herself to "our deeper dismay" and of failing to provide an imaginative expression for that dismay. In other words, to avoid comment is to acquiesce to (and therefore silently to condone) the present predicament. Yet if Lifton is correct in saying that ours is "the age of numbing" (*Life* 80), it should come as no surprise that such avoidance occurs.

Despite Schell's polemic about the poles of inefficacy and dishonesty in the art of the nuclear age, however, poets do have options other than to avoid or acquiesce to nuclearism. Among those who refuse to accept Schell's view, for instance, is David Dowling, to whom such a notion of art seems "both high-minded and simplistic." "Examples abound," argues Dowling, "of works of art created out of a mood of apprehension or despair—Picasso's *Guernica*, Beckett's *Waiting for Godot*—which are neither mendacious nor powerless. Even the prospect of the end of time has produced such masterpieces as the Book of Revelation or Messaien's 'Quartet for the End of Time' "; indeed, Dowling concludes, "Lurking in Schell's personification of art ('It') is a nostalgic notion of Renaissance humanism and the optimistic celebration of Man" (73).[13] Another critic, Rob Wilson, in writing on the "nuclear sublime," agrees with this assessment, insinuating that Schell vastly underestimates the flexibility and tensile strength of art: "We need to wonder whether or not, at some point, within postnuclear history, quantitative changes in speed and force could produce qualitative changes in the subject. That is, even within this recycled discourse of the sublime, can't we find new formations and affects, commensurate with (if not resistant to) this space-age threshold of nuclear force?" (236).

More traditionally humanist in view, Frank Kermode has argued that we need not look to the space age for evidence of the mind's ability to "find new formations and affects" in encountering annihilation, because we can look to the past. In *The Sense of an Ending*, Kermode openly dismisses the notion that the nuclear threat must produce its own art: "It would be childish to argue, in a discussion of how people behave under eschatological threat, that nuclear bombs are more real and make one experience more authentic crisis-feelings than armies in the sky. There is nothing at all distinguishing about eschatological anxiety; it was, one gathers, a feature of Mesopotamian culture, and it is now a characteristic, often somewhat reach-me-down in appearance, of what Mr. Lionel Trilling calls the 'adversary culture' or sub-culture in our society" (95). Though he does so in a sometimes condescending tone, Kermode proffers imaginative solutions to the nuclear threat in the variety of apocalyptic texts already to be found in the literary canon, arguing that "it is by our imagery of the past and present and future, rather than from our confidence in the uniqueness of our crisis, that the character of our apocalypse must be known" (96). Writing some fifteen years before Schell, Kermode seems to have the hysterical tone of *The Fate of the Earth* in mind when he criticizes the "element of convention in the dominant mood of crisis and apocalypse," charging that when literature responds to the nuclear threat, "novelty becomes the inflation of triviality; the apocalypse is signalled by trivial games, mostly not original. Millennial renovationism declines into antithetical multiform influx; there is more noise than information" (121).

While Kermode may be right about how the fear of annihilation breaks down longstanding hierarchical tropes of artistic and moral value, that he assumes such a collapse in meaning will precipitate "the inflation of triviality" suggests a clinging to an unchanging heritage, despite the degree to which events in the current century have, in fact, trivialized that heritage.[14] Furthermore, to recognize the technological reality of the power of nuclear weapons does not necessarily mean they elicit "more authentic crisis-feelings than armies in the sky"; it is to endow our era with a reality not more, but *equally* as valid as that of civilizations who functioned according to an alternate set of premises. Not to accept that our time regards nuclear bombs as more threatening than the appearance of comets is to undervalue ourselves and our perceptions in the same way Kermode suggests we tend to belittle the past. Joseph Dewey, who praises *The Sense of an Ending* as "indispensable" (11) in its dismissal of antibomb hysteria, still considers Kermode's "reassurances," in the context of the world's nuclear arsenals, "a bit naive" (41). "Pretending that the world has not been altered by the secrets of Los Alamos," writes Dewey, "or even protesting in the streets the existence of the arsenals" fails to accept the peculiar and "complicated history" of the bomb, which can no longer "be made to go away" (41). Instead of concentrating as Kermode does on the preoccupation with endings brought on by apocalyptical thinking, Dewey explores the "apocalytpic temper" of the present, a term he defines as "a response, voiced often by a highly literate, imaginative minority, to a culture suddenly convulsed by evidence of a radical discontinuity in its history" (10). This term aptly identifies a shared cultural heritage without obscuring the critically unique features of nuclear anxiety in the twentieth century.

While most critics, then, do not readily subscribe to Schell's statement about the undermining of art in the nuclear age, neither do they accept the Heideggerian dictum that poetry has the power to transcend technology and change history. As a third alternative, Adorno, for instance, without dismissing art's raison d'être in the nuclear age as Schell does, advances a more indirect function for poetry. In an age in which Hegelian transcendence has been "abolished altogether" and metaphysics is either in its "last, already lost defensive position" or "sur-

vives only in the meanest and shabbiest" of forms (402), neither positivist science nor conclusive despair can be philosophically validated.
"Metaphysics cannot rise again," argues Adorno, because "the concept
of resurrection belongs to creatures, not to something created, and in
structures of the mind it is an indication of untruth." Consequently,
metaphysics "may originate only with the realization of what has been
thought in its sign" (404). Adorno suggests here that metaphysics, or the
"philosophic need," may find its roots in the post-Hegelian world neither in love nor in any other false construction of transcendence, but instead in the kind of "anti-metaphysical invective" found in Nietzsche's
work or in nihilistic art, for instance—that is, in those linguistic expressions "amid untruth" that "will not let truth go": "Art is semblance
even at its highest peaks; but its semblance, the irresistible part of it, is
given to it by what is not semblance" (404). By "semblance," Adorno
means both art as appearance, as a formal presentation in the world, and
art as mimetic, re*sembling* the world. But art's "semblance" derives
from what is *not* semblance, namely, the uncertain presence of the
world itself.

Nonetheless, Adorno adds, "What art, notably the art decried as nihilistic, says in refraining from judgments is that everything is not just
nothing. If it were, whatever is would be pale, colorless, indifferent"
(404). Unlike Heidegger's praise for the unique power of poetry to speak
of nothing, and unlike Wyschogrod's argument for the power of poetry
to express love even if through the loss of the beloved, Adorno assigns
poetry the role of provocation rather than of truth-telling. Although it
may appear as "folly," poetry may paradoxically undermine that which
it signifies, even while creating the potential for its meaningfulness. Instead of asserting the truth of nothingness, "semblance is a promise of
nonsemblance" (405), thereby provoking thought about nothingness
without affirming it. In rephrasing this idea to address both Schell and
Kermode, we might agree that poetry need not assert a timeless truth in
order to avoid telling a lie; rather, it can do better by expressing the uncertainty of a world that itself hangs suspended between mutable truths
and insufficient lies.

This idea of uncertainty and nuclearism inevitably leads to a discussion of poetry, annihilation, and deconstructionism. In his book specifically about the "nuclear referent," J. Fisher Solomon also criticizes
Heidegger's attitude toward poetry, as well as his aversion to any kind
of more explicit analysis of "concrete political dilemmas," for failing to
"lead us to a realistic political criticism." "Poetry is not going to solve

the concrete problems of the nuclear age," writes Solomon. But what concerns Solomon even more than his opposition to Heidegger's anti-materialistic, uncompromising approach to the "atomic age" is what he considers Jacques Derrida's equally impractical deconstruction of it: "Where Derrida, for example, *has* exposed the metaphysical tendencies in Heidegger's text, he does not really oppose that text or attempt to escape it." That is to say, whereas Heidegger "contemns" the "ontic" or real world of technologically created dangers in favor of the higher realms of thinking and poetry, Derrida—based on his deconstructionist assumption that "any attempt to ground history or being in some supreme category or power outside the categories of Western metaphysics is futile"—merely "defers" it (241–43).

The central text of Derrida's that Solomon has in mind—indeed, his cause for writing *Discourse and Reference in the Nuclear Age*—is Derrida's contribution to a 1984 Cornell University symposium on nuclear criticism, "No Apocalypse, Not Now (full speed ahead, seven missiles, seven missives)," a seminal piece for nuclear criticism. In a style sometimes thick with deconstructionist terminology, sometimes whimsical, Derrida develops his argument through a series of reflections on the nature of nuclear weapons themselves (as well as on how we understand them in the "archival" terms of our history),[15] gradually leading to the fifth of his "seven missives": "The only referent that is absolutely real is thus of the scope or dimension of an absolute nuclear catastrophe that would irreversibly destroy the entire archive and all symbolic capacity, would destroy the 'movement of survival' . . . at the very heart of life. This absolute referent of all possible literature is on a par with the absolute effacement of any possible trace; it is thus the only ineffaceable trace, it is so as the trace of what is entirely other, '*trace du tout autre*' " (28). In other words, in a more nuanced analysis of what Schell calls "the second death" of civilization that would accompany all individual deaths in a nuclear holocaust, Derrida asserts that with those individual deaths would also occur the irreversible destruction of "the entire archive" of what we have come to accept as what we know, together with "all symbolic capacity" and the "movement" to survive. This threat of "the absolute effacement of any possible trace" renders nuclear annihilation "entirely other" to the mind. Consequently, "the only 'subject' of all possible literature, of all possible criticism, its only ultimate and a-symbolic referent, unsymbolizable, even unsignifiable . . . is, if not the nuclear age, if not the nuclear catastrophe, at least that toward which nuclear discourse and the nuclear symbolic are *still beckoning:*

the remainderless and a-symbolic destruction of literature. Literature and literary criticism cannot speak of anything else, they can have no other ultimate referent, they can only multiply their strategic manuevers in order to assimilate that unassimilable wholly other" (28).

For Derrida, potential annihilation has become the "ultimate referent" in the nuclear age. Yet as ultimate as annihilation may be, it still has no more of an absolute or determinate standing for him than "nothingness" does for Adorno. Indeed, *because* our annihilation has taken on the definition of "that unassimilable wholly other," there can be no certainty of its actually occurring; as Derrida states as his sixth missive, "*An absolute missile does not abolish chance*" (29). Rather, our knowledge of the future has been suspended in uncertainty, and history itself participates in what he calls " 'destinerrance' [—a wandering that is its own end]" (29). But even "destinerrance," argues Derrida, "no longer gives us the assurance of a sending of being, of a recovery of the sending of being"; that is, the "randomness and incalculability" that are an "essential" element of "destinerrance" are not just factors of uncertainty that affect the "margin of indeterminacy" of a "calculable decision" but are instead factors that may "escape all control, all reassimilation or self-regulation of a system that they will have *precipitously. . .* but irreversibly destroyed" (29).

In the nuclear age, to risk disorder or chaos has come to be the equivalent of risking annihilation, in that a missile sent, a word spoken, a head nodded, can have irreversible consequences for the very source from which it originates—or so we have come to realize. It is such a mode of being, of what Derrida calls "the aleatory destinerrance of the *envoi*" (or chance wandering of the sending of being), that "allows us to think . . . the age of nuclear war" (29–30), to create those conditions for annihilation that we have. We have always thought uncertainly about the direction of history, about its bearing on what we have stored in the archive of knowledge. "But," Derrida argues, "this thought has been able to become a radical one, as a thought left over from the 'remainderless,' only in the nuclear age" (30), in that only now can we, must we, scrutinize its metaphysical basis.

In doing so, of course, we arrive not at a metaphysics nor at a referent, but at a paradox. In his poststructuralist examination of nuclearism and art, Peter Schwenger identifies this same Derridean paradox of the "*envoi*" not only in a missile and a missive ("The Post Nuclear Post Card") the way Derrida does, but in deterrence diplomacy as well, where "the missile is aimed, but its real aim is precisely not to attain that toward which it is aimed. The more believable it is that the missile will reach its target the less likely it becomes that it will do so; its aim becomes false the more it rings true" (10). Even if launched, Schwenger adds, a missile cannot escape paradox but becomes even more paradoxical: "If a missive, it bears a message that, upon reaching its destination, annihilates it; in a sense, then, it can never reach that destination. It can never deliver a message that is annihilated along with the addressee and, quite likely, the sender" (10). For Schwenger, there is no nuclear referent, finally, nor "deconstructive processes that endlessly postpone closure," nor even endings, really, but only what he calls "undecidability itself, a 'burning' of logocentrism which is, nevertheless, an *effect*" (18) yet includes a return inquiry to its origins.

To return to Derrida's essay, then, where he establishes the pre-eminence of this unnamable nuclear referent and then describes the way it paradoxically deconstructs, rather than shapes, our understanding of temporal differences, he provides yet a further paradox in his final missive: "*The name of nuclear war is the name of the first war which can be fought in the name of the name alone, that is, of everything and of nothing*" (30). Since nuclear annihilation can only be thought of as "wholly other," or "a hypothesis, a phantasm, of total self-destruction," it "can only come about in the name of that which is worth more than life" (30). But for Derrida, the deep irony of what such a name would be is that, with annihilation, even the name of that which is worth more than life "can no longer be borne, transmitted, inherited by anything living, that name in the name of which war would take place would be the name of nothing, it would be pure name" (30–31). The only possible objective a nuclear war can have is nothingness, that which cannot be named.

In summary, then, in characterizing the crisis for poetry in the age of annihilation, Wyschogrod's conception of poetry is especially useful on two scores: first, by casting our knowledge of annihilation as an a priori, though not as transcendent, truth, she creates a theoretical *context* for a nuclear referent without valorizing that referent. Second, her recognition of the place of the expression of love, as a part of "techne" and "poesis," opens the possibility for merging in poetic language the concerns of an individual's passions with the larger reality of global annihilation. Yet she assigns meaning for that language primarily within the realm of social interaction, rather than to universal or immanent truth. On the other hand, beyond Schell's and Des Pres's subversion of the efficacy of poetry, Adorno undermines any adherence to poetic language as purposefully restorative (or positivist) through his negative dialectic, by which art cannot authentically represent the post-Auschwitz world without at least gesturing toward how that world dangles on the verge of extinction. Nonetheless, rather than dismiss poetry as pointless, Adorno discerns a more paradoxical function for it, as an expression of nihilism that serves, in effect, to suspend nothingness itself as an absolute referent. As an "anti-metaphysical invective," therefore, poetry helps maintain the vital link between potential meaning and potential meaninglessness. Finally, though the whimsicality and self-referentiality of Derrida's writing might suggest a cold distance from the post-Auschwitz world that so deeply engages Lifton, Adorno, Wyschogrod, and others, if we allow ourselves to take him seriously, his essay on the nuclear referent binds even more tightly the pervasive threat of nuclear annihilation to the demand that poets respond because, he asks, what else is there for them to do? In fact, as Schwenger interprets Derrida, "the 'unassimilable wholly other' of nuclear holocaust . . . is akin to the otherness that lies both beyond and within any text," with the task for literature being how to participate in that "ultimate deconstruction" without becoming nothing but more "fuel for the holocaust" (69).

By extrapolation from Derrida's deconstruction of the nuclear referent, and as an enhancement of Schell's paradox—as I see it—the challenge to the poet in the nuclear age consists of how, on the one hand, to confront and express the overwhelming sense one has of potential technological annihilation, not only of individuals but of the archive of human knowledge, as a subject of one's art, without, on the other hand, denying that there can ultimately be no meaningful name given to that subject except the "non-name of 'name' " or nothingness itself. In other words, if in the realm of nuclearism the most important subject to write about is unnamable, is nothingness itself, in what way other than by writing nothing at all is a poet to approach it? Is there any way, or ways? Or does nuclear annihilation, in fact, render poetry of the sort Heidegger praises so highly obsolete, leaving room only for the trivial meanderings of those too psychically numb to nuclearism to address it?

From the evidence in contemporary American poetry, there is no question that poets have sought (and, I contend, found) ways other than waxing hysterical or remaining silent when faced with nuclearism. While it may be true that poetry in the United States does not enjoy the kind of sanctified pre-eminence Heidegger assigns it, neither does it suffer quite the deconstructive stasis that Derrida insinuates threatens nuclear age literature.

For instance, by reading deeply into Derrida's own methods, Schwenger uncovers in literature and art the very sources of hope needed for reconstituting thought itself and posing a counter to nuclear disaster. One promising version of literature for him consists of what he calls "the sacrificial text" (such as Thomas Pynchon's *Gravity's Rainbow*), an art that in its deconstructive technique manages to "dismantle the ego's construction" and therefore, by displacing the principle of self that underlies our capacity for nuclear war, establishes "patterns . . . of a text that extends beyond the borders of self." By enabling individual "identity" to "give way before a crucial difference" (89), the sacrificial text opens the way for cultural (and therefore presumably political) change. Another type is the speculative text (such as Tim O'Brien's *The Nuclear Age*) which, by encountering "the blank abyss" and eventually finding the "right words" to express its overwhelming presence, "will not cover the abyss but manifest it, and evoke that which is beyond articulation" (121). While such a text, he admits, may provide "no statement . . . , no political program, no conceptual system, scarcely anything that could be called content," instead, by its unpredictable moves toward paradox, it "explodes" in the mind so that, "at least momentarily, we approach Otherness," an otherness akin to that found in the bomb as well as in "a future that is other than the present in which we try to make our home" (121–22). This art-induced "explosion in the mind" can serve as a "metaphor for imagination's disastrous force" and, "in the very space of disaster," provide us opportunity "to imagine a future" (122).

While Schwenger makes a formidable argument for nuclear-age literature's radical suspension of even the most basic premises, therein opening the way for new "modes of thinking" emerging from deconstructive texts, as William J. Scheick and Catherine Rainwater point out in their critique of him, he may too easily accept that hope automatically lies in change, when in fact change itself "is merely a *condition* of human experience, a process beyond any objective designations of good or bad" (354). Indeed, they add, "to designate any aspect of change as inherently good is—*contra*-deconstructive theory—to confine structurally what is only a neutral, non-evaluable process of repetition and difference" (354). Although mostly left to supply his own ethics not readily available in Derrida, Jacques Lacan, and Maurice Blanchot, his primary sources, Schwenger relies heavily on the self-referentiality of deconstructive methodology, even while creating a valuable theoretical space for *constructive* change.

Taking a more pragmatic position than Schwenger, Solomon, on the other hand, soundly disagrees with Derrida's formulation of the "suspension of calculation and belief in the face of the 'unheard-of.' " Rather, in emphasizing the need to think more "realistically" about the nuclear threat than Derrida does, he proposes what he calls "potentialist realism" or "potentialist metaphysics," a theory he builds on Aristotle's definitions of actuality and potentiality, wherein "the futurity of the nuclear referent is bound to the present not only by a tie of logical possibility but by one of empirical potentiality as well, a potentiality that *can* be calculated through the calculus of probability" (28–29). We can, Solomon argues, say *something* meaningful as well as make useful distinctions about potential nuclear annihilation without merely uttering nonsense or noise, because "our apprehension . . . of the nuclear referent is determined not only by our archival imagination [as Derrida would have it] but also by our knowledge of an extra-archival world that is as real in its dispositional potentialities as in its actuated formalities" (29).[16] In a rigorous attempt to establish a nuclear criticism that avoids the pitfall of infinite regression, an inherent danger in deconstructionism,[17] Solomon argues for the *political* necessity of making meaningful distinctions that influence *political* decisions, as well as the urgent need for critical theorists to "speak to power on a common ground," not just in their own self-perpetuating forms of discourse, if they hope realistically to have any impact on nuclear policy. "The place for nuclear criticism," Solomon concludes, "is the place of realism, a space from which nuclear criticism could compare and evaluate the various 'beliefs' that have been represented in the political debate surrounding the nuclear referent, arguing that not all beliefs are equal and not all possibilities the same" (274–75).

By extension, we can apply Solomon's thesis to poetry: Despite his contention that "poetry is not going to solve the concrete problems of the nuclear age," in its creative linguistic variety, poetry can embody the same range of "beliefs" that Solomon finds in general public discourse. Further, by opening itself to internal scrutiny, as Schwenger would have it—that is, by employing language for the deliberate purpose of self-revelation rather than self-protection or deception in the way language is habitually used in "non-creative" modes of discourse— poetry can in fact articulate the foundations for a change of whatever kind and imaginatively participate in "the very sliding signs, the radical instability of language" which forms the basis of Schwenger's principle of hope. In doing so, as art, it can embody Schwenger's "postal principle, which is a principle of motion [that] thus becomes also a principle of preservation" (22), while in its accessibility it can also explore the limits of the "common ground" Solomon seeks. In other words, without necessarily having to address itself directly to those in power (though some poems do just that), poetry can nonetheless "imagine the real" in a way that opens, rather than closes, language's possibilities to express the present, even in the shadow of its own eradication. And whether it witnesses change or not, in its precise though complex presentation of the present, more than in its transcendent or imaginative rendering of the future, it can create options for that future that may include survival.[18] Without having to lay claim to universality or transcendence, poetry can still, to paraphrase Theodore Roethke, learn by going where it has to go—not only as an agent *for* change but as an agent *of* change.

Contrary Ways of Nothingness in Two Poems by Gertrude Stein and William Carlos Williams

At what point did American poetry become aware of potential nuclear annihilation? Concerning science fiction, both Paul Brians and Dowling date the era of the depiction of nuclear annihilation from the publication of R. Cromie's *The Crack of Doom* in 1895 (Brians 4; Dowling 2). With poets, however, I hesitate to set a pre-1945 date, not because poems about apocalypse and annihilation do not exist, but rather because tracing them back in time would inevitably lead to the Bible or further.[19] It would not be difficult to trace the stylistic, symbolic, and thematic characteristics of most contemporary poems on nuclear anxiety to powerful predecessors of eschatological poetry in English, including such prophetic nineteenth-century works as Byron's "Darkness," Browning's "Childe Roland to the Dark Tower Came," and Hardy's "The Darkling Thrush." Those poems, of course, draw on earlier portraits of the world's end, for as Kermode rightly asserts, "The apocalyptic types—empire, decadence and renovation, progress and catastrophe—are fed by history and underlie our ways of making sense of the world from where we stand, in the middest" (29). Indeed, for most readers, many of the most prominent modernist poems are in fact also treatments of nothingness, whether as an apocalypse, a cultural barrenness, or a state of individual angst, notably Eliot's *The Waste Land* (1922) and "The Hollow Men" (1925), Yeats's "The Second Coming," and Archibald MacLeish's sonnet "The End of the World" (1926), with its eerily prophetic description of global holocaust, as well as several poems by

Wallace Stevens, including, for instance, "The Snow Man" (1921), which I discuss in chapter 5.[20] Less well known predecessors of contemporary verse, however, might include several poems in Weldon Kees's first collection *The Last Man* (1943), a book inordinately preoccupied with not only the death of individuals but, to use Schell's phrase, the "second death" of culture and time itself.

In one poem, "To the North," Kees laments the lack of things from the past worthy of praise, forcing the mind to "crouch, suspicious, veer away,/ And focus into idiot light" the terrors of the present, "Where the horror of history from cave/ To camp to the coffins of yesterday/ Burns to a single ash" (28). But in a closing that echoes MacLeish's sestet in "The End of the World," Kees's poem not only attempts to imagine annihilation, but, in wondering about the "grave/ Of Time," raises the question of how to do so:

> Where is the grave
> Of Time? What would you picture for decay?
> A horse's hoof, white bones, a lifeless tree,
> Cold hemispheres, dried moss, and a blue wave
> Breaking at noon on shores you will not see.

To depict devastation, Kees's poem uses prototypical images of lifelessness that anticipate both the material proximity to and psychic distance from annihilation which Adorno posits as part of any "human" response to the world after Auschwitz, a response I shall explore further in chapters 2 and 3. The point here is not that Kees's poem prophesies nuclear war, but that like *The Waste Land* and "The Second Coming" it employs the kind of language, imagery, and metaphor later poets have inevitably drawn on and swerved away from in conceptualizing annihilation.

Beyond Kees's work, though, two important poems that lay a practical framework for approaching post-Hiroshima poetry in the United States are Gertrude Stein's "Reflection on the Atomic Bomb" and William Carlos Williams's "Asphodel, That Greeny Flower." While Stein's prose poem addresses the potential bankruptcy of imagination awaiting the poet who takes on the nuclear threat (implying therefore a resistance to it), Williams demonstrates quite conversely how that threat can permeate poetic subject matter itself, implying therefore that we must imagine it before we can resist it. Despite their widely different approaches, though, both poems clearly protest the threat of annihilation, even as they imagine the nothingness it projects.

Composed in 1946, "Reflection" begins with Stein recalling how, when asked for her thoughts on the atomic bomb, she said she "had not been able to take any interest in it" (*Reflection* 161). Applying a self-enclosed logic similar to Derrida's in "No Apocalypse, Not Now," Stein argues about the bombs, "What is the use, if they are really as destructive as all that there is nothing left and if there is nothing there nobody to be interested and nothing to be interested about." The use of the word "there" here is reminiscent of Stein's famous line about her home in Oakland, California—"There is no there there"—but the operative word is "interested"; why be interested when there is "nothing to be interested about?" On the other hand, if the bombs are "not as destructive as all that then they are just a little more or less destructive than other things," which means they cannot have the power of annihilation: "There are always lots left on this earth to be interested or to be willing." By stating her view in dichotomous terms, as well as in the energetic, playful syntax that characterizes all her work, Stein dismisses the apparent uncertainty of the bomb's power by reassuring us that it is in fact not so uncertain but merely what it is, and "nobody else can do anything about it so you have to just live along like always."[21]

Here begins the poem's subtle message to resist the predominant aura of the bomb's power. With the power to annihilate, it eliminates all interest; without the power to annihilate, it is "not any more interesting than any other machine, and machines are only interesting in being invented or in what they do, so why be interested." Once invented, the bomb has no more interest than "everybody's secret weapon," but "that it has to be secret makes it dull and meaningless." To Stein, "it's the living that are interesting not the way of killing them," because any interest in destruction can only be sustained with "a lot left living."[22] In what starts as a poem that shrugs off the bomb as not even worth passing attention, Stein ends with an affirmation of life not only authoritative in tone, but delightful in its imaginative play with the tropes of reason. She closes her reflection almost as though she were reciting a fairy tale:

Alright, that is the way I feel about it. And really way down that is the way everybody feels about it. They think they are interested about the atomic bomb but they really are not not any more than I am. Really not. They may be a little scared, I am not so scared, there is so much to be scared of so what is the use of bothering to be scared, and if you are not scared the atomic bomb is not interesting.[23]

> Everybody gets so much information all day long that they lose their common sense. They listen so much that they forget to be natural. This is a nice story. (*Reflection* 161)

Contending that Stein tries to combat militarism with aestheticism, Rob Wilson finds her tone, despite its overt irony, "morally untenable, a modernist illusion of private superiority smugly sustained" (252). Similarly, Dewey considers its "ennui" representative of the "bored response" of the Lost Generation upon discovering itself "radically out of place as history had spontaneously created the Last Generation" (7–8). However, if one object of creative writing is less to shape public policy than to imagine an alternate "way of nothingness," Stein succeeds in gaining her reader's compliance—in that, were it not for the fear they induce, atomic weapons would command less attention than combine harvesters, since what they produce is nothing at all. Yet at the same time, she directs her rhythmic sentences toward "common sense," in order to tease us out of the assumption that atomic weapons are a "natural" part of the world. Her fairy-tale style, in fact, arguably subverts the self-assured tone of most scientific and technological "experts" by reducing their ideas to nothing but "information" in the way a feminist reconstruction of language can undermine the self-sustaining power of patriarchal rhetoric. This stylistic defense of Stein's prose poem is not to make a greater claim for its scope or universality than it makes for itself; it is, after all, only a "reflection." But in her probing of nothingness and in her undoing of dichotomous paradigms, she establishes one fundamental role for the imaginative writer (outside of science fiction) in the nuclear age: to confront annihilation's otherness without capitulating to its seductive power.

In his major love poem, "Asphodel, That Greeny Flower," originally meant to be included in Part V of *Paterson* and the final poem in *Journey to Love* (1955), Williams establishes a more heroic role for the poet than Stein does: to explore how annihilation has become an integral part of the self. Composed after he had had two strokes and struggled with his mental health, Williams's thirty-page poem, which Robert Lowell praises as "a triumph of simple confession" (*Prose* 44), grapples with the subject of the poet's infidelities, as he entreats his wife Flossie not to allow her love for him to die. "I cannot say/ that I have gone to hell/ for your love/ but often/ found myself there/ in your pursuit," writes the impassioned elder poet to his wife of over forty years, "I do not like it/ and wanted to be/ in heaven" (314). With its sustained image of the asphodel, together with its rich allusions to art and literature, and its slowly emerging image of light, the poem weaves a complex argument for nurturing and revering love in the face not only of life's and the poet's failures but of death:

> I have learned much in my life
>> from books
>>> and out of them
> about love.
>> Death
>>> is not the end of it. (314)

In a defense of the need for a poet to test the boundaries of life, Williams invokes the imagination's power to sustain beauty as well as love, going so far as to recall "Helen's public fault" as the source that "bred" the *Iliad* (315). Given the perennial power of Homer's epic, even death cannot bring love and art to an end.

However, in Book II Williams introduces what *does* have the power to annihilate art and love. First, though without wishing to make inordinate claims for poetry's place in nature, he affirms its place, writing, "The poem/ if it reflects the sea/ reflects only/ its dance/ upon that profound depth/ where/ it seems to triumph" (321). But then, suddenly, he interrupts this reverie:

> The bomb puts an end
>> to all that.
> I am reminded
>> that the bomb
>>> also
> is a flower
>> dedicated
>>> howbeit
> to our destruction.
>> The mere picture
>>> of the exploding bomb
> fascinates us
>> so that we cannot wait
>>> to prostrate ourselves
> before it. We do not believe
>> that love
>>> can so wreck our lives.
> The end
>> will come
>>> in its time.

Meanwhile
    we are sick to death
        of the bomb
and its childlike
    insistence.
        Death is no answer,
no answer—   (321–22)

By describing the bomb (like love) as "also" a flower—akin to the asphodel with its combination of original sweetness and, over time, "cu-
rious odor,/ a moral odor" (312)—Williams accords it as central a place
for his sensibility as it is marginal for Stein's, even anticipating Lifton's
diagnosis of "nuclear fundamentalism" by almost three decades ("We
cannot wait/ to prostrate ourselves/ before it"). He laments that "we do
not believe/ that love/ can so wreck our lives" as the bomb can, but the
pun on "that" here as both a relative and a demonstrative pronoun creates an ambiguity that ironically equates love of the bomb's destructiveness with physical love (which, the poet realizes, can also destroy).
Yet no matter which love he has in mind, Williams registers his dismay
at his own time's preoccupation with the wrong kind of power. Thinking again of Homer, he goes on to castigate us for not recognizing (as
Wyschogrod, for instance, proposes) that the potentially more enduring
power is interpersonal love:

There is no power
    so great as love
        which is a sea,
which is a garden —
    as enduring
        as the verses
of that blind old man
    destined
        to live forever.
Few men believe that
    nor in the games of children.
        They believe rather
in the bomb
    and shall die by
        the bomb. (322)

Given the complex, secular portrait of love in Williams's poem, embodied in the ambiguous, mushroom-cloud image of the asphodel (as op-

posed to the more classical and layered rose, for instance), the bomb as a counterforce to human interaction not only represents a rupture in the love between his wife and him, nor is it merely symbolic of mass death, but by the end of Book II, it also comes to encompass "all suppressions,/ from the witchcraft trials at Salem/ to the latest/ book burnings"; though we "come to our deaths/ in silence," the bomb "speaks" and "has entered our lives/ to destroy us" (324). In short, it is ubiquitous, not just as an image of individual death or technological oppression, but as an agent of psychic annihilation.

The remarkable fluidity with which the image of atomic annihilation enters "Asphodel," a poem whose author was "at heart apolitical"[24] (Mariani 651), is testimony to the profound impact it has had on the American poetic imagination. More significantly, though, its image appears in one of Williams's most eloquent acclamations of the power of love and, with love, of poetry itself. "While Williams wished to show that poetry was as *true* and as important as science," comments Lisa Steinman, "he wished also to rescue poetry from competing with science for the truth" (104), so instead he carves out a charged poetics that gives poetry a critical role to play in post-war America, a role that includes exploring, as "Asphodel" does, "the interconnectedness between the multiple spheres in which he and his readers live—the personal, the political, the biological, and the historical" (108).

It is in Book I, for example, where Williams argues that the "news/ of something/ that concerns you/ and concerns many men" can only be found in "despised poems," adding, "It is difficult/ to get the news from poems/ yet men die miserably every day/ for lack/ of what is found there" (318). And in the poem's Coda he dramatically celebrates the power of light—not only Einstein's light which "for all time shall outspeed/ the thunder crack" (335), not only the light at Flossie's and his wedding over forty years earlier when he "thought the world/ stood still" (336), but light as the very embodiment of love and the imagination, light that though "inseparable from the fire" still "takes precedence over it" (333):

> Do not hasten
> > laugh and play
> in an eternity
> > the heat will not overtake the light. ʳ
> > > That's sure.
> That gelds the bomb,
> > permitting
> > > that the mind contain it. (334)

Love and "that sweetest interval,/ when love will blossom," (334) enact the greatest of the creative powers of the human spirit. Annihilation is not inevitable, Williams is insisting, and the destructiveness of the bomb can be gelded, but only if the imagination "contain it," rather than it subduing the imagination. Despite its power to end all things, the bomb can be *both* resisted *and* imagined, because, as Williams proclaims,

> Only the imagination is real!
> I have declared it
> time without end. (334)

By intermingling the image of the bomb with the most intimate of his concerns, Williams grants it a central place in his imagination, where he might "contain it," rather than attempt to isolate it the way Stein does. Taken together, though, the self-consciously dismissive humor of "Reflection" and the heroic dignity of "Asphodel" represent disparate yet complementary approaches to nuclearism, in that both ultimately seek sanctuary from the threat of nothingness not just by denying or defying it but by enlisting the imagination to help grasp its implications. Only that which involves "the living" is "interesting" to Gertrude Stein, and for Williams, "Light, the imagination/ and love" are the things "in our age,/ by natural law,/ which we worship" and which "maintain/ all of a piece/ their dominance" (335). For both poets, the atom bomb threatens to eradicate the field the mind plays in and so must be resisted, by the mind if by nothing else. Undoubtedly, the most effective way for the mind to resist annihilation is to keep thinking, to "laugh and play/ in an eternity"—not only by "imagining the real," but by realizing the imaginary as well, that is, by going the way of nothingness imposed by the technology of the bomb.

Only in that twofold manner can we create a full vision by which we might see our way through nothingness into somethingness, a vision that will allow us to think through, and thereby to contain, "the unthinkable." To adapt William J. Scheick's definition of nuclear criticism in this context, we might say that the poetry of annihilation offers "a re-minding, a hoped-for reinterpretation of communal memory . . . that would contribute to a revision of human consciousness" appropriate to the tenuous reality of contemporary nuclearism. But such revision requires more than "a mere leap of faith; it requires a deliberate leap of the human mind into the seemingly far-fetched . . . , a fetching from afar . . . , a seeing anew, within the matter-of-fact rational boundaries of the ordinary" ("Nuclear" 6). Though others may be more adept at putting ideas into action, by following the example of Stein and Williams, poets are among those best equipped to speculate on nothingness, to fetch from afar, and to imagine ways that bring that vision into focus. It remains now to see how they have begun to do so.

TWO

Nuclear Protest Poetry

"All We/got/to Do Is Keep/on/poeting": Nuclearism and Protest

Nuclear protest poetry, that which speaks *against* nuclearism, is undoubtedly what first comes to mind as nuclear-age poetry. Sometimes erroneously referred to as "political" poetry, as though any other kind of poem had no political or ideological relevance, protest poetry in general gained notoriety in the United States during the Vietnam War era, building on the polemical style of the Beat poetry of the 1950s.[1] Since that time, literary magazines and presses throughout the country have frequently printed special issues and anthologies of creative work attacking the political establishment on behalf of a variety of causes, including the "anti-nuke movement," as it has often been called to its own detriment.[2] Despite its limited audience, this poetry has inspired citizens and nurtured solidarity among political activists, if nothing else. But in a country whose readership of any poetry remains small in relation to the size of its literate populace, what influence, if any, has it had on those in power or those who consult policy makers? Since protest poetry intends to speak *directly* to those responsible for nuclear proliferation, for instance, it is difficult not to wonder about its audience. Does protest poetry reach only the converted, or does it have a broader impact on public opinion and state policy?

Arguments for and against the political efficacy of poetry predate the nuclear age by several millenia,[3] and, short of a sociological investigation, it is impossible to verify the practical social consequences of any art. In our time, debates over the conflict between poetry and propaganda have been stirred again not only by the specter of nuclear war but by the public awareness of other social issues, including ecological threats, human and civil rights abuses, imperialist incursions, ethnic strife, economic injustices, and racial oppression. Meanwhile, discussions about the role of protest poetry in the United States tend to focus on the division between the private nature of poetry and the public nature of political discourse, on the poet's obligation to language and music rather than to ideology and praxis, and on the struggle between spirituality and social engagement in poetic expression[4]—with virtually no one suggesting that, despite the minimal success at best any poem might have in altering policy, poets should cease writing about nuclear or other issues.

How have nuclear protest poets seen their poems functioning, then? From what they say, American poets tend to see themselves as playing anything from an activist role of promoting (usually left-wing) views in order unabashedly to sway readers (and through them legislators), to a more humanistic role of producing "a personal kind of expression, and work which not only expresses concern for life and living, but does so with the artist's skill" (Sklar 6). This range of positions is particularly evident in a collection of statements made by a diverse group of poets in 1982. On 26 May of that year, Galway Kinnell (whose poem "The Fundamental Project of Technology" remains one of the most oft-cited poems in protest of nuclear weaponry) organized a benefit reading entitled "Poets against the End of the World" at Town Hall in New York City in anticipation of the nationwide June 12th rally for a nuclear freeze. Hoping to display as broad a sampling of the spectrum of American poets as possible, both ethnically and aesthetically (though not, apparently, politically, since neither pro-Reagan nor pro-military poets were present), Kinnell and his committee invited thirteen poets to read their work and later to contribute to a written symposium. In explaining his motivations for the reading, whose participants ranged from W. S. Merwin and Josephine Miles to June Jordan and Simon Ortiz, Kinnell noted that the nuclear issue "isn't political in quite the same sense that poems about El Salvador or South Africa are. It is possible to approach the nuclear issue from a very basic point of view that has nothing to do with public policy. It has to do with one's feelings that one wants to live. So, it's a kind of issue that a so-called very political poet and a so-called very nonpolitical poet could join together on" (Daniels 295), since their joint project is "to affirm the sacred character of life" (Kinnell 301).

In their responses to the symposium, several activist poets on Kinnell's slate tend to disagree with his largely humanist position. Jane Cooper, David Ignatow, and Stanley Kunitz reinforce what Kinnell believes, each expressing hope that her or his poetry might raise political consciousness of nuclearism by providing imaginative ways to wrestle with the nuclear dilemma. But in contrast, rather than unite poets and poetries, Amiri Baraka hopes the nuclear threat might politicize "those spawned on the elitism of literary reaction of the 'new criticism' or structuralism" so they might join with the protest poets and "come together around other important issues, such as the struggle for democracy by the oppressed nationalities and women and hopefully one day against monopoly capitalism/imperialism itself" (Kinnell 304). Simon Ortiz similarly defines protest poetry as an open critique of state policies when he writes, "The fighters against repression and exploitation in Guatemala and El Salvador are struggling against those same economic interests that Native Americans in the U.S. have fought. This is what must be understood by everyone who is concerned about the continuance of life. If we don't, we will not be able to fully comprehend what the present nuclear threat means and how it is used against us" (Kinnell 315–16). Also, June Jordan, though more succinctly than Baraka and Ortiz, asserts her belief that "life demands an always vigiliant dedication to justice and that justice depends upon the absolute support of self-determination everywhere in the world. As I am a poet I express what I believe, and I fight whatever I oppose, in poetry" (Kinnell 308). Unfettered by Kinnell's self-consciousness about protest poetry, Jordan frankly equates literary work with political action.

Between Kinnell's universalism and Jordan's activism stand poets who attempt to reconcile humanist poetics with dissident politics. Lacking Jordan's resolve, a more resigned Philip Levine nevertheless feels obliged to protest nuclearism in poetry, though he holds little hope that it might change matters. Thinking of the men in the Pentagon, Levine confesses, "I do not believe in the power of my poetry or any poetry I know to touch such men in a way that would prevent them from obeying the order to attack or retaliate. . . . I hope I am wrong" (Kinnell 314). Yet he still feels compelled to voice his opposition. Taking a less somber view, Denise Levertov sees the writing of protest poetry as only one of many activities individuals can do to precipitate change, such as writing letters or staging public rallies. "Poets should never moan and groan over not having produced political poems—it may simply not accord with their muse," Levertov reasons. "But in that case, they should find some other useful thing to do in relation to their political concern" (Kinnell 312), including using whatever "prestige" they have to influence their admirers. Rather than get sidetracked by the uncertain impact of protest poetry, Levertov realizes that her literary efforts, like other political actions, are sometimes effective and sometimes not. Etheridge Knight, too, disregards arguments over the nature of protest poetry by collapsing dichotomies: "The poet as individual, and the people, as collective—or community—*whatever* affects, or disaffects, them—be it a poem or a pistol, is political," writes Knight, so that, in keeping with Levine's sense of the necessity of protest, it is incumbent upon the poet to accept his or her political responsibility: "Because it/is/activity, the politics of Pound and Eliot/is/preferable to nonpolitics. And just as surely as celibacy/is/a sexist position, nonpolitics is the most rigid of all political stances. And the most dangerous" (Kinnell 309). By inverse logic, Knight concludes that not to write protest poetry is tantamount to complicity with the state, so in order to exercise one's political convictions "all we/got/to do is to keep/on/poeting" (Kinnell 310).

In adopting this attitude, Knight echoes W. H. Auden's essay "The Poet & the City," in which he argues that "in our age the mere making of a work of art is itself a political act," and any protest poem, "even if it is not terribly good, even if it appeals only to a handful of people," serves to "remind" the state both of the interior lives of its populace and of the fact that that populace is watching it, ready to dismantle it the moment its offensive machinery gets out of hand (51). Rather than judge nuclear protest poetry according to whether it influences policy, then, or whether it aesthetically "transcends" nuclear issues, we are better off examining *how* it articulates its resistance to annihilation. While it may neither enforce nor precipitate sociopolitical change on a broad scale, it could do so—at least as effectively as any other citizen action in a democracy[5]—so we must consider what as art it stands *for* as well as what it stands *against*.

In this light, discerning whether nuclear protest poetry is "terribly good" depends to some degree on its ability to overcome solipsism in order to confront political realities. James Scully, for instance, draws a distinction between "protest poetry," which "tends to be reactive, victim-oriented, incapacitated, lacking the theoretical and practical coherence that could give it muscle and point," and "dissident poetry," which "does not respect boundaries between private and public, self and other" and "talks back" in order to "act as part of the world, not simply as a mirror of it" (5). The difference between such poetries for Scully depends less on conflicts in ideology than on a poet's ability to make meaningful connections "between social empowerment and valorization and human definition." What matters is that the poet engage nuclear politics directly and forcefully, rather than be overly preoccupied with his or her personal sense of victimization.

Here from a small press anthology is an example of what Scully might call a "protest poem" by Margaret Key Biggs:

> Dirty Words
> I was caught up
> with a bunch of graffiti freaks
> whose highs come from
> the ubiquitous scrawling
> on bathroom walls.
> A clean wall was more disgraceful
> than the draft, to them.
> For my initiation
> they found a virgin wall,
> gave me a new can of spray paint,
> and told me to write
> the vilest, filthiest words
> I could summon.
> With great care I wrote:
> WAR—NUKES—MELTDOWN (Shipley 8)

Unafraid of using a stock metaphor ("virgin wall") or excessive phrasing ("The vilest, filthiest words/ I could summon"), Biggs clearly cares more for rendering her subject accessible and shocking her reader than for engaging the subtleties of language. In fact, the poem focuses more on her reaction to the nuclear presence than on the weapons and power themselves. Yet by depicting the act of spray painting the bare wall, almost as a crude sexual gesture, Biggs's open-faced language reperforms on our "virgin" minds what the spray painter performs on the wall; the poem tarnishes us with its nuclear awareness.[6] Consciously enlisting disruptive imagery, Biggs endeavors to effect real change in our attitude by villifying the nuclear establishment and shaking us into seeing it as pornographic. But given the flatness of the language, her poem does not sufficiently acknowledge the complexity of its own protest. In its eagerness to identify an enemy, it can be dangerously polarizing, rather than promoting the peace it seeks. Moreover, in protesting against the violence of nuclear bombs, by enacting the symbolic violence of hateful graffiti (such as that used in the anti-Semitic desecration of tombstones, for instance), is Biggs not inadvertently employing some of the methods of nuclearism she finds so offensive? Or as an open protest, does her language only induce shock, not condone violence? (And as a related question among activists themselves, is the use of violence against nuclear powers justifiable?)

Veteran protest (or "dissident") poets such as Sonia Sanchez, Gary Snyder, Allen Ginsberg, and Denise Levertov may handle nuclear issues with more aplomb than writers such as Biggs, yet the protest in their work is no less ambiguous. Even one as understated as Robert Creeley, when asked to respond to a policy of nuclear proliferation (a policy of which no poet I have read has come out unironically in favor), asks his readers to act against the status quo. In "On Saul Bellow's Thesis, That We Think Our Era's Awful Because We'll Die In It," Creeley's language remains characteristically succinct, yet in this poem, as in most protest poetry, after introducing the idea of extinction ("And there won't even be a you left // to contest this most meager provision/ your life"), the final couplet subtly but unquestionably places a responsibility on "you," namely, "the one presumably who's living" this life, to begin living by "contesting" for what meager provision there is in an age of impending extinction (Sklar 104).

In the same anthology in which Creeley's poem appears, the well-known activist (though not so well-known poet) Daniel Berrigan argues for taking social responsibility through reverse logic. His poem "Biography" opens by telling us that he was "born alive" on St. Gregory's Day in 1921 but "born dead" on "Hiroshima Day, 1945." Then through a se-

ries of contrasts, he calls himself a "casualty of Hiroshima" who is
"marked now/ by the stigma of those fires": "Presumably dead, I have
nothing to lose to death. Pre-/ sumed living, I have nothing to refuse life.
Or so I hope" (Sklar 180). He concludes, in other words, that we have
nothing to lose in resisting nuclearism, since fundamentally it has already overcome us. Without hesitation, Berrigan is urging us to join the
antinuclear cause.

Taking a more declamatory position, Sonia Sanchez's "Reflections
After the June 12th March for Disarmament" uses a rhetoric reminiscent of civil rights and peace movement speeches during the 1960s and
70s. The poem is developed over nineteen "verse clauses," each one
starting with "I" and ending with a semi-colon until the final one. The
first ten of these (with slight variations) use the anaphora "I have come
to you tonite," as Sanchez provides a litany of the sufferings and ac-
complishments of African-Americans, in order to argue that "those
years/ were not in vain, the ghosts of our/ ancestors searching this american dust for/ rest were not in vain, black women/ walking their lives
in clots were not/ in vain" (65). Then, yoking together the history of nuclear warfare and the history of slavery, the eighth clause identifies an
enemy, the "inhumanitarians in the world." They may have been called

> explorers, soldiers, mercenaries,
> imperialists, missionaries, adventurers,
> but they looked at the world for what
> it would give up to them (66)

In the tenth clause, Sanchez calls not just for the "stoppage" of nuclear
power plants and weapons, but "to stop the proliferation/ of nuclear
minds, of nuclear generals/ of nuclear presidents, of nuclear scientists,/
who spread human and nuclear waste" (67). Then the next three clauses
accelerate the poem's urgency by dropping the "have" ("I come to you
because") and speaking to the world's needs, rather than its threats. And
the last five switch to "I am here":

> I am here to move against
>   leaving our shadows implanted on the
>   earth while our bodies disintegrate in
>   nuclear lightning;
> I am here between the voices of our ancestors
>   and the noise of the planet,
>   between the surprise of death and life;

. . . .

I am here to say to you:
  my body is full of veins
  like the bombs waiting to burst
  with blood.
  we must learn to suckle life not
  bombs and rhetoric
  rising up in redwhiteandblue patriotism (68)

Sanchez's oral poetry is undoubtedly enhanced not only by its performance but by the dynamic tension of its context—hundreds of thousands of people gathered in the name of nuclear disarmament. Moreover, it affirms the necessity for collaboration among those engaged
in various "liberal" causes, anticipating, for instance, Jesse Jackson's
"rainbow coalition" during the 1984 presidential election campaign.
But because few, if any, of her listeners or readers are likely to identify
themselves as the "inhumanitarians" in her poem,[7] she inspires agreement, setting up an opposition to the "nuclear minds" which may finally valorize them by demonizing them. Regardless, the strength of
Sanchez's poem lies in its clarity and mood—a "nuclear mind" *could*
understand it—and there is no unintentional complicity in her method,
as in Biggs's poem.

Another occasional poem composed not for an actual event but an
imagined one, Alan Williamson's "Recitation for the Dismantling of a
Hydrogen Bomb," while contrasting Sanchez's poem by opting for a
conversational, rather than an incantatory, voice, nevertheless further
underscores the shared commitment of nuclear protest poetry to exert
power for social change. Composed virtually as a prayer, Williamson's
poem addresses the underground nuclear missiles themselves, personi-
fying them as spirits to be exorcised. He meditates on their potential to
be used or survived and compares them to other "things too big for us
[which] have been sung to sleep/ once we knew we couldn't, or no
longer wished to,/ kill them" (*Muse* 64). Through the conceit of a person with cancer who attends "a class where doctors . . . / . . . teach those
in permanent pain to focus/ on one word, and cross their legs in the right
way,/ as if singing, silently, to the thing in themselves," Williamson invokes the power of music "to sing" the missiles as a hidden disease out
from their underground silos. Then extending this conceit, he sees international missile treaties as "surface anesthesia/ for our tireless fear
of each other" which may eventually allow for the surgical dismantling
of the missiles "like taking up hands/ against some larger shape of ourselves" (*Muse* 65). Finally, he says to the bomb,

Go to sleep in us, as once, they say,
God went to sleep, and we trembled, not only that nothing
any longer overarched us, but that we
must contain what had. (*Muse* 65)

Though not as didactic in his call for disarmament, Williamson shares
with Biggs and Berrigan an unambiguous repulsion for the weapons and
with Sanchez a faith in poetry's power to help eliminate them. His use
of the word "contain" recalls William Carlos Williams's assertion that
the imagination must "contain" the bomb, before it possesses us, but
Williamson further compares the weapons to God, as he imagines their
demise.

More complex protests against nuclearism than in these poems can
be found in the sustained work of socially conscious poets. Enthusiastic readers of Gary Snyder's "eco-poetry" and "ethnopoetics," for instance, argue for its radical quality across volumes, even when they believe that its vision lies in private insight more than in public prophesy.[8]
As Charles Molesworth has argued, "Only [Charles] Olson . . . compares
with [Snyder] in terms of a mythic imagination, and only Levertov has
as broad and deep a political consciousness"; nevertheless Molesworth
still questions Snyder's "authority other than that of the aesthetic
realm" (105). Resting as it does on an interpretation of Zen Buddhism
not only for its mood but for its method, Snyder's verse requires a
sophisticated familiarity with Eastern, nondualistic metaphysics to
be fully appreciated, despite his accessibility and broad political consciousness. Nevertheless, in comparing Snyder with Adrienne Rich, as
poets who both assert the need for a radical revisioning of ideology,
Molesworth argues that "neither Rich nor Snyder should be totally
faulted for failing to provide—or even echo—a plan for achieving their
post-historical visions" (33) when, as poets, their object is to see "the
political in some larger context" and remind us "that politics must be
rightly ordered if the ultimate values are to be recognized and preserved" (41).

Unlike other protest poets, instead of naming the forces he opposes,
Snyder often protests them by deliberately leaving them unnamed. That
is not to say, as Des Pres has faulted in the work of others, that he fails
to make them the subjects of his poems, but rather that he creates a conspicuous space for them as absences.[9] From the late 1950s poem "Bomb
Test" to the most politically charged passages of *Turtle Island* (1974),
this elliptical method is especially evident in Snyder's approach to the
nuclear threat. Opening with an image of dead fish floating "belly-up,

for real," "Bomb Test" traces the path of radioactive uranium "From cirrus clouds to the seamounts,/ Through all the food chains,/ Shrimp to tuna" (*Left* 63), in effect emphasizing the fishes' viewpoint as a way of condemning atomic fallout. Yet by dispensing with any imagery of bombs or power plants themselves, the poem refuses to acknowledge and thereby subverts their power.

Later in *Turtle Island*, in an attempt to be more explicitly topical, while still maintaining "the Buddhist (non)conception of the Void" (Norton 168), Snyder addresses nuclearism again, but again with an aside, as he thinks of it as a counterforce to his central concern, "the energy-pathways that sustain life." "Spel Against Demons," for example, begins with a diatribe: "The release of Demonic Energies in the name of/ the People/ must cease// Messing with blood sacrifice in the name of/ Nature/ must cease" (*Turtle* 16), as, like Blake, Snyder opposes scientific with natural forces. With more verve than, yet with as much commitment to his cause as, other activists, he describes militarism as "self-indulgence in anger" and associates it with the demonic, calling those who pointlessly slaughter others not "wolves and eagles" but "hysterical sheep." However, rather than instruct us to take up arms against this sea of troubles, Snyder suggests more spiritual measures:

> The Demonic must be devoured!
> Self-serving must be
> > cut down
> Anger must be
> > plowed back
> Fearlessness, humor, detachment, is power
>
> Gnowledge is the secret of Transformation! (*Turtle* 16)

A page later this poem ends with an image of a Buddhist diety, "ACHALA the Immovable, Lord of Wisdom, Lord of Heat," otherwise known as *Fudomyo-o* and "regarded as an incarnation of the Mahavairocana Buddha or the Great Sun Buddha," the one who, according to the poem, "saves tortured intelligent demons and filth-eating/ hungry ghosts" and whose "spel" is the mantra that closes the poem (*Turtle* 17). Elsewhere (not in *Turtle Island*), Snyder translates ACHALA'S mantra as "I DEDICATE MYSELF TO THE UNIVERSAL/ DIAMOND BE THIS RAGING FURY DESTROYED" (Yamazoto 236). As a rallying cry for action, this mantra is not likely to find legions of followers. In fairness to Snyder, though, it is true that both "humor" and "detachment" are qualities he thinks necessary to overcome the demonic forces that threaten world destruction, and both qualities are evident in even his most polemical verses, including "Spel Against Demons." Still, unless readers are predisposed to Buddhist ritual, the imaginative reach of this diatribe tends to diminish its political efficacy, despite its visionary stance.

A poem in *Turtle Island* less oblique in its opposition to potential annihilation is "LMFBR," in which Snyder identifies the "Liquid Metal Fast Breeder Reactor" in a nuclear power plant with "death himself," who "stands grinning, beckoning" with his "plutonium toothglow" (*Turtle* 67). But again he imagines the massive concrete reactor in terms of a diety—in this case, as Kali, the six-handed, fang-toothed, blood-stained Hindu goddess who is the embodiment of destructive power:

Kali dances on the dead stiff cock.

   Aluminum beer cans, plastic spoons,
plywood veneer, PVC pipe, vinyl seat covers,
      don't exactly burn, don't quite rot,
      flood over us,

      robes and garbs
      of the Kali-yuga
      end of days. (*Turtle* 67)

The litany of lifeless products of Western technology here is depicted as the mere embellishments of an Eastern monster whose only cause is horrid death. In practice, Snyder's encompassing vision of the myriad of modern threats to all forms of life rarely bothers to single out nuclear power and war as distinct from fossil fuels, chemicals, strip mining, air pollution and other scientific or industrial products, so even to categorize him as an antinuclear poet is to narrow the scope of his project and to misrepresent it. As he argues in his "Plain Talk" manifesto, "Four Changes," to "stop all germ and chemical warfare research and experimentation" and to "work toward a hopefully safe disposal of the present staggering and stupid stockpiles of H-bombs, cobalt gunk, germ and poison tanks and cans" are practical goals that go hand in hand with establishing programs of recycling bottles, cans, and newspapers (*Turtle* 95). Because Snyder seems to believe so fully in his protest *for* life, rather than *against* extinction, not only are his poems void of explicit confrontations with nuclear annihilation, but they can only see its threat as part of a universal life cycle: "The power within," he concludes at the close of *Turtle Island*, "—the more you give, the more you have to give—will still be our source when coal and oil are long gone, and atoms are left to spin in peace" (114). As with poets from Kinnell to Ortiz, the protest here is, simply, that we *must* survive to see such a time. How, politically, to prevent nuclear weapons from annihilating us is not finally Snyder's purview as much as to cultivate a world where they are absent. In this way, Snyder's protest approaches prophesy.

What may be the most remarkable political diatribe, as well as the most famous nuclear protest poem, is Ginsberg's "Plutonium Ode." Like Sanchez's poem, this poem was composed explicitly for a public event, the blocking of a train carrying "waste fissile materials" away from the Rockwell Corporation's Nuclear Facility and Plutonium factory in Rocky Flats, Colorado. However, rather than direct his words at the state or nuclear power industry, Ginsberg, like Williamson and Snyder, addresses himself to the element plutonium itself (the fissionable material used in a nuclear warhead) as a new kind of god "named for Death's planet through the sea beyond Uranus/ whose chthonic ore fathers this magma-teared Lord of Hades" (11). Composed in three parts— and accompanied in Ginsberg's *Plutonian Ode and Other Poems, 1977– 1980* by a photograph of Ginsberg, Peter Orlovsky, and "friends" sitting on the tracks in front of the train on the day the poem was completed— the ode invokes the god of the 24,000-year cycle of the Great Year of Antiquity and compares that cycle to the half-life of plutonium decay, in order to "dare" the "Reality" of plutonium so that the poet himself might "embody" its very power and "enter with spirit out loud into your fuel rod drums underground on soundless thrones and beds of lead" (14). Once there in spirit, the poet likens his own "jubilant tones" to "honey and milk and wine-sweet water" to be "poured on the stone block floor" of the nuclear reactor, while he also scatters his syllables like "barley groats . . . on the Reactor's core" (14). Even more confident than Williamson in the spiritual efficacy of words, Ginsberg closes part one thus: "I call your name with hollow vowels, I psalm your Fate close by, my breath near deathless ever at your side/ to Spell your destiny, I set this verse prophetic on your mausoleum walls to seal you up Eternally with Diamond Truth! O doomed Plutonium" (15). By the resolute act of the poet's saying so, the evil of plutonium has been conquered.

In his second strophe, Ginsberg turns away from plutonium to an image of the "Bard" contemplating the nuclear facility before him in the particular year (1978) he is there, in order again to turn attention away from the threat of plutonium and toward the earth itself. Then in his fi-

nal strophe he calls on his audience to invoke the power of poetry with
him, in order to defeat, through the sheer art of declaration, the father
of Death, "Destroyer of lying Scientists" (13) and murderer of all others:

> This ode to you O Poets and Orators to come, you father
>   Whitman as I join your side, you Congress and American
>   people,
> you present mediators, spiritual friends & teachers, you O Master
>   of the Diamond Arts,
> Take this wheel of syllables in hand, these vowels and
>   consonants to breath's end
> take this inhalation of black poison to your heart, breathe out
>   this blessing from your breast on our creation
> forests cities oceans deserts rocky flats and mountains in the Ten
>   Directions pacify with this exhalation,
> enrich this Plutonian Ode to explode its empty thunder through
>   earthen thought-worlds
> Magnetize this howl with heartless compassion, destroy this
>   mountain of Plutonium with ordinary mind and body speech,
> thus empower this Mind-guard spirit gone out, gone out, gone
>   beyond me, Wake space, so Ah! (16–17)

Ginsberg's unquestioned faith in poetry's power to resist the destructive force of plutonium is as fierce and inspiring as Whitman's faith
in the hearts of the American people. Boldly echoing Whitman's ca-
dences and his operatic apostrophes to the earth, this poem has probably reached more Americans than any other I discuss, if the thousands
at Ginsberg's readings around the country are any indication. Furthermore, as with most nuclear protest poetry, Ginsberg's high moral tone
has played a major role in promoting pacifist sentiment among univer-
sity-educated liberals and others. Indeed, through practitioners as char-
ismatic as Berrigan, Sanchez, Snyder, Ginsberg, and Levertov, nuclear
protest poetry has been heard by more people than any other poetry
composed in the United States, with the exception of feminist and
African-American poetry. Although it has been disregarded by U.S. pol-
icy-makers at least as much as dissident poetry has throughout the rest
of the world, its distinctive contribution is less as an active force for political change than as the embodiment of the kind of galvanizing power
of resistance needed among the diverse citizenry in a democracy from
which that change ultimately must come. As a first way of nothingness,

it articulates the conscience of American activism. What the work of Levertov in particular illustrates, I believe, is that although poets may have no greater a political role to play in the United States than anyone else, because of their ability to register a persistent voice against annihilation, as well as to cross boundaries of discourse within their work, nor is their role a lesser one.

"Steel of Utterance": Denise Levertov's Vision of the Nuclear Age

No other poet has been more closely associated with the antinuclear movement in the United States than Denise Levertov. Unlike poets who occasionally compose a protest poem, Levertov has written a wide range of antinuclear and other protest poems for over thirty years. Included among those poems as well are a wealth of other politically engaged poems that do not overtly express opposition to the threat of nuclearism or civil abuse by the state. In fact, because her *life* has been intricately wrapped up in her public efforts to halt the production of nuclear arms, many of Levertov's poems inevitably embody that experience in the same way that any private experience informs a poet's sensibility. As a result, often her lyric poems treat her experience as a political activist in a language that is sometimes quite personal, sometimes visionary.

Levertov attempts to explain this congruence of public action and the private nature of lyric poetry in her 1975 lecture, "On the Edge of Darkness: What Is Political Poetry?" where she writes,

> A striking characteristic of contemporary political poetry is that, more than in the past, it is written by people who are active participants in the causes they write about, and not simply observers. It's a reciprocal phenomenon: people who are already poets in any case become involved in some aspect or aspects of these interrelated struggles, and it follows that they write poems concerned with the causes they believe in; these in turn inspire others, both to participation and to the writing of poems. Whether these poems are good or not depends on the gifts of the poet, not on the subject matter. But what is interesting historically is the greater interplay between these poets' actions and their writing.
>
> For many of us who are thus involved, it is possible that our sense of political urgency is at times an almost hectic stimulus. . . . [I]f one is led by a resulting commitment to the attempt to combat what threatens us, and thus to the experience of comradeship in actions involving some risk, such as civil disobedience, then one is

living a stirring life which—if one is given to writing poetry—is almost bound to result in poems directly related to these experiences.
(*Light* 120–21)

Even in a country where most artists are as politically inactive as they
are in the United States, this argument—namely, that the writer whose
life is "permeated by a sense of unremitting political emergency" must
try to "attain to such osmosis of the personal and the public, of assertion and of song, that no one be able to divide our poems into categories"
(*Light* 128)—predates both Levertov and the age she lives in.[10] But as
with other aspects of contemporary culture, it is radicalized by the conditions of nuclearism. In other words, for Levertov, as for Derrida, the
threat of technological annihilation breaks down the distinction between the personal and the public ultimately by insinuating the re-
moval of each arena of existence as a reference point for the other and
by coercing the poet to question the fundamental nature of the poetic
act. The poet has the obligation, then, not only to confront that political reality in her poetry but to protest those forces that restrain human
freedom.

Despite this acknowledgment by Levertov of the psychic terror inherent in the potential of a complete collapse of meaning and structures
of meaning, due to nuclearism, and partly because of her religious faith,
she has always informed her poetry with the praiseworthy of the world,
the "immanent" in objects when seen and expressed in precisely the
right way. Even in poems that treat nuclear annihilation—including
such mid-career poems as "Another Spring" and, more obliquely, "The
Novel," together with the later poems "An English Field in the Nuclear
Age," "Mass for the Day of St. Thomas Didymus," "The Cry," and
"Making Peace"—she has continually and stubbornly insisted, by using
visionary language and idiomatic form, that her poetry shape and praise
human existence, not incorporate tropes of despair. Consequently, as a
protest poet, Levertov utters her loudest opposition to the nuclear
threat not through her repeated warnings of impending holocaust, nor
as Ginsberg does in "Plutonian Ode" through the aggressive exer-
tion of language itself, but through praise, through insisting that
somethingness, not nothingness, be her subject. Given this pose, the
poetic dilemma she has encountered—perhaps more intensely in degree, though not in kind, than other nuclear protest poets—has been
finding an authentic voice in which to sound her alarm at the "unremitting emergency" of the nuclear threat without becoming either

histrionic or relentlessly disillusioned, so as not to appear as a poet of praise whose world has gone sour.

In attempting to explain her development from her early "romantic" poetry, through her self-conscious adoption of the projectivism of Williams and Olson, to her openly political work since the late 1960s, Levertov's readers have offered both sympathetic and critical appraisals. William Aiken, for example, considers her experimentation with versification to have reached its apex in the late fifties, when she asserted that the sensual image as the focus of content and the breath as the fundamental linguistic unit are the chief sources of a poem's resonant, even spiritual qualities. As she became increasingly concerned with broader issues, her artistic method remained unchanged, creating in Aiken's view "a running contradiction of precepts she had earlier set down regarding poetic content, form, and intention" (136). By contrast, Kerry Driscoll calls this same period of the 1960s, when Levertov published *The Jacob's Ladder* (1961), *O Taste and See* (1964), and *The Sorrow Dance* (1967), the start of "the blossoming and maturation of an inherently empathic sensibility" (148). Driscoll argues that, by turning to the horrors of the world and placing itself "in the antithetical positions of oppressor and oppressed" (153), Levertov's poetry assumes "primitive, almost shamanistic, overtones; through the power of song, she not only keeps the 'devil' within herself in check, but sets an ethical and aesthetic example for society at large" (155). Driscoll believes that such an act by a poet, whether it moves others to action or not, whether practically effective or not, is "revolutionary" (155).

In his book on postwar poets, James Breslin defines the opening up of Levertov's field of vision during the sixties as an aspect of her "magical realism," without making any larger claims for her political effectiveness nor, by exclusion, her irrelevance. While acknowledging a number of strong individual poems written during this period, Breslin observes, "Levertov is moving toward a vision she has not yet fully articulated and which she cannot yet consistently embody in her style" (161). In *The Psycho-Political Muse,* Paul Breslin argues that the source of the "running contradiction" that Aiken finds in Levertov's political verse can be found in her poetic roots, that is, in projectivism's focus on "the value of the poetic process, rather than on the poem as the made thing." In this view, to focus on the art rather than on the world outside it encourages in the poet a kind of omphaloskepticism which, by its nature, cannot handle larger social issues, let alone apocalyptic ones (202–3). In other words, the same self-consciousness that leads to sensual triumph in such Levertov poems as "O Taste and See," "The Ache of Marriage," "A Psalm Praising the Hair of Man's Body," "The Rainwalkers," and "Song of Ishtar" is liable to betray her when she handles frightening social issues by drawing attention not to their political conditions but to the poet's psychic distress about those conditions.

Speaking also to Levertov's tone, in criticizing her books of the early 1980's, Sandra Gilbert attributes what she suggests is the failure of Levertov's protest poems not to her poetics but to her polemics. "Levertov's most revolutionary gesture," Gilbert argues, "is probably her persistent articulation of joy" (201) but this strength, she adds, is diminished whenever Levertov approaches political subjects from too partisan a perspective: "Because she has little taste or talent for irony, her comments on social catastrophe lack, on the one hand, the sardonic ferocity that animates, say, Bly's 'The Teeth Mother Naked At Last'. . . and, on the other hand, the details of disillusionment that give plausibility to, say, Lowell's 'For the Union Dead' " (213). Gilbert advises Levertov to avoid "mere cries of rage and defiance" in favor of expressing "rebellious *caritas*" (214). Such advice may be warranted in general political discourse, but because nuclearism is not merely a political evil to be opposed but rather could ultimately remove the dichotomy of good and evil altogether, I wonder if Gilbert's criticism of Levertov is not too glib in its failure to distinguish nuclear from other ideological problems, as well as in its simplified view of political activism. Even Edith Wyschogrod, in arguing for a philosophically viable route out of the nuclear nightmare, acknowledges that love is a means of living with, but not necessarily a solution to defeating, the menace of man-made mass death. Levertov shares Wyschogrod's circumspection.

In her thorough assessment of Levertov's political poetry, Lorrie Smith characterizes Levertov's achievement as one of overcoming the tendency toward polarities in thought and feeling that are the norm in other protest poetry. Building on the conflict in form between the lyric and the didactic,[11] Smith sees Levertov's development as a fall from innocence, an "intensely personal working out of the very traditional confrontation of evil in the world" ("Songs" 159). For a poet of praise such as Levertov, Smith notes, "the tension of trying to maintain integrity— to balance the fundamentally mystical imagination with a larger sphere of events and issues—is betrayed in recurrent patterns of unresolved polarity and paradox" (159). Examining Levertov's Vietnam poems, Smith traces her shift away from polarities "toward a more complex paradigm of dialogue—both spiritual and social—to bridge her knowledge of evil and her yearning for peace" (168). In her mature work, Levertov no longer entertains illusions about the power of poetry to change political structures, says Smith; rather, she considers her role "to celebrate what is valuable, and protest what is unconscionable" (171).

As convincing as Smith's analysis is, we still need to ask the same question of Levertov we ask of Snyder: Can we accept her spiritual resolve (that which mitigates both her joy and her outrage) as an authentic response not just to politics in general, but to the radical implications of nuclearism? As a protest poet, Levertov might take her place next to Berrigan, Sanchez, and Ginsberg, as they make their stand against the ideological forces they see driving us toward extinction. But if, on the one hand, Levertov's projectivist poetics cannot adequately embody the world and, on the other hand, she finds her most powerful expression in poems more spiritual than ideological, then like Snyder what she offers is, primarily, a spiritual vision of an otherwise political concern (namely, annihilation). What her nuclear protest poetry most poignantly offers, I believe, is *not* a revolutionary vision that alters our fundamental thinking, but a voice of radical calm and political fortitude in an age in which public hysteria about annihilation is commonplace.

Though Levertov was actively protesting nuclear proliferation during the fifties and sixties, none of her poems from this period directly concerns the nuclear threat. In an interview with Smith, she downplays the political nature of her earlier verse, citing only the sequence "During the Eichmann Trial" in *The Jacob's Ladder* and "Another Spring" in *O Taste and See*, and calling the latter "very oblique" in its politics (Smith, "Interview" 596). In that poem, however, evidence of both Levertov's vision of annihilation and her determined resistance to it emerge. "Another Spring" opens

In the gold mouth of a flower
the black smell of spring earth.
No more skulls on our desks

but the pervasive
testing of death—as if we had need
of new ways of dying? No,

we have no need
of new ways of dying.
Death in us goes on

testing the wild
chance of living
as Adam chanced it. (*Poems* 88)

Characteristically, Levertov evokes the sensual image of the flower here and juxtaposes it sharply against the "skulls on our desks," a traditional *memento mori* image as well as, perhaps, an allusion to the scientist as the impersonal experimenter on life. (Might these skulls also be an allusion to the Nazi doctors as in Plath's "Lady Lazarus"? If so, they are certainly more subtle, less flamboyant.) Despite the renewal of spring—indeed, embedded in spring's "gold mouth"—our technology finds "new ways of dying" as a set of variations on the old ways. In the elliptical manner of the projectivists, Levertov phrases the second sentence (like the first, in fact, actually a fragment) as a rhetorical question, which sets up her protest in reply: "No," followed by an emphatic stanza break and the echo of the phrasing, only now as a statement. In projectivist terms, the poet has reacted to the juxtaposition of the opening images, moving from a reflection on them to a qualification of her thought: "Death in us goes on// testing the wild/ chance of living/ as Adam chanced it"; risking death is, as it has always been, an extreme way of affirming life, itself a "wild chance," an uncertainty. In an ironic inversion of seasons, the skulls can almost be seen as seeds, spreading death instead of life to the wind. Yet by polarizing death and life, Levertov conceives of them as interdependent for meaning, or "Manichean" (Smith, "Songs" 159). Thus she restores the primeval significance not only of death (and by inference, genocide), but of life, "the black smell of spring earth."

This sharp contrast deepens through the remainder of the poem: as the flower's "gold mouth" reappears as "Golden-mouth, the tilted smile/ of the moon westering," the "black smell" of line two becomes "the black window" through which or in which the moon is viewed, and the "skulls" return as "Calavera of Spring," the moon being seen as a bright gold skull. Only, in Zen-like fashion, the oppositions are now reversed, with the gold within the black, rather than the black within the gold, and the poem has turned: whereas it begins with the poet finding death in the midst of rebirth, it closes with a focus on life in the midst of darkness:

Do you mistake me?
I am speaking of living,

of moving from one moment into
the next, and into the
one after, breathing

death in the spring air, knowing
air also means
music to sing to. (*Poems* 88–89)

In these lines reminiscent of Olson or Creeley, the subtle pauses created by the line breaks after "into," "the," and "breathing" create a sense of the poem itself coming into being before our eyes, moment by moment, in an evolutionary growth of language. Its sense of wholeness is attenuated no doubt by the shifting to "breathing/ death in the spring air" (rather than "life"), as a reminder of the poem's opening concern— especially given the crucial prominence of "breath" in Levertov's poetics, such that "contaminated" breath cuts to the core of her vision of life in language (Paul Breslin 200–201). Yet this poem closes with life and death in tension with each other, and with "music to sing to" getting the last word, so to speak.

While vividly depicting the threat of self-annihilation in "Another Spring," Levertov adopts a fairly traditional view of the struggle between creative and destructive forces that does not yet voice the "unremitting emergency" posed by nuclearism. Not that this "very oblique" poem protests nuclear arms, exactly, but its faith in the power of the "air" we serenade not to be irreversibly polluted by the "death" we breathe in it is implicit here and elsewhere in Levertov's poems from this period. However, in "The Novel," another poem whose theme is both the process of artistic creation (a novel) and the sensibilities that comprise that creation (the man and woman as characters both within and outside the novel), Levertov's sense of "erasure" or nothingness takes on a distinctly nuclearistic quality. Speaking of the couple "cramped in their not yet/ halfwritten lives," she says,

They live (when they live) in fear

of blinding, of burning, of choking under a
mushroom cloud in the year of the roach.
And they want (like us) the eternity
of today, they want this fear to be
struck out at once by a thick black
magic marker, everywhere, every page. . . . (*Poems* 136)

Two of the symptoms Lifton has identified among the psychological effects of life under the nuclear threat are rendered here: (1) that the threat of annihilation contributes to our sense of futurelessness and therefore undermines our sense of the continuity of life: "And they want (like us) the eternity/ of today"; and (2) that the power of annihilation stirs awe in us, inducing a kind of bomb worship, here equated with the annihilating power of the "thick black/ magic marker" blotting out the lives both within and outside the world of the novel.

Nevertheless, as in "Another Spring," this poem turns in its last three stanzas toward reasserting, as equal to the power of annihilation, the power of creation, whether as a tentative "vision" that "breaks in on the cramped grimace,/ inscape of transformation" (the last phrase of which begs interpretation), or as part of the novel in which "By scene, by sentence, something is rendered/ back into life, back to the gods" (*Poems* 137).[12] This assertion that language can make meaning, as well as that humans can live meaningful lives—albeit a modest, hesitant, even quavering assertion—is echoed throughout Levertov's work of the sixties. It culminates in the poem at the end of *The Sorrow Dance*, "Living," in which the sense of an ending mimics the sense of a beginning which closes "Another Spring" and "The Novel," literally inverting the effects of those earlier poems:

> The fire in leaf and grass
> so green it seems
> each summer the last summer.
>
> The wind blowing, the leaves
> shivering in the sun,
> each day the last day.
>
> A red salamander
> so cold and so
> easy to catch, dreamily
>
> moves his delicate feet
> and long tail. I hold
> my hand open for him to go.
>
> Each minute the last minute. (*Poems* 240)

◇ After publishing poems related to her experiences of protesting American involvement in Vietnam in *Relearning the Alphabet* (1970), *To Stay Alive* (1973), *The Freeing of the Dust* (1975), and *Life in the Forest* (1978), Levertov established herself among the prominent protest poets of her day and garnered a devoted following. Since that time most of her books (which now appear almost every other year) include a separate section made up entirely of topical, if not always protest, poems: Part

V, "Age of Terror," in *Candles in Babylon* (1982), part II, "Prisoners," in *Oblique Prayers* (1984), part IV in *Breathing the Water* (1987), part II in *A Door in the Hive* (1989), and part VI, "Witnessing from Afar," in *Evening Train* (1992). Levertov's abiding awareness of nuclear annihilation finds its way into all these books, and not surprisingly, her vision has become increasingly complicated: There is less resilient joy in these poems which, on the whole, assume a moderate tone—neither defeatist nor cynical, to be sure, but seasoned by a deeper dread of nuclearism. With her "political outrage" now "tempered" (Smith, "Songs" 168), however, has Levertov's fundamental view of annihilation also been altered?

In her critique of Levertov's "An English Field in the Nuclear Age," Denise Lynch suggests that it has. Similarly to "Another Spring," this poem juxtaposes opposites—not life and death, but everything and nothing—with the poet's task to "render" both the presence of the immediate field before her and the "isolate Knowledge" of its potential absence in the nuclear age. Both what is and what could be (or could *not* be) press themselves upon the poet's imagination simultaneously. Yet Levertov further recognizes, in the poem's most prominent participial clauses, that "no one" else can "partake nor proffer vision unless"..."it/ *be* wrought." Paradoxically, though, "there is no sharing save in the furnace,/ the transubstantiate, acts/ of passion" (*Candles* 79). In other words, a vision must be whole to be identified by others, but others can only share in that whole if they also share in its coming into being—notwithstanding whether it be through the "rites of alchemy ('furnace')" or the ritual of the "Eucharist ('transubstantiate'), wherein the spirit is reborn in matter, just as the poet's vision must be wrought in language" (Lynch 40–41).

Lynch adds, "The poem's structure corresponds to this theme. Its recurrent parentheses require pauses longer than the usual line breaks and capture the rhythms of a mind interrupting itself and, by reflecting on its own creative engagement with a perishable universe, holding 'dread' at bay" (41). Such an explanation of Levertov's poetics recalls Derrida's idea of the "strategic manuevers" one must employ "in order to assimilate that unassimilable wholly other" (28), namely, extinction itself, as like Snyder she invokes the unnamable without having to name it. Without question, Levertov's form in "An English Field" is less neatly symmetrical than in "Another Spring," primarily because the thing in this poem that represents the threat to the "haze and halos of/ sun-bless'd particulars" is neither in the English field nor even in the poem.

Instead, it is that which, outside the poem, threatens the making of the poem—namely, annihilation.

But what is Levertov's vision here then? What is this thing to be "named, spun, tempered, stain of it/ sunk into steel of utterance" (*Candles* 79)? In its very coming into being, the poem graphically and syntactically divides lines of self-consciousness (on the left margin) from lines describing nature and the world (parenthetical lines on the right side) until both sides merge in the middle of the page to form the final twelve lines, including the image of the "air" that "searches/ warm bare shoulders" (the poet's? Think of the double purpose of "the spring air" in "Another Spring") and the image of the "gold mirrors of buttercup satin" springing up among "long-dried cowpads" (79). Both nature and artifice "assert eternity as they reflect/ nothing, everything, absolute instant" (79–80). The "steel of utterance" welded by the poet contains both matter and spirit, everything and nothing—all together, for at least as long as the poem lasts, in its saying and in its existence, creating a final but highly significant qualification missing from Levertov's earlier poems.

Although the graphic use of white space, the sophisticated interplay of various levels of diction, the balance of self-consciousness and imagery, and the sober yet assertive voice of "An English Field" create a more convincing portrait of living under the nuclear shadow than does "Another Spring," it still does not strike me as a "revolutionary" poem. Its real achievement lies in how Levertov brings together, as she always has, those sensual, psychological, and moral forces that test an individual's equilibrium and gives them a unified shape—for instance, in the authoritative way she closes with a sense not of triumph but of relief. But does this poem actually change our way of thinking about impending annihilation? Its complexity does distinguish it from Levertov's more self-evident nuclear protest poems, such as "Rocky Flats," for example, which employs many of the same manuevers (even the image of breathing) that "Another Spring" and "An English Field" do, but which avails itself of such clear polarities, especially in its closing image of the "spores of the Destroying Angel" (*Oblique* 38), that it pales in comparison to documentary films on nuclear war and even to a fund-raising letter I received from Physicians for Social Responsibility that described the numerous safety violations at the Rocky Flats plant. For all its complexity, "An English Field" neither stirs us to action, nor converts our way of thinking, nor offers an unexpected vision. To be sure, it recognizes the need for such a vision, a "steel of utterance"—thereby announcing itself as protest art—but its strength lies less in its ideological assertion than in its calming reassurance that "this minute at least was/ not the last" (*Candles* 80).

Levertov's "Age of Terror" in *Candles in Bablylon* and "Watching Dark Circle" in *Oblique Prayers*, by ending with questions, seem honestly in search of a genuine change in thinking, rather than merely a change in power; with striking sincerity, they create a calm similar to that in "An English Field." Beyond them, poems such as "Mass for the Day of St. Thomas Didymus" and "The Cry" begin, if somewhat tentatively, to assert a belief that accommodates the fear of extinction and acknowledges the inadequacy of "rhetoric" to "fit/ that *unrendering*" (*Oblique* 45), even while they refuse to be silenced (to paraphrase the title of yet another Levertov poem). Notably, the core of this belief in "The Cry" is expressed in terms of spiritual *and* physical rebirth once again, with a "newborn cry/ demanding/ with cherubim/ and seraphim/ eternity:/ being:/ milk:" (*Oblique* 46). Ending with a colon, the poem seems unfinished, and it courts meaninglessness, yet it also returns to Levertov's earliest concern with sensual matter and life.

The six-part "Mass for the Day of St. Thomas Didymus," one of Levertov's most ambitious poems, combines her personal alarm and political resolve in the face of potential extinction with her deepening Christian faith. She herself has described the composition of this poem as a period of self-conversion—a return to the religious faith of her childhood and a discovery of herself (by the time she had finished the poem) as spiritually transformed (Gery). It is here that she comes closest to voicing poetically a complete vision of ideological change, one which, if not utterly public in its expression, is meant both as a personal statement and a ritual sequence of universal prayers.[13] As Harry Marten has pointed out, the Apostle St. Thomas Didymus who inspires this poem, the "doubting Thomas" in John 20.24–29, is "an ideal choice to reveal the nature of Levertov's faith" (164). In demanding to see physical evidence of Christ's resurrection, St. Thomas embodies the essence of Levertov's embrace of matter as the source of the spiritual, while at the same time the response he evokes from Christ—who says, "Thomas, because thou hast seen me, thou hast believed: blessed are they that have not seen, and yet have believed" (John 20.29)—creates for her an opportunity to *protest* her own faith in spite of her modern (as well as postmodern?) skepticism. However, given the special congruence of the Biblical and political contexts of this poem, Levertov surprises us by directing her skepticism not just at the insubstantiation of Christ but also at our own potential annihilation.

Arranged in the sequence of a Catholic mass, the poem opens with a "Kyrie," asking mercy of the "deep unknown" (109), imagined as a "guttering candle,/ beloved nugget lodged/ in the obscure heart's/ last recess" (*Candles* 108). This unknown, however, is twofold in its power over us. As the poet explains: "We live in terror" both "of what we know" —that is,

> death, death, and the world's
> death we imagine
>   and cannot imagine,

—and "of what we do not know," that is,

> of the limitless, through which freefalling
> forever, our dread
> sinks and sinks,
>   or
> of the violent closure of all. (108)

What we know about death and the world's potential to destroy itself is cause for alarm and terror, but what we do *not* know about annihilation is equally terrifying. "Yet," Levertov ironically asserts, in recalling Christ's blessing of those "that have not seen, and yet have believed," "our hope lies/ in the unknown,/ in our unknowing" (109). To believe in the potential of nothingness, despite our inability to see it, is strangely akin to believing in God's power, because of the indeterminability of both.

In part ii, "Gloria," Levertov maintains this odd parallel between nothingness and godliness, praising the unknown as a source of hope by placing it in a hierarchy of increasingly significant images: wet snow, a shadow cast by her neighbor's chimney on a particular gray day in October, the "invisible sun" behind the clouds, "god or the gods," and finally the unknown itself,

> that which imagined us, which stays
> our hand,
> our murderous hand,
>   and gives us
> still,
> in the shadow of death,
>   our daily life. (109)

Obliquely, Levertov equates the uncertainty of our power to annihilate ourselves, an uncertainty that has so far deterred us from apocalyptic war, with the uncertainty of the reach of unearthly powers. But unlike in "The Novel," and in contrast to a less sophisticated poet who might unintentionally deify nuclear powers, she implies no bomb worship in this equation because she remains focused on the unknown itself, even in part iii, where she expresses unambiguously her creed that "the earth/ exists" (110). Returning to the image of the candle, she addresses God as "Thou/ unknown I know," whom she then asks to "help . . . my/ unbelief" not by becoming manifest in itself but by allowing the "belovéd, threatened world" to go on existing. She acknowledges that she interrupts her belief with doubt and interrupts her doubt with belief; nonetheless, as long as the world survives, the possibility to experience faith will, beyond doubt, continue. And so she closes her "Credo" simply: "Be, that I may believe. Amen" (110), even though the use of the auxiliary verb "may" *still* leaves room for unbelief.

Part iv, "Sanctus," depicts the means by which the world may go on existing. Here the poet praises as holy "all that Imagination/ has wrought, has rendered," asserting that whatever we manage to name is able "to give/ to the Vast Loneliness/ a hearth, a locus" (111). Through prayer—and by extension, through poetry—"all the gods,/ angels and demigods," as well as "eloquent animals" and "oracles," may "send forth their song towards/ the harboring silence," thereby creating meaning amid nothingness. Yet Levertov uses an appositive to indicate how "the ecstasy of their names" is one and the same as "the multiform/ name of the Other, the known/ Unknown, unknowable" (111), as she merges being and nothingness in the name of the spirit. In the "Benedictus" section that follows, she blesses this spirit, again providing a litany of images as the sources wherein the spirit's name is written:

in woodgrain, windripple, crystal,

in crystals of snow, in petal, leaf,
moss and moon, fossil and feather,

blood, bone, song, silence,
very word of
very word,
flesh and
vision. (111–12)

Despite the positive, almost pantheistic faith in the immanence of things expressed here (and again seventeen lines later), the "Benedictus" is twice broken by a series of questions, bringing into this section,

too, St. Thomas's doubt which interrupts belief. Levertov asks whether
the word by which the spirit is named is "audible under or over the
gross/ cacophony of malevolence" (112). Yet not only is she concerned
about the limited power a mere "vibration/ known in the fibers of/ the
tree of nerves" has to express the universal spirit, but beyond the frailty
of the word in the world she wonders about nothingness itself: "What
of the emptiness/ the destructive vortex that whirls/ no word with it?"
(112). The "known/ Unknown, unknowable" may be the entirety of "all
that Imagination has wrought," but it may just as well be "emptiness."
The latter part of "Benedictus" reiterates this argument, where the poet
blesses "that which utters/ its being," because wherever it does—as
"the stone of stone,/ the straw of straw"—"there/ spirit is" (112–13).
"But," she asks again, "can the name/ utter itself/ in the downspin of
time?/ Can it enter/ the void?" (113).

Instead of remaining in suspension, however—between the spirit of
both being and nothingness, and the annihilation of spirit always beside
it (albeit in the form of questions)—as in "An English Field," Levertov
reconciles her uncertainty by uttering it and letting it go:

Blesséd

be the dust. From dust the world
utters itself. We have no other
hope, no knowledge.
The word
chose to become
flesh. In the blur of flesh
we bow, baffled. (113)

The "Benedictus" both affirms spiritual existence and accepts that for
us to know the spirit demands that the flesh, itself endangered, continue. For human beings, the spirit depends on flesh, despite the spirit's
transcendent qualities. Inevitably attached as we are to material being,
implies the poem, in the wake of the spirit we can only "bow, baffled."

Virtually as long as part v, making these last two sections the longest
of the poem, part vi of "Mass," the "Agnus Dei," further explores the
idea of the dependence of the spirit on its worldly utterance. Here, Levertov turns, logically, toward the incarnation of Christ. In speaking of
her own Christianity, she has noted, "I now define myself as a Christian, but not a very orthodox one, and I think that there is a way of looking at Christian faith as involving the cooperation of man. I think that's
part of the meaning of the incarnation" (Smith, "Interview" 603). The

opening of "Agnus Dei" perpetuates this focus on the significance of earthly being and its name(s), by questioning the existence of the "Lamb of God" in the most literal sense. As Audrey Rodgers has noted, this final section of "Mass" creates a sudden contrast to the rest of the poem through its enhanced use of colloquial speech in which "the rhythms of the liturgy are supplanted by a persistently questioning voice" (175). First Levertov wonders about the vulnerability of "infant sheep" who are "afraid and foolish" and have "neither rage nor claws,/ venom nor cunning" (*Candles* 113). How can such a "pretty creature, vigorous/ to nuzzle at milky dugs," be a symbol of God, she asks, and "What terror lies concealed" (113–14) in our chanting the *Agnus Dei?* Does the metaphor of the lamb unwittingly suggest "an ignorance/ smelling of ignorance" (114)? If so, the poet reasons as she develops her line of thought through interrogatives,

> God then,
> encompassing all things, is
> defenseless? Omnipotence
> has been tossed away, reduced
> to a wisp of damp wool? (114)

The coming of Christ, by implication, was not so much a revelation of God's sovereignty as a reminder of the human responsibility to keep the world going, to utter the names of immanent things so that the spirit might continue. It is we, who seem to want "only to sleep till catastrophe/ has raged, clashed, seethed, and gone by without us" and who "in shamefaced private hope" had heretofore sought to be "given/ a bliss we deserved for having imagined it," who must in fact "protect this perversely weak/ animal," the Lamb of God, rather than the other way around. It is we, the poet protests, who "must hold to our icy hearts/ a shivering God" (114).

Though expressed through questions, Levertov's urging of the individual to assume social responsibility in the "Agnus Dei" is filled with as much conviction as that of other nuclear protest poets. But the difference in her work is the carefully wrought commingling of the spiritual with the social, of the private resources of self with the public forum of political action. The inverted image of the Lamb of God here derives as much from the tradition in religious poetry from George Herbert through Rilke as it does from secular verse; yet it strives unquestionably to provide guidance to the living, to give us reason to act *in concert* and *against* those forces that threaten us with annihilation.

As conclusive evidence of the poem's directedness and despite its being a poem "for the Day" of doubting Thomas, "Mass" ends as do earlier and later Levertov poems, not with questions but with its own quiet
resolve:

> So be it.
>   Come, rag of pungent
> quiverings,
>   dim star.
>   Let's try
> if something human still
> can shield you,
>   spark
> of remote light. (115)

Despite the remoteness of the "spark" of hope, rather than cower under
the burden or despair that human beings have to protect that spark as
our only indication of "god or the gods" in the nuclear age, Levertov
calmly asks us to try—to continue through song and belief, utterance
and action—to nourish the earth and, "in each minim mote/ of its
dust," to believe in "the holy/ glow" of the spirit's unknown candle immanent within (110). Our nuclear future may remain as unknown to us
as the mystery surrounding Christ's incarnation. Yet Levertov believes
we have the spiritual, as well as the political, obligation to the worldly
shaping of that future: to "bow, baffled," perhaps, but to bow nonetheless.

◇ In *Breathing the Water* (1987), Levertov further explores nuclearism
while still protesting it. In "During a Son's Dangerous Illness," for example, she contrasts the horror of potential annihilation with that of
losing her son: While to imagine her son's death as preceding her own
is "unthinkable," as it would leave her in the "desolation of/ survival,"
she realizes it is "infinitely smaller but/ the same in kind" (35) as global
annihilation, which would mean the loss not only of her own progeny's
future, but of all pasts and futures. While this poem does not presume
to imagine the full impact of such a loss (Derrida's "unassimilable
wholly other"), it employs the concept effectively in casting in a new
light what it means for a parent to lose a child, since both losses are presented as anomalies in the natural course of human experience. In a
comparable poem, "The Batterers" in *Evening Train* (1992), Levertov
depicts a man nursing the injuries of a woman he has beaten as a con-

ceit for the human maltreatment of the earth. Suddenly the man recognizes how much he cherishes the woman and fears her death, while the poet wonders in the final strophe, "Earth, can we not love you/ unless the end is near?" (71). In both these later poems, the contrast between a human loss and the loss of the earth works to enlarge our conception of both kinds of loss simultaneously—an example of the metaphorical approach to nuclear annihilation I shall examine in more detail in chapter 3.

Finally, "Making Peace" again illustrates the kind of political courage Levertov has, as again she expresses a "steel of utterance," or radical calm, that by itself may not transform our thinking but instead emphasizes the need for, and gestures toward the possibility of, just such a transformation. Like "The Novel," "An English Field," and "Mass," the poem uses as its guiding conceit the making of art or the naming of things, that is, the creative process of coming into being—this time using the writing of poetry as a metaphor for "making peace":

> A line of peace might appear
> if we restructured the sentence our lives are making,
> revoked its reaffirmation of profit and power,
> questioned our needs, allowed
> long pauses . . . (*Breathing* 40)

But rather than elaborate on that "restructuring" or actually employ it in the poem (as I shall argue in chapter 5, the poems of "destinerrance" do), this poem trails off with its ellipsis points, followed by the same closure found in Levertov's earlier poems:

> A cadence of peace might balance its weight
> on that different fulcrum; peace, a presence,
> an energy field more intense than war,
> might pulse then,
> stanza by stanza into the world,
> each act of living
> one of its words, each word
> a vibration of light—facets
> of the forming crystal. (*Breathing* 40)

The conditional verbs here ("might balance," "might pulse"), together with the varied line lengths and the delicately unfolding syntactic units, lend this poem a dignity that fills it with a sense of purpose—despite the overt partisanship that leaks out, once, in the catch-phrase "profit and power" (in contrast to the resonant double entendre of "sentence")—that is, as a clear protest *against* nothingness and *for* the making of peace.

Understandably, a poem such as "Making Peace" functions well as inspiration for those who find in Levertov a rich source of consolation for, and reaffirmation of, their own efforts to avert nuclear war. Unlike the abiding skepticism toward spiritual faith found throughout "Mass for the Day of St. Thomas Didymus," however, this poem's tone does not induce us actually to rethink "our needs" so much as it reminds us of the importance of doing so. Ultimately, a truly "revolutionary" poet must follow the "long pauses" Levertov asks for with a poetry that in form and focus dismantles our basic assumptions, while undoing the social or cultural ideology of nuclearism more extensively than hers does. Such poetry may not be as readily recognized as "political" as hers and that of other nuclear protest poets; indeed, it may seem deliberately at times to withdraw from politics in order to delve into the "personal," cultural, or psychic experience of imagining annihilation, without any apparent concern for state policy. Consequently, with its consummate political awareness, its wide-ranging moral conscience, and its resistance to annihilation, Levertov's protest poetry goes an essential way of nothingness among the chorus of voices in our uncertain age: As a poetry that has, for over thirty years, been welding the alloy from which other poets might forge a more fully revolutionary vision, her "steel of utterance" should prove unshakable enough to earn their and our deep regard.

THREE

The Apocalyptic Lyric

"Talking of the Danger": Nuclearism and Metaphor

In the half-century since the Manhattan Project, the culture of nuclearism has seeped into virtually every corner of the public and private
consciousness of Americans. Not only have films of the devastation at
Hiroshima and Nagasaki, as well as of the scores of above-ground nuclear
tests before they were banned in 1963, imprinted an indelible image in
the popular mind of what a nuclear war might look, sound, and smell
like; not only have groups such as the Physicians for Social Responsibility and the Union for Concerned Scientists provided excruciatingly detailed speculations on the physical, biological, medical, psychological,

and even meteorological effects of nuclear war; but as with other inter-nationally debated issues in this century, the idea of nuclear annihilation and its accompanying apparatus of visual and linguistic tropes have been embraced by and absorbed into American culture at large. To whom, then, do we turn to scrutinize the domestic, aesthetic, and spiritual ef-fects of nuclearism? Do they not fall within the purview of theologians, artists, and poets? In chapter 1, I demonstrated how nuclear annihilation has not only become a preoccupation of poets but has provoked some to investigate how Western consciousness itself has altered. In this chapter I want to look more specifically at its impact on the making of metaphors *through* which poets imagine individual experience.

The extent to which nuclear references, from the image of the atomic mushroom cloud to the terminology of nuclear diplomacy, have infil-trated American life is so wide-reaching it hardly needs comment. Paul Loeb, for instance, discusses with horror the unself-conscious adoption of the language and imagery of nuclear weaponry in Hanford, Washing-ton, where the significance of the atomic weapons industry, the area's only major employer, "becomes trivialized when images from it are used for businesses with such names as Atomic Foods, Atomic Body Shop, Atomic Lanes (a Richland bowling center), Atomic Plumbing, Atomic Health Center and Atomic TV Service; when nuclear symbols decorate banks and delivery trucks and the ads of a collection agency which brags 'we don't use atomic bombs but our blast is equally effec-tive'; when you can live on Proton, Argon or Nuclear Lane, send kids to a school where the principal calls their mushroom cloud emblem 'a symbol of peace' and praise God for the FFTF [Fast Flux Test Facility]" (172–73). Even the Hanford High School football team, nicknamed "The Bombers," features an exploding A-bomb as its logo. Though extreme in number, these commercial and communal adaptions of the language of nuclearism encapsulate the broader American attitude toward the im-agery of annihilation.

In her book *Missile Envy*, an energetic but sometimes disjointed polemic against the military-industrial complex, Helen Caldicott diag-noses these symptoms of the popularization of nuclear weapons as a psychopathology or cultural illness, which she explains in terms of Carl Jung's theory of the anima and the animus. While lambasting the nu-clear industry, Caldicott describes the American military's continual desire for new, widely diverse missile systems as a manifestation of male feelings of "inadequate sexuality and a need to continually prove their virility plus a primitive fascination with killing" (319). Not only the phallic imagery of missiles and bombs, argues Caldicott, but "the names that the military uses are laden with psychosexual overtones: missile erector, thrust-to-weight ratio, soft lay down, deep penetration, hard line and soft line."[1] Such Freudian metaphors for describing weapon systems, she suggests, obscure their destructive capabilities while simultaneously informing them with a disproportionate virilism.

Looking more deeply into the psychology of weapons-making than Caldicott does, Spencer Weart in his cultural history of nuclear anxiety provides exhaustive evidence of how, well before the development of nuclear physics, atomic energy had already come to stand for "all the powers of science, powers for the better—or perhaps for the worst" (16). Because of the caution with which scientists conducted atomic research in the 1920s and '30s, for example, their work was enshrouded in a "secretiveness" that, when combined with "the widespread suppression of the natural curiosity about matters such as sex and birth," led to the popular association of nuclear science with age-old myths about the unknown forces controlling life (56–57). Over time, observes Weart, nuclear imagery has become the modern receptacle of a host of "universal anxieties and hopes," including "peeking at forbidden secrets; punishment through abandonment or other victimization by an authority; a corresponding all-destructive rage; homicidal and suicidal urges and the accompanying guilt; struggle through chaos; heroic triumph over peril; miraculous life and regeneration of self; world rebirth through a marriage of survivors; [and] entry to a joyful community" (424). Collectively, these anxieties find in nuclear imagery what Weart calls "the myth of transmutational power from beyond the mortal sphere" (424), a myth that, because the impact of nuclear devices can be physically calculated, has taken on the additional prominence of inhabiting both the visible (natural) and invisible (symbolic) dimensions of experience. The popular nuclear imagery surrounding us, while it may in itself have few direct social effects, "harnesses a particular set of traditions, social tensions, and personal impulses, joining them into an alliance to work upon minds" (425). In the ambiguous presence of this imagery, with its promise of rebirth coexisting with that of annihilation, Weart concludes that "our secret thoughts have come into the open at last, taking form in metal so that we can deny them no longer" (425). Despite the particular recondite quality of nuclear technology (a quality that Wyschogrod argues ultimately has no mythological basis), or perhaps *because* of that quality, we continue to locate in its imagery all sorts of explanations for ourselves, our fears, and our world.

Weart makes an indisputable case for the centrality of nuclear imagery in the contemporary imagination. However, we still continue to find ways to deny its importance. As Lifton notes in his account of psychic numbing, our minds have a strong (even healthy) tendency to diminish our fear of nuclear weapons and energy by trivializing and thereby domesticating the language with which we speak about them: "Rather than feel their malignant actuality, we render them benign. In calling them 'nukes,' for instance, we render them small and 'cute,' something on the order of a household pet. That tendency was explicit in the naming of the two atomic bombs dropped on Japanese cities—the first 'Little Boy' suggesting a newborn baby or small child, the second 'Fat Man' after Winston Churchill. (So universal is the bomb-related impulse toward numbing that even Japanese survivors domesticated their bomb by referring to it with the not-unpleasant-sounding term *pikadon*, or 'flash-boom')" (Lifton and Falk 106–107). Lifton reasons that, together with the "nuke-speak" used by nuclear experts, this popular belittling of the language by those who discuss nuclear issues (including nuclear protestors) anesthetizes us from their destructive power: "Quite simply, *these words provide a way of talking about nuclear weapons without really talking about them*" (Lifton and Falk 107). But if we cannot use these words to talk meaningfully about self-annihilation, what words can we use?

One way of speaking about nuclearism, as I discussed in chapter 2, is to speak out against it. Furthermore, as Weart points out and as the abundance of intelligent research into nuclearism over the last fifteen years proves, the continued display of nuclear imagery has begun to render them "so bizarre that more and more people, facing the propaganda that exploits the images, have begun to ask whether the messages are realistic and relevant" (425). Many poets—even those less actively hostile to the nuclear complex than the protest poets—have, from time to time, also voiced their objections. More often, however, given their other concerns, this second group of poets find themselves thinking *through* the imagery of nuclearism as it impinges upon contemporary experience. Stylistically, a major difference between the protest poets and this second group is the accepted prominence of the private, meditative voice, or what might be called the post-Romantic "I," in their verse. In opposition to what Des Pres observes about the implied protest in these poets' work, what I here refer to as "the apocalyptic lyric" in fact seems less interested in saying No to the bomb than in creating accessible, nontrivializing metaphors for the otherwise inconceivable devastation and extinction of nuclear war.

In characterizing this "subjective" literary response to nuclearism, Rob Wilson has described the widely diverse portrayal of nuclear imagery in post-World War II writing as a generic extension of American artists' struggle with "vastness" since before the eighteenth century. Situating postnuclear culture within the tradition of "the American sublime," "a poetic genre that implicates the lyric ego in the production of America as site of the sublime," Wilson argues that historically this genre, "rooted in Puritan and Romantic persuasions and political unconscious ambitions," has been "deconstructed by the nuclear horizon," because the impact of nuclear technology has called into question "the long-standing American sacralization of force that a poet like Whitman all too unconsciously embodied" (9). In a section of his book entitled "Beyond the Natural Sublime," Wilson traces the way postmodern poets transfer the source of vast power from pastoral to urban landscapes as they "try to theorize these emergent modes of American sublimity—commodity-infinitude, simulacrous immensity, mass death, nuclear weaponry, black holes, the colonization of outer space into tourist attractions, viral infiltration—within an urban space . . . that is itself another instance of mass empowerment gone off the deep end into waste, death, disaster" (226). Together with scientists, politicians, and other power makers, American poets are complicit in this unconscious aggrandizing of nuclearism, since "nuclear power . . . seems to emanate from the innermost depths of American poetics articulating self-rapture and national empowerment like a first fate, a fact of nature" (227). The post-Transcendentalist lyric ego, for Wilson, contributes to the proliferation of nuclear culture.

However, the difference between nineteenth-century and postmodern poetics in their expressions of the sublime is that whereas the "natural sublime" entailed an implicit dialogue between the "idealist" poet and the wilderness being observed, the nuclear sublime entails a dialogue between the disenfranchised poet and technology. In other words, having inherited a poetics that responded to the threatening vastness of the natural landscape and tamed it through a self-empowering art, postmodern poets have been faced with applying that subjectivist poetics to the alternate scenario of a power "that threatens to efface not only subjective traces but entire reference systems" (234). Outside the political complications inherent in this dramatic shift in venue for the lyric poet, the additional stylistic problem it creates involves the potential *qualitative* failure of the earlier poetics of the sublime "to domesticate this astonishing force through homey but inadequate metaphors of *mushroom, lightbulb, flower,* or *umbrella"* (235). In other words, in the same way critics have questioned the ability of projectivist poetics to handle radical politics in Levertov's work, Wilson questions the ability of post-Romantic, subjectively metaphoric language itself to encase (or "fictively dominate," to use Wilson's phrase) nuclear force in such a way as to gain a convincing intellectual or spiritual power over it (236).[2]

Despite this concern about the adequacy of American poetics to confront the threat of annihilation, a wide range of poets—in terms of style, range of talent, and theme—have taken on the challenge of extending or reshaping subjectivist poetics in order to invent metaphors that (to recall Williams's words) might "geld the bomb" by helping "the mind contain" nuclear reality, rather than be subdued by it. But to measure the relative success of these poets is not easy, it seems to me, for two contrasting reasons: first, as Lifton suggests, to invoke familiar imagery to depict the nuclear threat, as a way of rendering the "unthinkable" thinkable, ironically risks anesthetizing us to the very thing described, rather than opening us to its unique nature—thereby creating exactly the opposite effect of the one desired. For example, in the anthology *Meltdown: Poems from the Core,* Bill Hopkins has a poem entitled "Radioactive Lover," in which he portrays radioactive fallout as a living substance or "sperm" permeating the landscape much like The Blob from Outer Space or the Black Plague (Shipley 10). Like hundreds of artworks depicting nuclear powers, Hopkins's poem readily uses familiar images to capture what is essentially an unfamiliar experience. The shortcoming of such depictions is that once the association with the familiar is established—even, as in this case, with the supposedly frightening but finally conventional imagery of horror movies—it distances us from the technological reality of the nuclear threat and perpetuates its fantastic dimensions, rather than induces us to see its proximity to ordinary life. On the other hand, to assume that only *un*familiar imagery, extreme metaphors or hysterical language can capture the sense of difference entailed in nuclear annihilation is equally problematic, because the very strangeness of such metaphors may fail to touch us other than intellectually—thereby (as in Lawrence Freedman's characterization of the debates of nuclear strategists) leaving us only with a sense of annihilation as an intellectual concept rather than as a force shaping our existence.[3]

Ultimately, poets may reach the conclusion that the subjective lyric so predominant in the United States in the last half century is inadequate to address conditions such as world hunger, imperialist incur-

sions, environmental decay, dangerous technologies, genetic engineer-
ing, and nuclear annihilation in other than a limited, self-centered, or
self-parodying manner. Yet despite the profound implications of these
global issues on the value of the individual life, rather than trivializing
personal experience or eliminating it altogether (at least until the end
of a nuclear war), they permeate that life in a way that demands reimag-
ining or "re-minding" (Scheick, "Post-Nuclear" 76) even our most private experiences, if we do not want to live entirely disassociated from
our broader perceptions. As Adorno argues in his account of consciousness after Auschwitz, though our awareness of global annihilation may
cause us to experience "a sense of being not quite there" as the only authentically human existence, to take refuge in absolute despair or nothingness is as shortsighted as to deny annihilation's real presence in our
lives (363–64). So in risking misrepresentation of the subject of annihilation yet at the same time in attempting to refashion its prevalence
through metaphors of personal experience, the poets of the apocalyptic
lyric keep bringing home to us that nuclear annihilation is not only a
"universal" threat but, emotionally and spiritually speaking, a highly
individuated (if not a strictly subjective) one as well. Their poems strive
to shock us into recognizing the extreme violence of the nuclear threat
(though not, in most cases, for gratuitous reasons), yet they do so in
terms that by lyric conventions draw attention to our humanity. In following this second way of nothingness, these apocalyptic poets[4] stretch
(and sometimes strain) their metaphors so that, at their best, they
deepen our sense of annihilation, particularly by the way they alter our
sense of personal experience itself.

◇ In the apocalyptic lyric, metaphors for nuclear war, power, and annihilation are basically employed in two corresponding ways, either as the
indirect, implied subject of familiar imagery (the tenor of the metaphor)
or as the imagery itself (the vehicle) used to evoke some other, more familiar subject. Of the former model, well-known examples from the
1950s and 1960s set the range: William Stafford's "At the Bomb Testing
Site," for instance, with its perspective of the "panting lizard" waiting
for history to change in the desert as it watches "an important scene/
acted in stone for little selves/ at the flute end of consequences" (41)
speaks with an understated power best evoked through obliquity, as it
diminishes the global significance of atomic testing without trivializing it. In "When the Vacation Is Over for Good," Mark Strand depicts
nuclear war as a kind of grim fairy tale, in terms less of its inevitable

devastation than of its unpredictable strangeness "like summer/ At its most august except that the nights were warmer/ And the clouds seemed to glow"; speaking in the guise of a storyteller he ultimately admits to being "still unable, to know just what it was/ That went so completely wrong, or why it is/ We are dying" (5). Philip Levine also tells a tale of sorts when he depicts the aftermath of Hiroshima in an extended metaphor in "The Horse." Still alive, yet "without skin, naked, hairless,/ without eyes and ears" (11), the horse represents the spirit of the *hibakusha* which has fled the devastated city. Although the survivors, their mouths open "like the gills of a fish caught/ above water," continue to speak about the lost ghost of the horse, the poem's speaker realizes that the horse never existed and will not return; even the survivors themselves will forget about it, the poem concludes, once their "rage" has "gone out of/ their bones in one mad dance" (12). In six short stanzas Robert Lowell's "Fall 1961" uses no less than seven metaphors for the poet's sense of uncertainty, fear, and sheer exhaustion under the nuclear threat—from that of the swinging pendulum and "tock, tock, tock" of the grandfather clock he watches as he thinks how "our end drifts nearer" to his simile for the arms control debate: "We are like a lot of wild/ spiders crying together,/ but without tears" (*Life* [*For the Union*] 11). And in "For the Union Dead," one of the most remarkable poems of the last fifty years, Lowell links the prominent display in a downtown Boston bank of a "commercial photograph" of "Hiroshima boiling// over a Mosler safe" (as an image of postwar capitalism) to the troubled tradition of American puritanism, when with bitter irony he cites the caption to the photograph: "the 'Rock of Ages' " (*Life* [*For the Union*] 72). Finally, in "Advice to a Prophet" Richard Wilbur subverts images of mass destruction with figurative images of nature, so that we might better sense what it is we risk losing in a nuclear war, which is not only the natural world but our appreciation of that world. "What should we be," asks Wilbur, "without/ The dolphin's arc, the dove's return,// These things in which we have seen ourselves and spoken?" (*New* 182–83).

Whether resorting to nature, fantasy, or high culture, all these poems employ images from the world of the familiar and then distort that imagery to convey the skewed or illogical character of nuclear technology. In taking this approach to the bomb's massive power, they recall Stein's "common sense" claim that the nuclear threat by itself is neither "natural" nor "interesting" in the ways we have convinced ourselves it is. However, as I hope to illustrate in the second part of this chapter, it is partly because of that same threat that basic assumptions in the work of a poet like Wilbur, assumptions about both nature and nothingness, have also changed during the nuclear age.

Recent variations on Stafford's often anthologized poem include Ted Kooser's "In the Kitchen, at Midnight," in which he expresses envy of the cockroach's ability to survive a nuclear blast (*Sure* 45), and Sherod Santos's updated "Near the Desert Test Sites," which mocks the "pampered opulence" (77) of the tacky 1985 landscape of Palm Desert, Nevada. And not unlike Strand, who employs Borgesian twists in "When the Vacation Is Over for Good" in order to suggest the cost of a nuclear confrontation, Baron Wormser invents his own fairy tale, complete with three different characterizations of death, in order to express exactly what extinction means, in "I Try to Explain to My Children a Newspaper Article Which Says that According to a Computer a Nuclear War Is Likely to Occur in the Next Twenty Years" (54). In a more literary vein, Eleanor Wilner's "High Noon at Los Alamos" initially imagines the "white fire" of the first bomb test in an image of the midday desert sun, but then conceives of nuclear war in terms of mythic poetry itself—the blast as the "signal fire that ends/ the epic" of world history, and the electromagnetic shock wave as "a curséd line/ with its caesura, a pause/ to signal peace, or a rehearsal/ for the silence" (67). Even more obliquely than Strand, Levine, Wormser, or Wilner, Tom Disch (who has written as much science fiction as poetry) in "An Allegory" uses the conceit of three lofty ballerinas on a stage ("these represent light") in order to convey the abruptness of nuclear extinction. The ballerinas

> seem to float. Wave
> or particle? we ask ourselves, when
> suddenly the theater
> is plunged
>
> in darkness, as some day zillions
> of years hence our universe
> will appear to fizzle out, much as if the same
> three famous ballerinas were to be seen
>
> walking down a midtown street in rush hour,
> too anxious or too old to interest
> anyone. Then
> the curtain call —
> we all stand up and scream. (49)

The hyperbolic "zillions" collapses the sense of an indefinite future into the immediate present, as Disch imagines annihilation as the blackout that ends the dance performance, while the audience's enthusiastic applause, suddenly, and horribly, becomes the cries of the annihilated. The distortion here is extreme yet plausible.

Echoing Wilbur's regard for nature, Kooser's "At Nightfall" considers "our madness" in bringing to an end the swallow's ability "to guide her flight home in the darkness" after the "hundred thousand years" (One World 37) it has taken her to learn it. Similarly, in its direct address to her horse, Maxine Kumin's "The Agnostic Speaks to Her Horse's Hoof" follows a pastoral, indirect route in fighting, if not despair, dismay at the catastrophic potential of technology. Finding herself on her knees in order to pry a splinter out of her horse Amanda's upturned hoof, the poet suddenly thinks of two kinds of apocalypse, biblical and technological ones. But to counter a sense of her own (and her horse's) insignificance, she urges Amanda, "Let us ripen in our own way," and goes on pulling out the splinter with a hoofpick, as she ends the poem in mock heroic fashion. Without denying her fear, she finds dignity in defiance:

> Let us come to the apocalypse complete
> without splinter or stone.
> Let us ride out
> on four iron feet. (Our Ground 134)

Even more striking in their nuclear detail than these poems, though, are a number of poems by Paul Zimmer, who, together with John Engels, is unique among American poets for having witnessed aboveground atomic tests. As a drafted infantryman in the U.S. Army, Zimmer was assigned in Spring 1955 to work in the public information office for the Atomic Energy Commission (AEC) at Camp Desert Rock, not far from the Camp Mercury, Nevada, bomb test site. Of the dozen or so bombs detonated during Zimmer's time at Camp Desert Rock, he observed eight firsthand, including one air burst or aerial shot, one underground burst, and half a dozen blasted from towers. During most of these bomb tests, Zimmer was stationed with his fellow infantryman in the "forward position" in trenches not far from ground zero where, after the blast and initial shock wave had passed over them, the soldiers were ordered to advance slowly toward the rising cloud until the AEC's geiger counters indicated too lethal a dose of radiation to proceed. As Zimmer has noted, being used as "guinea pigs" in order for the AEC "to observe how military troops—this is what they said—would react under atomic attack," the infantrymen themselves (most under twenty years old) were "of course, scared shitless,"[5] though they tried to maintain a tough facade.

In a prose passage from *Earthbound Zimmer*, Zimmer provides a compelling account of one bomb test. First he recounts his troop's being awakened before dawn, driven in trucks into the desert, and told to crouch and cover their eyes as the countdown proceeded. Then he describes the blast itself, followed by his troop's advance:

> The flash was like a sudden immense snap of electrical heat. I could see the bones in my fingers. I stayed low, trembling, smelling ozone in the air. From several miles away I could hear the shock wave rolling toward us like a stampede. When it roared over the trench top a few seconds later I could hear things tearing from the land. We rose at last to see the fireball blossoming lavender on its great column in the dawn light. The sun came up as we began to walk forward. I could see the debris of the blasted desert all around us, the bushes and cacti ripped up. We came across corpses of the dead and near-dead animals of the desert. A brightly colored bird ran crazily past me, trying to find its burned-out eyes again. Then just ahead of me a blinded rabbit sprang from a bush amidst the men and began zigzagging through them, bumping into their boots. "Son-of-a-bitch!" one of the men said, and kicked viciously at the rabbit. It rolled in the dust but rose to hobble again. The men began laughing at its frantic movements. "Son-of-a-bitch!" another man said, and this time kicked it squarely in its side. It flew through the air and landed softly amidst the roots of the fractured Yucca plants and cacti. The rabbit did not move again. We walked on toward the grey column of dust as it drifted into the shape of a Z in the morning crosswinds. (*Earthbound* n.p. [32])

What is so striking about this passage, despite its understated metaphors ("like a sudden immense snap of electrical heat," "like a stampede," "the fireball blossoming lavender," "the shape of a Z"), is Zimmer's emphasis not on the bomb, nor on his own physical and emotional response, but on the frantic activities of the bird and rabbit, turning our attention from the human to nature itself. Indeed, together with the image of the fireball which appears in later Zimmer poems, this wounded rabbit haunts his work as a reminder of what he regards "the ultimate human cruelty" of nuclear war ("Importance" 20). Robbed of its sight, the rabbit's aimlessness comes to signify in nature the aimlessness of the soldiers themselves. Yet rather than express compassion for their fellow sufferer, the soldiers divert themselves from their hostility toward the bomb (against which they are powerless) by turning on the rabbit (who is powerless against them). Identifying not with the poor "son-of-a-bitch" driven mad by the bomb but with the destructive force behind it—even the Z shape of the dust cloud alludes to the poet's name—the soldiers make a pathetic attempt to displace their own sense of victimization through the ritualized torture and death of the rabbit.

In other poems about both his immediate and long-term fears of exposure to the bomb tests, Zimmer (like Wilbur, Kumin, and Kooser) also uses the natural world for contrast, as well as for consolation. In the 1981 "Poem Ending with an Old Cliché," for instance, the death of the poet's cat, in whose eyes he has watched "the clouds come down," reminds him of the truism, "Life is precious," as he again recalls "the flash and ram of those explosions,/ The vaporized towers and mangled animals,/ Caved-in trenches and awesome dawn clouds" whose radioactive "secrets" he might still be carrying within his own body twenty-five years later (*Ancient* 23). However, instead of despairing at the power of annihilation, Zimmer in this case admits to his own powerlessness, while he still relies on his natural instincts to reinvest the "old cliché" with new meaning: "From down on my knees in fear/ Of early death, senility or loss;/ Even in happiness it cannot be forgotten" that "life is precious" (23). Here invisible radiation reminds Zimmer of the value of the lives it endangers.

Zimmer's preoccupation with war and mass killing predates his poems that explicitly recall the atomic tests, but as is best demonstrated in his "Imbellis" poems, the peculiar annihilatory power of nuclear weapons complicates what otherwise might have developed into a more traditional voice of pacifism. In the first nine Imbellis poems composed during the war in Vietnam (*Republic* 11–19), through his trademark persona "Zimmer" who appears in so many of his poems and the menacing figure of "Imbellis"—a mythic figure who "born by mistake in a test-tube . . . has, as his name implies, war embodied within him" (Jellema 75)—Zimmer attempts to purge the cruelty he finds inside himself as a way of exposing it in others.[6] Although by the end of this early sequence Zimmer manages to kill Imbellis and return him to the agar jar where he was born, this violent character refuses to abandon Zimmer's sensibility, reappearing in several of Zimmer's poems in the 1970s, most significantly in a revised version of "The Sweet Night

Bleeds from Zimmer," where the poet connects Imbellis directly to his memory of the atomic tests.

As in other Zimmer poems, "The Sweet Night" is grounded in the imagery of nature. The first three strophes recall Zimmer's being cornered as a child by a bully who beats him until "the sweet night is bleeding from my skull." Then in the fourth strophe, the memory of the beating itself "in a dark place" is generalized into a night landscape filled with stars, which "descend to coil about my head,/ Buzzing about my gravity, sinking/ Their stingers in my lips and eyelids" (*Family* 20). "How could I have forgotten all these stars?" the poet asks himself, but in an abrupt shift in the fifth strophe, this memory suddenly stirs his memory of the test site, where an even grander assault on his person occurred. As Rod Jellema notes, at this point "The Sweet Night" switches from present to past tense verbs (76), and reminiscent of the prose passage from *Earthbound Zimmer*, the poem catalogues images of nature being blasted by the bomb, whose

> flash and shock wave rammed
> Sand in my face, uprooted cactus,
> Blasted the animals, birds from the sky.
> Afterwards, under the fireball
> And faint stars, we wanted to kick
> Dead rabbits, throw stones at each other,
> Call each other sons-of-bitches. (*Family* 20)

In the course of this poem, Imbellis has been transformed from a spirit of human cruelty who beats up a child to the spirit of annihilation, including self-annihilation, as embodied by nuclear weapons. Yet by focusing on images from nature, rather than on global holocaust, not only does Zimmer maintain a human scale, but particularly in the image of the soldiers throwing stones and calling each other (not the rabbit this time) "sons-of-bitches," he expresses each one's complicity with that larger spirit. The sixth strophe makes this complicity more pronounced, as Zimmer changes scenes again (though still in a natural setting) to the image of himself fishing at night on "a dark still lake"; he remembers catching a pickerel which "when I ripped it out . . . / Screamed like a wounded rabbit" (*Family* 21). Linking this fish's cry with the irradiated rabbit in the desert, the poet expresses his horror at discovering his own destructive urge, so he rows his boat "out of the dark,/ Churning the galaxies and nebulae" reflected in the lake water, thereby metaphorically wreaking as much havoc on nature by his escape from cruelty as by his participation in it, in either case "spoiling the perfect night." Realizing his own complicity with that which also victimizes him, Zimmer echoes the poem's opening line in his final strophe and remains "caught" in a dark place by Imbellis, who "won't back off and let me be." Unable to hide "under/ Mother's navel, behind father's penis," no longer able to see himself as inculpable, despite his sense of victimization, he recognizes the paradox that, if he acknowledges the opposing sides in himself, he has lost his identity. "I can't remember who I am," he laments. In closing, the poem fuses the images of Zimmer being pummeled, Zimmer with his face in the desert sand, Zimmer rowing out of the dark to escape his worst instincts, and by inference, Zimmer writing the poem—all into one image of

> Someone wounded and breathing hard,
> Trying to become the earth; sorry man
> Remembering each cruelty under the stars;
> Someone wagging submission forever. (*Family* 21)

"The Sweet Night Bleeds for Zimmer" marks a turning point for Zimmer, plunging him into the complexities of how internalized assumptions about war have led us to the brink of annihilation. In later poems, Zimmer continues to explore the bomb test imagery he cannot abandon, as nature itself for him becomes increasingly subject to the destructive force of nuclearism. In "Zimmer Sees Imbellis, the Bully, Rise from the Water," the poet's haunted memory of the bomb tests is abruptly stirred when Imbellis again surfaces, this time from the bottom of the lake where Zimmer is fishing and, with a silent rage like radiation, penetrates everything in the landscape. Helpless against this creature of annihilation, who "ruts and strikes flint," "shits in the waters/ Of our lakes," and "stalks our borders," the poet concludes, "We can do nothing but stand together" (*Great Bird* 15).

"Because of Duties, Zimmer Had Forgotten the Forest" also seeks consolation in nature—not in animals this time but in trees: The first stanza praises the beauty of dusk in a forest whose trees' "great canopies begin to grow the stars," yet in forgetting the forest for the trees, as it were, the poet prefers not "to dwell upon this splendor" but instead to build a wood fire to back its "glister away from my glare" (*Great Bird* 6). In the second stanza, though, the flames of that fire again remind the poet of the "ferocity" of those predawn bomb tests, leaving him finally "no comfort" throughout his night in the forest, until "dawn begins to piece itself through the leaves" and helps him to remember his "delicate kinship" to, rather than the apocalyptic suggestion of, burning wood. In a mood of reconciliation he concludes this poem, "no matter what we do to trees they love/ Us to the end, stroking our bones with root tips,/ Topping the markers to purify our graves." By invoking the forgiving power of nature, these and other Zimmer poems that allude to the bomb tests often close in a resigned, accepting mood as the poet searches for justification for having been branded in the Nevada desert.

Zimmer's more recent poem "But Bird" takes a somewhat different tact—first by contrasting the bomb tests not to the natural wilderness but to an image of jazz saxophonist Charlie Parker, and second by offering, instead of consolation, an ambiguity reminiscent of "For the Union Dead." Juxtaposing the scene in 1954 of one of Bird's last performances at Birdland in New York against the poet's own induction into the army, Zimmer alternates stanzas between descriptions of the generative power of Parker's music as "something to believe in" and those of the deathly atmosphere of the bomb tests as one of those "things you should forget" (*Big Blue* 35). On the one hand, Bird

> blew crisp and clean,
> Bringing each face in the crowd
> Gleaming to the bell of his horn.
> No fluffing, no wavering,
> But soaring like on my old
> Verve waxes back in Ohio. (*Big Blue* 35–36)

On the other hand, months later, when the poet finds himself in the Nevada desert, after the countdown,

> The bones in our fingers were
> Suddenly x-rayed by the flash.
> We moaned together in light
> That entered everything,
> Tried to become the earth itself
> As the shock rolled toward us. (*Big Blue* 36)

Jazz induces "soaring," while bombs induce cowering. Through three musical sets, "Bird was giving it all away,/ One of his last great gifts," but in the desert "when the trench caved in it felt/ Like death," even though afterwards

> we clawed out,
> Walked beneath the roiling, brutal cloud
> To see the flattened houses,

Sheep and pigs blasted,
Ravens and rabbits blind
Scrabbling in the grit and yucca. (*Big Blue* 36)

Once again Zimmer portrays the blinded rabbits, but instead of emphasizing the brutality of the soldiers who kicked them, he contrasts their
"scrabbling" against the unwavering melodies of Parker. Indeed, the final, unresolved irony in "But Bird" is that despite the life-giving performance of Parker, in contrast to the morbid passivity of the poet during the bomb tests, it is the bold saxophonist who disappears "Five
months later, dead," while paradoxically the timid Zimmer survives,
only to remember being "down on my knees,/ Wretched with fear in/
The cinders of the desert" (*Big Blue* 37). This conclusion suggests not
only the omnipotence of nuclear weaponry, but the equally magnificent
though fragile power of the beauty it threatens to annihilate. As Zimmer has expanded his ideas of nature in poems such as "But Bird" and
others [7] to include not only landscapes and animals but people and art,
he has also become increasingly pessimistic about the ultimate possibility of curbing the destructive power of nuclearism. Nevertheless,
with more poignancy than before, his more recent work conveys just
how much he believes the endangered world is to be treasured. His
bomb-test experience manifests itself not only in a fear of the natural
world's annihilation, but in a deepening, sobered appreciation for the
most vulnerable qualities of life, as well as for the beauty without which
that life would have no justification.

With a dark irony similar to Lowell's and Zimmer's, poets who grew
up during the early years of the Cold War have also responded to atomic
proliferation and testing, often with more extreme metaphors than
Lowell's or Zimmer's. Toi Derricotte's "Aerial Photograph Before the
Atomic Bomb" (part one of "Fires in Childhood") recalls the poet's
childhood fascination with a *Life* magazine photo of Hiroshima taken
just before it was bombed. Puzzling over the panoramic view of the
doomed city, turning it around like a "kaleidoscope or prism," the
young girl in the poem identifies with "the town lying under," as Derricotte introduces the frightening simile of a sleeping child about to be
raped, "before the spasm/ of stopped breath, the closure at the/ scream
of the throat, before the body is awakened/ along its shocked spine to
bursting/ light, the legs closing, the arms,/ like a chilled flower" (15).
"This was a heat/ I had felt already in our house," she confesses, casting the bombing in frighteningly intimate terms. With a fascination
similar to Derricotte's, Kay Murphy's "Hiroshima Photo" examines the

image of a young *hibakusha* shortly after the blast, but rather than focus on the child's smiling image, Murphy employs a dramatic monologue to convey the innocent fear of both the girl in the photograph and the girl looking at it: "If you look/ closely, there's a squint in my eyes/ from the sun," says the poet in the *hibakusha*'s voice, "and a slight blur/ from the rising number of casualties" (5).

In less domestic settings, poems such as David Bottoms's "A Model Shelter" (48), Greg Pape's "Drill" (39), and Jim Powell's "Home Free" remember the fallout shelters and the "duck and cover" civil defense exercises of the fifties and sixties. In the manner of a post-Romantic meditation on a childhood memory, Powell expresses how those exercises, performed nationwide to assure schoolchildren they could indeed survive a nuclear attack, would stir them instead to imagine "an aftermath/ of freedom, . . ./ a frontier of long orchards/ and no parents calling" where "we could be wild Indians/ prowling behind the vanished fences/ of a new suburban wilderness" (5). Typical of the domestic ideology of the time, these highly publicized exercises for survival encouraged a whole generation "later, to think it made us different:/ we could call ourselves/ the first to ripen toward the light/ of a general annihilation/ we could believe we shared" (6). But in a reversal that occurs through memory, Powell concludes that the real lesson for children behind those cheerful acts of self-defense was not to trust national security, as we might expect, but to "trust/ nothing . . . to the next day./ It might not come. We dwelt on that" (7).

In a less discursive style than Powell's, Stephen Dunn's "The Cocked Finger" also expresses the "terrible dullness" that has inured the post-war generation to nuclearism:

I've gotten used to the rapes,
the murders. I eat dinner
and watch them on Channel Six
and nothing shocks me,
not even kindness,
not even, though I'm afraid,
the bomb.
The finger that might
touch it off is cocked
like an apostrophe
on the wrong side of a possessive,
an error so obvious
almost everyone can see it. (460–61)

The frankly banal simile of the misplaced apostrophe figuratively suggests that, despite the gross inhumanity of nuclear weapons, because almost everyone *does* see the error, no one pays attention to it.

Beyond metaphors for the social impact of a nuclear attack, what might be said about its aesthetic effects—its brilliant colors, deafening roar, and brutal physical power? As subject as anyone to bomb worship, poets are not immune to the allure of bright, irradiated clouds rising miles into the sky, as in Sharon Olds's "When":

> I wonder now only when it will happen,
> when the young mother will hear the
> noise like somebody's pressure cooker
> down the block, going off. She'll go out in the yard,
> holding her small daughter in her arms,
> and there, above the end of the street, in the
> air above the line of the trees,
> she will see it rising, lifting up
> over our horizon, the upper rim of the
> gold ball, large as a giant
> planet starting to lift up over ours.
> She will stand there in the yard holding her daughter,
> looking at it rise and glow and blossom and rise,
> and the child will open her arms to it,
> it will look so beautiful. (20)

In the understated manner of Stafford and Strand, Olds says nothing about the destructive force of the blast, her darkest image being of a pressure cooker. Instead, she imagines the scene from a domestic viewpoint by using familiar diction, commonplace imagery, and colloquial versification. Yet despite the line breaks that interrupt the syntax, thereby suggesting the suddenness of the explosion, most of the poem's impact as a statement of quiet abhorrence relies not on the form and imagery of the poem as much as on general cultural notions of what a blast is like—a fantasy that has become a source for endless poetic speculation, as in Maxine Kumin's "Out in It" (*Long* 65–66), C. K. Williams's "Downwards" (*Poems* 44), Jared Carter's "Electromagnetic Pulse" (*Millenial* 12), Richard Cole's "The Last Days of Heaven" (36), Dana Gioia's "The End" (*Daily* 51–52), and Elizabeth Spires's "Sunday Afternoon at Fulham Palace" (13–15). Like Olds's, these poems emphasize a nuclear blast as a rupture in the ordinary business of everyday life, so that the metaphor is one of a negation that abruptly creates the absence of the present. However, as Lifton warns, regardless of the tonal rejection of apocalypse in "When," the language in the poem unwittingly tends to valorize, even to deify, nuclear power without any indication that the poet suspects her own motives for doing so.

Despite these various efforts, the task of creating metaphors for the individual experience of nuclear annihilation in order to capture its implications as well as its potentiality is not as easy as we might think, because to have that experience is, de facto, to eliminate all other experience; and any poem that relies as much on subjective consciousness as Olds's poem does structurally poses the problem of presenting in too familiar a manner an image no human being (or idiom) could survive to talk about. In other words, poems such as hers do not finally portray the experience of nuclear *annihilation* but only of a nuclear *catastrophe* up to, yet not a second beyond, the moment of annihilation. Of course, any nuclear exchange may be sufficient cause for annihilation, but speculations on annihilation need not be limited solely to the moment of its occurrence.

◇ On the other side of poems that use metaphors for the imagery of nuclear havoc are those that employ the same imagery as a metaphor's vehicle, not to portray annihilation but to portray contemporary experience. Whether Michael Burkhard's "Someone," for example, is about a conflict between two lovers, the poet's bereft consciousness, or a nuclear holocaust is, for me at least, uncertain, but doubtless the imagery that permeates his poem derives from that wasteland we now associate with external, not just internal, annihilation—the "washed away" moment, the tree bearing "a song of ashes," the landscape devoid of "a village, horses drawn up, and the water there," and the "black sky out a window" which "will drift by" but "will be still as well" (16). In another example of this kind of metaphor, William Olsen's "Fireworks," a poem about suburban ennui, or "the nothingness of a night" on the Fourth of July "in the stalled heart of the country" (147), is steeped in the language of nuclear war to describe skyrockets, sparklers, Roman Candles, and fireworks as emblems of the repressed violence just beneath the surface of a dying American town. Speaking of the antics of neighborhood children, Olsen writes, "Each match flares up/ its very own holocaust on this street,/ illuminating kids who came from some place further/ even than the dark houses where nothing has changed for years," and the poem closes with those same children seen as the victims of their own "incendiary hearts": "All prior attempts at happiness have failed./

There are no scared children/ half naked on the naked lawn of ashes/ who walk armed into the vast oven of night" (148). For Olsen, the nightmare of our contemporary torpor is not, as it is for T. S. Eliot's Prufrock, like Dante's Inferno; it is like Dachau and Hiroshima.

In contrast to using images of nuclear war as metaphors for horror or ennui, and in a shocking inversion of poems that juxtapose images from nature *against* bomb imagery, Frederick Turner's "Early Warning" freely employs the language of "a missile strike" to describe the arrival of spring in Dallas:

> All along Hillcrest and Arapaho
> Rises, pinkwhite, a radioactive glow
> Of blanched pearblossom, apple, plum and quince,
> Black redbud cankered with flushed innocence.
> Don't drive there with the window open; you'll
> Fall sick with the flower-fumes. It's April Fool,
> It's mayday, mayday. Photochemical,
> The Carolina jasmine's cadmium fireball
> Batters the sidewalk with a yellow shock
> Releasing a sweet gas of poppycock. (*April* 39)

Rather than shun nuclear imagery as too terrifying to consider, Turner admits it into his imagination by deliberately, rather than inadvertently, trying to domesticate it. Unlike Olds's "When," however, which only alludes to an explosion, Turner's poem creates tension by testing the limits of its own metaphoric language: Does spring on the Texas plains, we might ask, really arrive in as dramatic fashion as a nuclear attack? That Turner encloses the poem in rhyming couplets, therein echoing the urbane wit of Alexander Pope, formally discloses his manipulation of language and creates an ironic distance between poet and landscape. When he spots an oncoming thunderstorm, for example, he reassures himself, "Yes, it's a cloud. The weathermap has grown/ A newborn thunderworld all of its own,/ Mushrooming up, neon and shadowhazy," and then he urges himself to prepare for yet another strike—of hail this time:

> It smells of black disk-brake powder, of guns,
> Of pyramids and glass and pentagons.
> Better take shelter in an underpass.
> City of all desires, city of glass. (*April* 39)

Unlike Lowell's layered ironies in "Fall 1961" and "For the Union Dead," this poem does not employ nuclear imagery primarily to undermine it. Rather, Turner plays indiscriminately with that imagery, at the seeming risk of valorizing it, perhaps to deflate its sanctified stature, perhaps to unveil our false sense of security from it. The aesthetic (and, some might add, moral) questions his poem raises—one reason why "Early Warning" may stir as much antipathy among readers as admiration—recall the questions critics have asked about Plath's use of Holocaust metaphors: How appropriate is it for a poet to employ the imagery of mass death in describing personal experience? Is there gratuitious violence in "Early Warning"? Or does the deliberately cavalier posture of the poem release us from the psychic trap of nuclearism? If nothing else, it strikes me that the poem's self-conscious mannerisms structurally articulate, if only humorously, real conditions that are otherwise on a scale intractable in our shared symbolic experience.

Adrienne Rich's "Trying to Talk with a Man," a far more serious poem than "Early Warning" and entirely unrelated to it in theme as well as in viewpoint, uses a nuclear metaphor in a surprisingly comparable manner. Two earlier Rich poems, "Night-Pieces: For a Child" and "The Demon Lover," anticipate her later use of nuclear imagery to depict subjective experience. In the former poem, the poet as a young mother anxious about her child suddenly wakes up in the middle of the night "in a dark/ hourless as Hiroshima/ almost hearing you breathe/ in a cot three doors away" (*Fact* 67) and then combines the primeval and the modern, when the mother imagines herself and her infant "swaddled in a dumb dark/ old as sickheartedness,/ modern as pure annihilation," as the two of them "drift in ignorance" (*Fact* 68). "The Demon Lover" also combines progeny and aimlessness with annihilation, when Rich records a dream about being bombed, and then adds:

The end is just a straw,
a feather furling slowly down,
floating to light by chance, a breath
on the long-loaded scales.
Posterity trembles like a leaf
and we go on making heirs and heirlooms. (83–84)

In this poem the spectre of nuclear annihilation has the contours of the emptiness in a self-enclosed relationship.

In "Trying to Talk with a Man," the title and language point not to the landscape of holocaust, as "Early Warning" does in its intentionally misleading way, but to the intimacy of a collapsing marriage. Yet like Turner, Rich juxtaposes the imagery of domestic life against the arid "condemned scenery" of a Nevada test site: the "underground river/ forcing its way between deformed cliffs," the "dull green succulents," the "silence of the place," "laceration, thirst" (*Fact* 149–50). Instead of using familiar images to portray extreme horror, Rich uses extreme images to express the deadening effects of a painful breakup between a man and a woman:

> Out here I feel more helpless
> with you than without you
> You mention the danger
> and list the equipment
> we talk of people caring for each other
> in emergencies—laceration, thirst—
> but you look at me like an emergency
>
> Your dry heat feels like power
> your eyes are stars of a different magnitude
> they reflect lights that spell out: EXIT
> when you get up and pace the floor
>
> talking of the danger
> as if it were not ourselves
> as if we were testing anything else. (*Fact* 149–50)

In this poem, not only does our shared notion of a nuclear explosion (together with the expectation that weapons tested will inevitably be used) convey the despair of the poet, but in a fashion more subtle than in either "When" or "Early Warning," Rich's poem weaves a distinctly subjective yet broadly human experience into the very fabric of our conception of nuclear weapons, together with our impotence in containing them. The personal dread created by a failed relationship equals the deep cultural dread associated with annihilation. "Talking of the danger" of one reiterates exactly "talking of the danger" of the other, because in both cases we are talking about ourselves and testing ourselves. As Turner and Rich both insinuate, only by acknowledging that it is we who are being tested will we begin to see our way through that danger.[8]

By metaphorically integrating nuclear imagery and the fear of annihilation with more private dimensions of experience, apocalyptic lyric poets may not always express direct opposition to nuclearism, but, at their best, they broaden the figurative scope of both political poetry and the personal lyric in ways that reflect the age in which they are composed.[9] "Trying to Talk with a Man" is finally neither solely about gender relations nor about nuclearism; it is about both. Once Rich's poem establishes its peculiar but intricate bond between these two critical concerns, our sense of both is irreversibly altered, as she speaks through the nuclear present. Whether or not the reconstruction of thought her poem embodies can lead to our survival is debatable, but without such a reconstruction we remain mired in our present inadequate modes of thinking.

The Sensible Emptiness in Three Poems by Richard Wilbur

Because of the uniform quality of Richard Wilbur's poetry over the years, changes in his vision are not as easily traceable as in the work of Rich, a poet who celebrates change. Yet despite the formal grace of his work, Wilbur is a poet of disparities as well as of unities. No more a religious poet, finally, than a sociopolitical or transcendentalist one, he joins images and ideas as much to explore what inevitably divides them as to illustrate their inherent connections, to impart "the proper relation between the tangible world and the intuitions of the spirit" (*Responses* 125). To read a poem by Wilbur—whose poems like those of the Metaphysical poets are ideally suited for careful scrutiny—is to be pulled simultaneously toward anxiety and consolation, toward despair and hope, and ultimately to be deposited somewhere in between. More than most of his contemporaries, Wilbur has maintained a conviction in the continuity of the world; his deliberately balanced work seems, in its very structure, to argue a belief in nature, as well as in the role of language in nature. But his art attempts neither to convince us through a will to belief nor to cajole us through cunning; he considers his role as an artist too modest to proselytize or pander. Still, the assumptions of the believer are everywhere evident—in his rhymes, in his precise diction and playful punning, in his acceptance of prevalent literary conventions, in his patterns of imagery, in his tone.

Writing within these self-determined confines, Wilbur has been regularly criticized, ever since Randall Jarrell complained that "he never goes far enough" (230), for having avoided the serious issues of the modern world, for being too oblique or emblematic in his approach to contemporary problems, or, in comparison to such poets as Lowell, Berryman, Plath, and Ginsberg, for not suffering enough.[10] Rather than measure him only according to others, however, Wilbur's more appreciative readers opt to take him on his own terms, as a poet originally provoked by his disturbing experience in World War II "to take ahold of raw events and convert them, provisionally, into experience," as well as to take "refuge from events in language itself" (*Responses* 118), specifically, in the language of poetry. "One must gauge the impact of the war on Wilbur," notes John Reibetanz, "not so much by looking for reflections of it in his poetry (the way we do with Lowell) as by observing the extent to which it has driven him into a world of his own making" (63). Unlike more dramatic or politicized poets, he is a poet less of action than of observation, for whom "images come in and vision flows out" (Bixler 11), a "quiet thought-provoker . . . sick of pretensiousness and extravagant claims, desiring instead a simple and direct appraisal of the 'world's own change' " (Cummins 14), and, most of all, "a true nature poet" who "always has had a kind of ecological prophecy to deliver" and whose "reverence for life—not as an abstraction but in its very holy and delectable particulars—makes his voice timely" (Salinger 10). As Bruce Michelson adroitly observes, "If one of the shortcuts of our times is to assume that complexity and intensity are by nature at odds with one another, then Wilbur can teach us something about nature and poetry. Wilbur is a poet of *our* times, in many valid meanings of that phrase, yet there is nothing typical about his voice. It takes time to learn to hear him" (35).

Whether palatable to readers or not, the conspicuous presence of form in Wilbur's poems does more than suggest a belief in the ability of language to convey meaning. It provides two distinct advantages. First, his explicitly formal structure provides him a kind of linguistic sanctuary within which he can speculate on any subject outside his immediate experience. Like Yeats, in other words, Wilbur accepts the "artificiality" of art. In an early essay in response to the "free" verse of Williams, he writes,

> In each art the difficulty of the form is a substitution for the difficulty of direct apprehension and expression of the object. The first difficulty may be more or less overcome, but the second is insuperable; thus every poem begins, or ought to, by a disorderly retreat to defensible positions. Or, rather, by a perception of the hopelessness of direct combat, and a resort to the warfare of spells, effigies, and prophecies. The relation between the artist and reality is an oblique one, and indeed there is no good art which is not consciously oblique. If you respect the reality of the world, you know that you can approach that reality only by indirect means. (*Responses* 220)

The military terms Wilbur uses here ("disorderly retreat," "defensible positions," "warfare of spells") underscore his perception of the separation of, if not the outright opposition between, art and nature. Furthermore, in such a confrontation, nature inevitably has the upper hand; consequently, the artist must defer to "that feeling of inadequacy which must precede every genuine act of creation" (*Responses* 220).[11] By Wilbur's definition the subject of art (be it concrete or abstract, a red wheelbarrow or eternity) always demands greater respect than art itself, thus demanding modesty in the artist.

The second advantage to imposing form on a poem is that it releases the poet from having to devise another way of incorporating the ineffable or infinite, that which lies outside the confines of language; at the same time, asserting the ineffable as "other" frees the poet to beckon toward it, to imagine it, even to yearn for it. Here Wilbur takes his lead from Emily Dickinson, who, he wrote in 1959, "elected the economy of desire, and called her privation good, rendering it positive by renunciation" (*Responses* 11). Wilbur describes Dickinson as one who "identified in her mind . . . distance and delight": "Not only are the objects of her desire distant; they are also very often moving away, their sweetness increasing in proportion to their remoteness," because for her "it was natural and necessary that things be touched with infinity" (*Responses* 11–12). Implicit in this argument is that formal restrictions established for Dickinson the right relation between the self and the inherently distant, be it "Heaven" (defined as "what I cannot reach") or a "vanishing point" toward which "all things are seen . . . either moving or gesturing" (*Responses* 12). In other words, by recognizing and even imitating the limits of perception, form provides an indirect means by which the artist can treat a subject beyond the self, while it simultaneously opens and extends the range of that subject to limitless possibilities, from the widest extremes of infinity to its equally inconceivable counterpart of nothingness.

Within these self-determined parameters of poetry, Wilbur has shown throughout his career a preoccupation with "delectable particulars," the "things of this world" that manifest for him a "tension" between "eye and mind," therein establishing "the irreconcilable oppositions of appearance and knowledge" (Woodward 227). In triumphant poems, such as "A Plain Song for Comadre" and "Love Calls Us to the Things of This World," Wilbur comes to celebrate the spirit of life reflected in ordinary things—whether in a cleaning woman's "stained suds" that "flash/ Like angel-feathers" (*New* 244) or in nuns' "dark habits," helping them keep "their difficult balance" (*New* 234). Yet it is wrong, I think, to assume that Wilbur does nothing but revel in these particulars, ignoring the larger issues of his time. His approach may be formal, but he is no less serious nor candid than Levertov; however, like Turner and Rich, he concentrates on their individual implications instead of fashioning an activist response to nuclearism.

In fact, in three poems written at roughly ten-year intervals between the 1940s and 1960s—" 'A World without Objects Is a Sensible Empti-ness,' " "Advice to a Prophet," and "In the Field"—Wilbur specifically confronts the potential annihilation of "the things of this world," not only their physical eradication, but their spiritual annihilation as well. Yet what becomes clear when placing these three poems in sequence is how Wilbur's sense of annihilation has changed in the course of the nu-clear age: his vision has become not only more somber but increasingly expressive of the necessary modesty of the human spirit. A poet com-fortable with Platonic modes of thinking yet lacking Platonic aspira-tions, Wilbur in " 'A World without Objects . . .' " ontologically deduces the existence of a world other than this one by examining the particu-lars of this one as the signifiers of an "other." The imagined annihila-tion of things gives them their meaning, the experience of which the poet then applies to ordinary existence. But the metaphoric paradigm discovered here Wilbur later puts to broader use, when he comes to ac-knowledge that not only does potential annihilation create meaning in nature (and therefore for us), but it also signals the finitude of nature it-self, consequently circumscribing nature's primacy over the spirit. In other words, what we learn from imagining the annihilation of nature and the world is not just that nature has meaning (since it has the po-tential *not* to exist and therefore *not* to have meaning),[12] but also that nature itself is an endangered source of meaning and cannot, therefore, be relied on nor looked to as the provider of truth—a troubling conclu-sion, to say the least, for any avowed nature poet to reach.

◇ Taking its title from a slight rephrasing of a passage from Thomas Traherne's "Meditation 65" in *Second Century*, " 'A World without Ob-jects Is a Sensible Emptiness,' " like most of Wilbur's early nature po-ems, looks to the physical world for spiritual value. As Donald Hill notes, the poem "affirms a sort of responsibility toward the physical world, one based on a belief in its blessedness and in its power to refresh us" (64). Divided into seven identically structured four-line stanzas, the poem progresses from its concrete image for the imagination (stanzas 1–2), to the poet's expressed desire for the utterly abstract, or a "sensi-ble emptiness," as revealed through his warning to resist such a desire (stanzas 3–5), to his final celebration of the apprehensible world, displayed in the image of the Nativity (stanzas 6–7). What interests me about this poem, in this context, is not just Wilbur's resorting to "the trees arrayed/ In bursts of glare," "the halo-dialing run/ Of the country creeks, and the hills' bracken tiaras" (*New* 283)—namely, the glittering things of this world—but the emergence in its middle stanzas of an image of nothingness and the poet's disposition toward that "sensible emptiness," not as a death wish but as that state from which the objects of this world gain their credence.

The poem opens with an image of "tall camels of the spirit," alluding to the journey of the wise men toward Bethlehem and, more broadly, to the mind's own journeying. As these camels pass "the last groves loud/ With the sawmill shrill of the locust," they are headed from the safety of the physical world to "the whole honey of the arid/ Sun," or "the land of sheer horizon" (*New* 283). The image of the desert here is equated to the absence of objects, "where the brain's lantern-slide/ Revels in vast returns." When all objects are annihilated, the imagination is not depleted but piqued, in the same way that a light in a vast void of space travels indefinitely. The camels are "hunting Traherne's/ *Sensible emptiness*": their search for the Messiah is expressed as a desire for the wholly abstract or, as it were, the wholly other. The relevant passage from Traherne reads: "The whole world ministers to you as the theatre of your love. It sustains you and all objects that you may continue to love them. Without which it were better for you to have no being. Life without objects is a sensible emptiness, and that is a greater misery than death or nothing" (Hill 62). For Wilbur, there is an undeniable attraction to this emptiness—which is "sensible" in its being " 'knowable'—apprehensible to the consciousness" (Hill 63), even though Traherne himself believes that to live in such a state would stir "a greater misery than death or nothing." As the third stanza explains, the camels, as "connoisseurs of thirst" in the desert, "long to learn to drink/ Of pure mirage"; to be released from the concrete world is the spirit's ambition, despite the poet's warning that such an emptiness is "accurst," shimmering "on the brink// Of absence" (*New* 283).

"Auras, lustres,/ And all shinings need to be shaped and borne," the poem continues. As with any vision, a "pure mirage" or a knowable emptiness must take on a shape; it must be recognizable to the eye or the touch, in the same way that the "aureate plates" above the heads of figures in Christian paintings identify them as saints. The lack of such a shape renders the vision inconceivable to the human mind. So in the next two and a half lines the poet urges his soul to turn away "from the fine sleights of the sand," suggesting in the play on the phrase "sleights of hand" that the desire for "sensible emptiness" is a cunning and deceptive one. He also tells his soul to turn "from the long empty oven/ Where flames in flamings burn," an apparent reference not only to the desert and to Hell but to the "greater misery than death or nothing" mentioned in Traherne's passage. Furthermore, that the oven is "empty" and that the "flames in flamings burn" both convey a sense of infinity, an absence of perspective for the spirit in this desert. Therefore, the poem turns "Back to the trees arrayed/ In bursts of glare" and those other sensible objects of the world "made/ Gold in the sunken sun." There is a definite retreat evident in the phrase "back to," even though the poet seems to consider it wise to "watch for the sight" of the Star of David, and even though he ultimately considers "light incarnate" or "Lampshine blurred in the steam of beasts" to be "the spirit's right/ Oasis" (*New* 284). As Raymond Benoit has argued, "Wilbur urges the Nativity upon us" at the close of this poem because "insight can only come from a plunge into the concrete" (64). Yet as Hill argues, although it is "clearly a rejection of the quest for visions, however beguiling, that are not firmly based in this life," the sharp contrast between the image of the camels themselves (as "slow, proud" and moving "with a stilted stride") and the less vivid imagery of the last four stanzas betrays the poet's uneasiness with his own conclusion (64–65). Despite the overt claim for the necessity of a world *with* objects, because of its strong orientation toward "sensible emptiness," the poem also implicitly acknowledges how imagined annihilation is valuable in setting those limits from which we can "turn . . . back" to the world, in all its newly measurable and sensible fullness.

Published nearly a decade after " 'A World without Objects. . . ,' " Wilbur's "Advice to a Prophet" reverses his earlier appreciation of the things of this world from the perspective of a sensible emptiness to an appreciation of that same emptiness from the perspective of the things of this world. Considered one of his most overtly political poems (Salinger 10; Hill 106),[13] "Advice to a Prophet" also reveals a Wilbur apparently even more confident than before in the power of the physical world (specifically, in nature itself) to provide meaning. At the same time, he seems less concerned about any allegorical resonance to that meaning—regardless of the fact that the image of the rose in the last two stanzas seems deliberately symbolic.

The first three of this poem's nine quatrains (their alternating pentameter and tetrameter lines counterpointed by the *abba* rhyme scheme) open with the poet's advising the "prophet" what *not* to tell us when warning us of our approaching doom. Nothing in the poem identifies the prophet as priest, scientist, or poet, subsuming all three under the traditional notion of the prophet as doomsayer, or a "mad-eyed" prophet such as Ezekiel or Cassandra. Such a prophet, the poet reminds us, will not come "proclaiming our fall but begging us/ In God's name to have self-pity" (*New* 182), that is, imploring us to put life above the sensible emptiness our minds seem to hanker after. We will not, he goes on to say in the second stanza, be swayed to self-pity by an account of the "force and range" of weapons of mass destruction, because any such description will "rocket the mind," thus actually feeding the imagination rather than curbing it. "Our slow, unreckoning hearts," on the other hand, "will be left behind," unable to accommodate our feelings to whatever unfamiliar notions our minds may grasp. Nor can "talk of the death of the race" carry much emotional weight, since we cannot really imagine a state of annihilation,[14] and we have no basis to "dream of this place without us":

The sun mere fire, the leaves untroubled about us,
A stone look on the stone's face? (182)

The tone and imagery here recall the "pure mirage" of " 'A World without Objects . . .' " ("the long empty oven/ Where flames in flamings burn"), but in this rendition Wilbur is thinking of an absence created by the elimination of any perceiver, rather than "the brink of absence," as that which a perceiver cannot fully understand. This shift in emphasis is a slight but crucial one: In the earlier poem the failure to be able to conceive of an immaterial state is expressed with a hint of resignation, but in "Advice to a Prophet" not to conceive of it means not to feel the full import of the prophet's warning. What has become more important than the preeminence of "light incarnate," of the things of this world, is the presence of the watcher of that light, of those of us who "cannot conceive/ Of an undreamt thing" but who, because we can dream, remember, and speak, can also attribute meaning to the things of this world.

The poem next urges the prophet to present his or her prophecies in terms we can accept, in terms of "the world's own change,"[15] and throughout stanzas four, five, and six he catalogues a variety of images from nature that "we know to our cost"—the dissipated cloud, the "blackened" vines, the disappearing white-tailed deer, the evasive lark, the lost "grip" of the jack-pine, and the flow of a burning river such as the mythic Xanthus, which was destroyed rather than surrendered to invaders. These earthly images, together with "the dolphin's arc" and "the dove's return" to Noah's ark, are all "things in which we have seen ourselves and spoken" (182–83). In this line Wilbur introduces the vital connection hinted at earlier between seeing, knowing, and saying, and as the poem approaches its climax, all of his concerns are heaped on one another: Not only does he ask the prophet to explain our apocalypse in terms of changes in nature, as well as the termination of those changes (Benoit 191–92), so that we might better comprehend its implications; he also links our experience of nature's changes both to our consciousness and to our acknowledgment of our consciousness, both to our seeing and to our speaking about what we have seen. Unlike " 'A World without Objects . . . ,' " "Advice to a Prophet" becomes increasingly preoccupied with our *perception* of the world more than with the things in it. Therefore, even though nature itself is prominent both as the source of the heart's understanding and as the source of our physical existence, the annihilation of nature is meaningless unless or until it is articulated in terms of the human experience of it:

> Ask us, prophet, how we shall call
> Our natures forth when that live tongue is all
> Dispelled, that glass obscured or broken
>
> In which we have said the rose of our love and the clean
> Horse of our courage, in which beheld
> The singing locust of the soul unshelled,
> And all we mean or wish to mean. (183)

Though urging the prophet to couch his prophecy in the context of nature, Wilbur in fact draws attention to our awareness of nature, as revealed by our speaking of it ("we shall call," "live tongue," and "we have said"). Once we *see* the relation between language and nature, he suggests, we will better *sense* annihilation as silence and understand that "with the worldless rose/ Our hearts shall fail us." Then in the final stanza, he further emphasizes our perception of nature ("the bronze annals") rather than nature itself ("the oak-tree"), as he isolates our sense of time's continuity by isolating, in what seems a deliberately awkward fashion, our vocabulary for that sense: "come demanding/ Whether there shall be lofty or long standing/ When the bronze annals of the oak-tree close" (183). "The final, urgent plea of 'Advice to a

Prophet' is that we not destroy vocabulary!" Wendy Salinger notes, "Wilbur's most moving political poem is at its heart about language" (17). It is about language, but specifically it is about feeling the *loss* of language (and through that the loss of perception) as our only means of appreciating the dangers of nuclearism. Annihilation, in other words, is a physical and psychic condition that encompasses the signifiers "lofty" and "long standing" together with whatever they signify, as well as everything else imaginable.

With its intricate interweaving of natural imagery and language, "Advice to a Prophet" ingeniously conveys how our experience of nature, perception, and language is the key to our grasping the implications of annihilation. But in his late sixties poem, "In the Field," Wilbur goes even further to demonstrate that not only is our source of meaning limited to our experience of nature, but even nature itself, now threatened by annihilation, cannot finally provide meaning, circumscribed as it is by its own potential absence from both our perception of it and from existence. There is merit to poet Henry Taylor's "suspicion" that "In the Field" may be "Wilbur's finest poem so far" (94), because it poignantly strikes a balance between an awareness of nothingness and a resolve for the continuity of the human project. Although Bruce Michelson considers the poem's tone one of "bemusement, edged with a certain scorn" (100) in the way it presents the mind at work, he finds in its disillusionment with science and its keen self-consciousness evidence of a "romantic or modern sensibility that rages . . . that the comely, comprehensible universe that mythology gave us has been overthrown by a wisdom which sustains neither poetry nor hope" (101). Despite this gloomy prospect, however, like most of Wilbur's poems, it proceeds with apparent inevitability, developing across twenty-four stanzas (with consistently varying line lengths in each stanza)—its strict form again reinforcing the poet's beckoning toward the ineffable, as Dickinson does. And in my view, the surprise of this poem lies in its unpredictably paradoxical closure.

"In the Field" divides into three parts: The first thirteen stanzas set the stage by depicting "our" walk in "this field-grass" (*New* 131) last night; stanzas fourteen through seventeen describe what we see in that same field today; and the final three stanzas, comprised of a single sentence, comment on our understanding of the difference between last night and today, a difference that is pointedly deceptive. "Last night, when out we stumbled looking up" (131), we were occupied less with the field than with the star-spangled sky above it, initially described in

terms of its astrological and astronomical history. For the knowledge-
able speaker of this poem, the "pine at the sky's rim" is at first considered only as an obstruction to a full view of the constellations, and he
proceeds to allude not just to various ancient names attributed to the
stars, but also to the mythic stories behind them. "But none of that was
true," he concedes in the next stanza, given how time alters human perceptions and our methods of explaining the universe:

> And did we not recall
> That Egypt's north was in the Dragon's tail?
> As if a form of type should fall
> And dash itself like hail,
>
> The heavens jumped away,
> Bursting the cincture of the zodiac. (131)

The more we learn about alternate systems of understanding the
constellations, the less compelling any one of them is bound to be,
since various systems and interpretations inevitably emphasize varying "truths." The idea of language as our primary access to experience, so prevalent in "Advice to a Prophet," here falls away, in the image of the "form of type" dashing itself like hail. All schemes are broken, or at least breakable, as "the heavens" themselves burst out of the
zodiac we have superimposed on them and shoot "flares with nothing
left to say/ To us, not coming back// Unless they should at last,/ Like
hard-flung dice that ramble out the throw,/ Be gathered for another
cast." (131–32). Unless we superimpose another set of relations, another
language, on what we are observing, the meaning of the night sky has
successfully escaped us. The simile of thrown dice reinforces the element of chance, if not haphazardness, in any method of understanding
the stars.

"Whether that might be so// We could not say" (132), the poet confesses, but the pronoun "that" here is ambiguous. Literally, its antecedent is the "cast" of the dice, as another system, zodiac, or language
to explain our perceptions of nature; whether or not such an alternative
might present itself, last night "we could not say." But the indefinite
quality of the pronoun idiomatically alludes as well to the whole idea
of language, to those "shot flares with nothing left to say." Put simply,
last night "we could not say" whether the sky has anything to say to us
at all. It is not that it is waiting for a language to explain it; it is just not
available to meaning.

Left, then, incapable of speaking to either of these unknowns, instead we

> trued
> Our talk awhile to words of the real sky,
>   Chatting of class or magnitude,
>   Star-clusters, nebulae. (132)

Indirectly, the poem implies that, by applying scientific jargon to what we observe, we are doing precisely what we "could not say" is possible in the previous stanzas. The verb "trued" seems deliberately ironic, especially in its proximity to the adjective "real" in the following line, as though to mock us for considering the sky of our scientific age somehow more authentic than the one at which the ancients gazed. Literally, we "leveled" our talk, or "squared" it, rather than remain speechless in the face of the uninterpretable universe. In addition, however, Wilbur injects a sense of human will here through his "ordinary evening-talk" (Michelson 101); that is, by speaking of the sky in the familiar terms of contemporary astronomy, we determine our own truth for ourselves, beyond the questionable understanding of our predecessors.[16] And we assign our own terms, despite the acknowledged circumscription of language, so that we might "talk" about the star Antares fleeing or disappearing "as in some rimless centrifuge/ Into a blink of red." Michelson reads the pace of these opening ten quatrains to be running "at a mental low idle, catching our bizarre ability to look straight at the infinite, at the imagination-shattering fact, and react with near-perfect banality" (101).

However, in the next stanza "the nip of fear" (a feeling, not an idea) once again silences us. That fear reveals to us that the imagination has extended beyond mere understanding (being touched by "the feel of what we said"), that it has mingled with our "schoolbook thoughts," and, most importantly, that it has

> faked a scan of space
> Blown black and hollow by our spent grenade,
>   All worlds dashed out without a trace,
>   The very light unmade. (132)

The attempt to speak of the disappearance of Antares "into a blink of red" has stirred the imagination not to frame nature into a finite universe, as we might have hoped, but paradoxically to "fake" annihilation, to "unmake" what we would have it make knowable—in other words, to reveal a sensible emptiness. In the field last night, this poem is saying, the more we tried to apply our conscious intelligence to our perceptions of nature, the more profoundly we were forced to confront our inability to master those perceptions. The result is an apocalyptic vision of the finitude not only of language and ourselves but of the context of experience, that is, of nature itself. Bereft, "then, in the late-night chill" with this devastating revelation about our language, ourselves, and our universe, "we turned and picked our way through outcrop stone" back indoors, away from the horrors both subjective and objective our evening walk has bestowed on us. The retreat here echoes the retreat at the end of " 'A World without Objects . . . .' " but without its sense of renewal in that retreat.

Then, abruptly, the poem shifts to "today," where "in the same field" not the darkness of "the very light unmade" but the brilliant sun "takes all," obscuring with its blinding light the blink of the stars, as well as their suggestion of annihilation. Rather than "those holes in heaven" that "have been sealed/ Like rain-drills in a pond,"

> we, beheld in gold,
> See nothing starry but these galaxies
>   Of flowers, dense and manifold,
>   Which lift about our knees— (133)

The despairing image a few lines earlier is suddenly countered dramatically by both the sensuous imagery of the field and the buoyant language in the next three stanzas: *beheld, starry, manifold, lift, white, daisy-drifts, chasms, strews, commit.* Rather than have to strain ourselves looking upward, while stumbling through the darkness, now we have a raised perspective so that the flowers "lift about our knees" and "you/ Sink down to pick an armload as we pass." Even the "few dead polls" of the hawkweed that have been loosed to the wind carry with them "the seeds of their return" in apparent triumph over death. All that surrounds us, all of nature, seems to have conquered "the nip of fear" in the earlier stanzas.

What soon becomes evident, however, is that, as beautiful and consolatory as the things of nature may be, Wilbur can no longer take refuge in them unequivocally, because among the lessons of the previous night is the confining yet unconfined willfulness of the imagination, whether treating darkness or light. To take "these flowers for some answer to that fright/ We felt for all creation's sake/ In our dark talk last night" would "no doubt" be as much a "mistake" (or *mis-take*) as was our attempt to "true" it earlier. Unlike in " 'A World without Objects. . . ,' " where imagined annihilation is presented as that experience beyond the sensual that ultimately allows us to value and praise the sensible fullness of everyday life; and unlike in "Advice to a Prophet," where it is through language's ability to value and praise nature's sensible fullness that we can grasp the horror of imagined annihilation; in "In the Field," imagined annihilation takes precedence over language, sensible experience, and nature, too. As though arguing against his earlier poems by refuting the power of "these galaxies/ Of flowers" to provide "some answer," Wilbur reveals, if not a full loss of faith in nature as a vial for the spirit, a profound skepticism. Despite the lightness of the imagery in these lines, that skepticism casts a shadow over this poem equal in its disconsolation to most of Wilbur's seemingly gloomier contemporaries. Indeed, his sentiment is more moving for being understated, nor does he dwell on his own fears, milking them to the point of numbing us to their effect.

What is clear by the end of the poem is that, despite the unexpected reversal expressed in the main clause of the final sentence, the rest of the sentence continues for two more stanzas, exacting what it is we are *liable* to conclude from the sensible fullness of nature. And despite its stated negation, the poem closes in a celebratory tone, as we erroneously take "to heart what came/ Of the heart's wish for life" (133). What surfaces in daylight, much as "the nip of fear" at night, is the desire to live and to sanction life, "staking here/ In the least field an endless claim"—namely, as the puns on "staking" and "claim" suggest, the claim of self-possession, of the inalienable right to go on living against all odds that the spirit has any redemption. If the stirred imagination envisions annihilation despite our desire not to confront that possibility, "the heart's wish for life," even beyond our conscious recognition of its finitude, "Beats on from sphere to sphere"—

> And pounds beyond the sun,
> Where nothing less peremptory can go,
> And is ourselves, and is the one
> Unbounded thing we know. (133)

As much as the imagination can fake "a scan of space" at night, it can also pound "beyond the sun" by day. The cataclysmic connotations of "blown black and hollow," "spent grenade," "worlds dashed," and "light unmade" in stanza twelve are here transformed into generative ones, and the "scan of space" that before insinuated annihilation now hints at transcendence: What, exactly, *is* the place "where nothing less peremptory can go"? Where only the absolute or the "non-sensible" can go? Where nothing less compelling than the full-blown, heart-warmed imagination can go? Where nothing less capable of putting an end to all doubts can go? In characteristically Wilbur fashion, the word "peremptory" carries with it all these meanings, paradoxically—especially when we remember that it is a "mistake" to take our good feelings too much "to heart." It may be wrong to accept "what comes" of our "wish for life" as "ourselves" and as "the one/ Unbounded thing we know." Yet the very "peremptory" nature of that wish compels us to do so. To imagine utter annihilation is no more or less avoidable than imagining something "unbounded," and although nature itself is bounded by potential annihilation, it teaches us that, in the imagination, nothingness has no greater claim on us than somethingness; the uncertainty of either only serves to reinforce the potential of the other. So while we cannot take refuge in nature, as we are permitted to do in " 'A World without Objects . . .' " and "Advice to a Prophet," we can still accept our self-interested inclination to do so. Indeed, as Ejner Jensen points out, the poem suggests that it is "heroic" (249) to do so.

◇ By tracing the development of Wilbur's concept of annihilation from a "sensible emptiness" to that ambivalent sphere "where nothing less peremptory can go," I mean to illustrate the increasing sophistication of his poetry and the relevance of his apparently benign sensibility to our time. He is neither static in his thinking nor indifferent in his imagining; rather, he is a nature poet in crisis who has accepted his own lyric heritage while through the manipulation of form and image he has represented the psychic interior of nuclearism. Also evident in his careful way of talking about nothingness, of finding the appropriate metaphors for it, is how the making of those metaphors itself has interfered with his vision, irrevocably undermining his innate reliance on nature. He vividly proves that, despite the urgency to speak, the poet in our time cannot really articulate what it means to live with uncertainty without his or her imagination being changed by that very endeavor. Because a protest poet like Levertov rigorously attends to the external threat of nuclear weapons and power, she bravely urges us to initiate a radical change in thinking, but it is within the figurative language of Wilbur's poetry that we begin to find that change taking place, despite its oblique relationship to the realm of political action.

In his 1966 essay "On My Own Work," Wilbur identifies two differences between his earlier and later poems: a change from "a certain preciosity" to a style "plainer and more straightforward than it used to be" and "a partial shift from the ironic meditative lyric toward the dramatic poem" (*Responses* 118). These changes are born out in the three poems I discuss here, as evident in the relaxation of the diction, the increasingly accessible imagery, and the shift from imagined landscapes in the two earlier poems to the "real" one in "In the Field." But to these two changes I would add a third: the increasing contemporaneity in Wilbur's voice. For all its playfulness and panache, a poem such as " 'A World without Objects . . .' " has few characteristics to distinguish it from its predecessors. Both "Advice to a Prophet" and "In the Field," however, clearly belong to the era in which they were composed, not merely in their willingness to create metaphors for annihilation, but in the way they diffuse the often loud and distracting superfluities of those who feel threatened in our world, in order to get to the heart of the matter—the stifled human spirit. In a time when high drama and crisis occur daily, when "the things of this world" seem subverted by the widespread maligning and endangerment of them, and when language itself is vulnerable to its own undoing, it should come as no surprise if a poet's cry sounds muffled, nondramatic, oblique, and paradoxical. After all, that voice is expressing itself in an atmosphere that demonstrates little patience for what it has to say. And for a poet like Wilbur, so completely committed to the continuity of the world despite its bent toward self-annihilation, the way of nothingness, the way of survival, has ironically come to require that he acknowledge nature's finitude as perhaps the *only* means to preserve the spirit it fosters.

FOUR

Psychohistorical Poetry in the Nuclear Age

Atomic Pasts and Nuclear Futures: Nuclearism and Cultural History

Besides protesting nuclear powers and besides constructing metaphoric bridges through individual experience and nuclear imagery, poets have also approached nuclearism by looking *around* it at the scientific, technical, mythical, psychological, and ideological context of post-Hiroshima America. In terms of technique, while some of these poets use lyric forms, others have adopted more expansive, even epic forms that offer them a less subjective, more discursive language. Moreover, the major qualitative difference between the first two categories and this one concerns its emphasis on social history and culture, rather than on current politics or subjective experience; this difference is analogous to the distinction between individual death in a nuclear war and what Schell calls the "second death" (*Fate* 114–21), or the resulting eradication in a nuclear holocaust of what Derrida calls the "archivization" of human history or the "movement of survival" (28). While nuclear protest and apocalyptic lyric poets concentrate on the impact of the nuclear threat on the global community or subjective consciousness, this third group—which I want to label "psychohistorical"—concerns itself more with a somewhat broader heritage, especially the endangered past and possible futurelessness of civilizations. Expanding their scope through time (and space) challenges, if not requires, these poets to find forms that are flexible enough to accommodate their far-reaching speculations on nuclear ideology, and while their take on the nuclear threat may not lend their poetry political efficacy in the moment, it does open them to a way of nothingness not readily evident in the first two groups.

The term "psychohistory" itself grew out of the collaborative work of historians, social scientists, psychologists, and psychoanalysts in the 1960s and 1970s, particularly the work of the Wellfleet Psychohistory Group (gathered in Robert Jay Lifton's and Eric Olson's *Explorations in Psychohistory: The Wellfleet Papers* [1974]). In *Decoding the Past*, Peter Loewenberg defines psychohistory as a method of research that "combines historical analysis with social science models, humanistic sensibility, and psychodynamic theory and clinical insights to create a fuller, more rounded view of life in the past. The psychohistorian is aware of the dynamic interaction of character, society, and human thought and action" (14). Specifically, such a psychodynamic investigation of cultural history values "the function of the unconscious in human behavior," "emphasizes the importance of origins, antecedents, and patterns of repetition" in acknowledging that "the present reality interacts at all times with and is related to the personal and social past of the person in the unconscious," and "recognizes that fantasies of the subject, rather than meaning externally ascribed, constitute the relevant determinant of the emotional meaning of an event, symbol, or image" (14–15). Interweaving post-Freudian, Eriksonian, or other psychoanalytic interpretations of historical phenomena, psychohistory has branched into at least two directions: the psychoanalytic and biographical study of major historical figures (psychobiography) and the psychodynamic reading of a group, community, or culture within its historical context.[1]

Though not without controversy in both methodology and application, it is this latter branch of psychohistory, what Bruce Mazlish identifies as the "psychic repository" of a group or the "national group psychology," that best delineates the poems in this third category. In speculating on "the American psyche" in particular, Mazlish defines a group's "psychic repository" as that "on which it draws unconsciously as well as consciously and which fundamentally shapes its sense of self, its identity, or character. This repository, in turn, can be known through an analysis of myths, legends, creeds, folklore, and literary constructions, as well as rituals, ceremonies, monuments, and so forth. These, of course, embody historical experiences, from which they gain their particular form and content" (*Leader* 267). As readers, we might do a "psychohistorical" critique of nuclear protest and apocalyptic lyric poetry (or of any poetry, for that matter). But with this third group, it is the poets themselves who step away from the immediacy of the nuclear threat in order to reconfigure it in the context of world history, national or group rituals, psychic (even parapsychic) phenomena, or myth—in a poetry that takes shape as its own brand of creative psychohistory. Instead of focusing primarily on the potential or imagery of nuclear annihilation, this poetry employs generic or mythic language, as well as figures from history, literature, mythology, or science. This difference in technique allows these poets not only to raise issues other than those created by the "unremitting political emergency" of nuclearism, but also to insinuate cultural responses to that threat without necessarily having to resort to polarizing or histrionic terms.

To understand why a psychohistorical perspective (with its emphasis on cultural history rather than on individuals) requires a different poetics, we need to recall Derrida's discussion of how the threat of "the total destruction of the archive, if not of the human habitat," renders nuclear war "the absolute referent." Derrida conceives of individual death as "a destruction affecting only a part of society, of tradition, of culture [that] may always give rise to a symbolic work of mourning, with memory, compensation, internalization, idealization, displacement, and so on. In that case there is monumentalization, archivization and *work on the remainder, work of the remainder*" (28). An awareness of this "archivization" always accompanies an individual's awareness of his or her own death, so that "all the resources of memory and tradition can mute the reality of that death, whose anticipation then is still woven out of fictionality, symbolicity, or, if you prefer, literature." Being at a "fictional" or symbolic remove from one's own death allows any individual's actual death (and the personal mourning that follows it) to be anticipated "phantasmatically, symbolically too, as a negativity at work" (28) in the ongoing process of history.

However, in the case of nuclear annihilation there arises a critical difference as to where the fiction of death lies, due to the elimination of the "archivization" by which we understand individual death: Whereas in individual experience the continuing culture and archival memory create a fictional, symbolic distance between each of us and our own deaths, in nuclear culture, annihilation (as an "a-symbolic referent, unsymbolizable, even unsignifiable") removes that symbolic distance, creating for Derrida something akin to Husserl's "fiction of total chaos" (28). To rephrase this concept in relation to poetry, whereas the nuclear threat may prompt a poet concerned with subjective experience to create a poem that negotiates the conflict between mass death and the complex archive of "symbolicity" (or conceptualization) of the meaning of individual death, it may further inspire the poet to reexamine the archive of history itself. This task involves revising, stretching, rethinking, or breaking out of the predominant "archivized" forms by which we normally articulate experience. So it comes as no surprise that some poets choose to circumvent the subjectivity of the conventional modern lyric in order to address the archive of history. Asserting this remove from predominant poetic forms does not keep psychohistorical poets from joining in resistance against nuclearism (in their work or their lives), but it gives them the opportunity to talk broadly about culture in an attempt to uncover what ideologies have combined to make nuclear annihilation possible in the first place.

◇ Shorter poems that draw attention to "archivized" forms in order to broaden their perspective on nuclearism are rare, perhaps because, although they may gain distance from conventional subjectivity through their explicit experimentation, they tend in their lyric closure to echo the same resistance to the political sources of power found in nuclear protest poems—even if they do not make that resistance their theme. This is not to suggest that the devices these poets use (satire, pronounced patterns of repetition, ritualized chanting, dramatic monologue, parody, collage, and so on) are unfamiliar in other venues. But because they are used so self-consciously as to be emblematic, they expose their own poetics as a social practice, in opposition to the intimate tone, immediacy, and idiomatic phrasing of the free verse that currently predominates in American poetry. Nonetheless, as psychohistorical poems, the examples I want to discuss here address not only nuclear policy but larger ideological values.

For instance, Ai's "The Testimony of J. Robert Oppenheimer," with its conspicuous subtitle of "A Fiction," belongs in a series of dramatic monologues in Ai's collection *Sin*, where she speaks in the grim voices of those in extreme historical circumstances—John Kennedy after his assassination, Joseph McCarthy fantasizing about unlimited power, a leftist dying in Madrid during the Spanish Civil War, an aging journalist remembering Vietnam in 1966, the Atlanta child killer in 1981—so Oppenheimer's "testimony" (presumably before a Senate Committee on atomic warfare in the 1950s) takes its place in the landscape of horrors that comprise for Ai our recent American legacy. Though portraying widely different characters in her monologues, Ai makes no attempt to vary their voices from poem to poem, and the speaker in "The Testimony of J. Robert Oppenheimer" makes his confession in the same frenzied tone of the other poems, as though recalling a nightmare. Still, Ai's characterization of Oppenheimer, the "father" of the atomic bomb, is not unlike other psychobiographical accounts of him by those such as Brian Easlea (86–92; 124–31) and Lifton (*Future* 164–67): Her poem opens with the physicist praising the bomb as evidence of modern "enlightenment" (64). Yet because this is a confession, the speaker also acknowledges his guilt for having pursued truth too scientifically, a guilt he then tries to rationalize:

To me, the ideological high wire
is for fools to balance on with their illusions.
It is better to leap into the void.
Isn't that what we all want anyway?—
to eliminate all pretense
till like the oppressed who in the end
identifies with the oppressor,
we accept the worst in ourselves
and are set free. (65)

As a scientist, Ai's Oppenheimer embodies the cultural urge to know beyond speculation. But in the second strophe, he equates this obsessive drive, this desire for "the big fall smooth as honey down a throat," with prenatal desire, as he sighs, "Anything that gets you closer/ to what you are./ Oh, to be born again and again/ from that dark, metal womb,/ the sweet, intoxicating smell of decay/ the imminent dead give off" (65–66). As Spenser Weart has also observed about nuclear psychology, this poem insinuates that the drive for atomic wisdom reflects a desire to return to the womb. Yet in the last strophe, Oppenheimer confesses his ultimate frustration with the futility of pursuing a truth that "is always changing,/ always shaped by the latest/ collective urge to destroy," and he feels trapped by his own "urge" to know, calling his soul "a wound that will not heal" (66). He looks at the country around him, "our military in readiness,/ our private citizens/ in a constant frenzy of patriotism/ and jingoistic pride,/ our enemies endless,/ our need to defend infinite," and mocks us that "we do not regret or mourn" but "like characters in the funny papers" just "march past the third eye of History" (67). By the end of the poem, Ai portrays Oppenheimer not in order to imagine a nuclear holocaust but to question the popularly held assumption that history is progressive. Behind the veneer of Oppenheimer's guilt-ridden confession, she disrupts that notion, and she reconfigures nuclear annihilation not as a violent climax but as a slow spiritual decay:

We strip away the tattered fabric
of the universe
to the juicy, dark meat,
the nothing beyond time.
We tear ourselves down atom by atom,
till electron and positron,
we become our own transcendent annihilation. (67)

As a dramatic monologue, with its obsessive tone, its focus on the past rather than the future, and its Browningesque psychoanalysis, Ai's poem distracts attention from the phenonmenon of nuclear war, turning instead to the ideology behind that phenomenon, and, by implication, condemning that ideology. By contrast, in a similarly indirect, though somewhat less successful attempt, Molly Peacock's satire "Don't Think Governments End the World," composed in iambic pentameter with an *abab* rhyme scheme, begins by proposing that "The blast/ the burnings, and the final famine will/ be brought on *by mistake*": It will have been initiated by some troubled personality sitting at the control panel "who couldn't get through his head/ that his mother couldn't love him" (61). In the poem's third stanza, however, as the rhythm and rhyme scheme start to break down, Peacock exonerates both this unstable man and his "childish" mother from blame, explaining that if he had only known what to do to prevent annihilation, "he'd have done it to please her," who in response "might have said,

'That's nice dear,'/ and we wouldn't be dead." To this point the poem's dark humor scoffs at the haphazardness of the nuclear future. Unfortunately, though, rather than leave it at that, in the final lines, Peacock turns suddenly serious:

> Aren't you scared of your life in his hands?
> But of all the men whose hands you'd hope to be in,
> name the one you're sure of. The history of nations
> is cold; the world burns by generations. (61)

By extending her jab about parents' influence on their children to spell out its implication about the impersonality of "nations," Peacock robs the poem of its satiric edge in favor of an explicit protest against nuclear ideology, thereby telegraphing its political punch. It is not that her subject matter is not deadly serious, nor that her insinuation about gender has no basis, but the neatness of the last sentence tidies up the poem at the expense of its own cool irony.

Using highly ornate forms, Allen Grossman and Peter Meinke go a rhetorical step beyond Ai and Peacock in order to suspend the very discourse of nuclearism. Grossman combines the language of atomic blasts ("The cold black cloud, the phallic whip, the curse") and the famous line from the Bhagavad-Gita that Oppenheimer is said to have uttered after the first bomb test at Alamogordo ("I have become Death, shatterer of worlds") to create a haunting (if somewhat impenetrable) villanelle, "Villanelle of Keeping." Though his poem makes no explicit reference to Alamogordo or to atomic warfare, it places itself undeniably in nuclear history, even while stepping outside that history into apocalyptic mythology:

> The earth remains, and cures.
> (Everything will perish, except this face.)
> Battered by absence the tablet earth endures
>
> Storms of unwriting; and the lines still bless
> The narrow light, the morning star in tears.
> "I have become Death, shatterer of worlds."
> Battered by absence the tablet earth endures. (76)

With its repeated counterpoint lines of "I have become Death, shatterer of worlds" and "Battered by absence the tablet earth endures," the poem becomes, rather unexpectedly, a mantra of hope, a prayer for the potential of the earth, if not for the continuity of life on it. While Grossman draws no clear psychohistorical conclusions from his juxtaposition of spiritual language and modern myth, his poem plays each one's cultural resonance against their depletion as artifacts under nuclearism.

Meinke's "Atomic Pantoum" develops an even more intricate deconstruction of nuclearism's language than Grossman's poem by using the Malayan-French pantoum form that, in enacting the steps of a detonated bomb, creates a dizzying effect through repetition. The intricate pattern of echoed lines allows Meinke to stage a metamorphosis from the recitation of the technical steps of a blast to an invocation of a fundamentalist revival, a metamorphosis first apparent with the introduction of the word "choir" in the third stanza:

> In a chain reaction
> the neutrons released
> split other nuclei
> which release more neutrons
>
> The neutrons released
> blow open some others
> which release more neutrons
> and start this all over
>
> Blow open some others
> and choirs will crumble
> and start this all over
> with eyes burned to ashes (15)

With its frenetic tone, Meinke's rhetorical flourish resembles Ai's, and ultimately his poem, like hers, suggests that there is a religious fervor underlying our obsession with nuclear weaponry. The only variation in the poem from a strict adherence to the pantoum structure (including the reversal of the first and third lines of the first stanza as the fourth and second lines of the last stanza) is the addition of the word "like" at the end, creating a nuclear simile for human beings, rather than bombs, so that what begins as a poem that recounts a technological operation closes:

> Curled and tightened
> blind to the end
> torching our enemies
> we sing to Jesus
>
> Blind to the end
> split up *like* nuclei
> we sing to Jesus
> in a chain reaction (16, italics added)

Instead of opposing nuclear policy or shaping metaphors, Meinke's poem and others like it[2] explore the rhetorical strategies of the nuclear world at the risk of seeming to endorse it. Although they clearly don't, their psychohistorical view finds links between that world and cultural identity and so breaks down the symbolic isolation of nuclear technology from the world of material experience.

◇ More ambitious examples of psychohistorical poems than these lyrics are those that employ longer, more comprehensive forms. Surprisingly few poets have tried longer forms, but of five who have—Dick Allen, Marc Kaminsky, Celia Gilbert, Frederick Turner, and James Merrill—all use history, the history of nuclear weapons as well as cultural history, to provide themselves a larger thematic, as well as structural, canvas. The forms they adopt vary widely—from Allen's camp narrative, Kaminsky's lyric sequence, and Gilbert's collage, to Turner's science fiction epics complete with knights and battles and Merrill's Dantean epic portraying a series of otherworldly conversations via a Ouija board—and the variety in their diction makes them in other respects hardly comparable to each other. Yet their efforts are connected by their mutual interest in nuclearism in contemporary history. The diversity in their application of long forms suggests, finally, not that they have little in common but rather, as is widely held among critics, that there exists no predominant epic form in the United States.

Admittedly, Dick Allen's *Anon* hardly touches on global annihilation in itself, but its late sixties antihero, Anon, proceeds, against a backdrop of futility cast by the nuclear threat, from innocence to experience through the poem's quickly moving chapters. As the poet argues in his preface, "The children of our age have understood: there is very little doubt that Western civilization, as we apprehend it today, is doomed. The end may come in the nuclear holocaust made so familiar by our cinema, or more likely in pollution and cannibalism" (*Anon* xv). Yet in keeping with the popular literature and music of the time, behind this pose of despair resides an almost naive optimism, as, in a sardonic voice, Allen adds that after "a green spell of many centuries" (during which "the knowledge we have amassed will be preserved in time capsules and the new monasteries"), future historians will study our age as a utopian period (*Anon* xv–xvi).

By implication, the story of Anon addresses that future. But even though Allen's post-Beat Everyman ends up the last man on earth, the Williamsesque vitality of his poetry, the persistent, sometimes excessively bawdy humor, and the caricatured inhabitants of Anon's universe finally undermine any sense that Allen actually believes that the human race will be annihilated. Indeed, reflecting the absorption into American culture of the doomsday mindset also evident in such 1960s films as *Seven Days in May, Doctor Strangelove,* and the James Bond movies, Allen's mock epic captures more of the sixties youths' obsessive search for personal liberation than of the Cold War repression that piqued it. Moving freely through history, for instance, Anon at one point finds himself aboard the *Enola Gay* flying over Hiroshima. But a few pages later, when he expresses concern about the destructive capacity of the hydrogen bomb, his spiritual advisor Whangdoodle (a "Wobblie" and long-haired folk singer strumming his guitar) urges him not to be anxious and instead to live for the moment:

"That's your hangup, friend,"
said Whang.
"The point is don't

worry over that. What's true is true.
The only moment that you have is now.
The scene's the scene. The play

does not exist." (*Anon* 79)

Although the parodic tone of Allen's poem often mocks the hippie philosophy that its characters such as Whang espouse, despite its irony, as Allen himself recognizes, it is "imbued with a sense of the 60s, the excitement of breaking taboos, using an 'oral' form."[3] And because of its energy and optimism, it does not even pretend to offer the more complete vision of the nuclear age promised in its preface. As a satire like Peacock's "Don't Think Goverments End the World," though, the book derides nuclearism as yet another stupidity of late bourgeois capitalist America.

In a far more serious response to the bombing of Hiroshima, Marc Kaminsky's *The Road to Hiroshima* uses a sequence of dramatic monologues to recall the imagery of the 1945 attack. In a style that imitates the understatement of traditional Japanese verse, Kaminsky depicts the bomb's physical damage, the residual medical and emotional effects on the *hibakusha,* and, most poignantly, the sense of nuclear emptiness associated with the victimized city since the bombing. As he admits in an afterword, for his subject matter he relies heavily on extant literature about Hiroshima (most notably, John Hersey's *Hiroshima,* Masuji

Ibuse's *Black Rain*, Michihiko Hachiya's *Hiroshima Diary*, and Lifton's *Death in Life*). So although he would have us understand his poems as (in paraphrasing Marianne Moore) "imaginary journeys with real push-carts in them" (111), most of those "pushcarts" are already available elsewhere—not as poems, perhaps, but in imagery as striking as his. For those familiar with the tragic legacy of the Hiroshima bombing, for instance, Kaminsky's dramatic monologue in which a minister describes peeling the skin off the hands of an A-bomb victim he is pulling out of a ditch graphically conveys the horror of the attack's aftermath (62), but as he portrays it, it is neither unprecedented nor particularly distinctive as poetry.

To be sure, Kaminsky does not just dwell on death and gore but also celebrates the *hibakushas'* instinct to survive. Given the vividly descriptive quality of his sources, however, what purpose does his creative adaption of Hiroshima serve when the originals themselves have such implicit power as literature? In both the first and last poems of the book he asks himself a similar question, at first indicting himself for merchandising the bombing and later wondering whether he is exploiting the victims for commercial or spiritual reasons, as he puns on *profiteer* and *prophet* (107). Yet in both poems he closes by avowing his obligation (to whom? the people of Hiroshima and Nagasaki? to human history?) to bring the horrors of this past to life again. Not to complete his sequence, he concludes, would be a betrayal of himself and all he loves, as the book intends to purge the poet (and his audience) of guilt, if not responsibility, for the bombings. In this way, *The Road to Hiroshima*, despite taking a dramatic approach as a psychohistorical sequence, follows the way of nuclear protest poetry: Its explicit preoccupation with the Hiroshima catastrophe is not for the poet's profit, surely, but for encouraging the missionary impulse among antinuclear activists by reminding them of the human effects of the bomb's devastation. Although the book attempts to recast the bombings in the light of literary and spiritual history, it finally offers little new psychosocial insight into American or Japanese thought.

On the other hand, Celia Gilbert's "Lot's Wife," though like Allen's narrative and Kaminsky's sequence unquestionably opposed to the ideology of the bomb, devises a more unusual historical contrast to Hiroshima (and Nagasaki). Admittedly not book length (no longer, in fact, than Levertov's "Mass for the Day of St. Thomas Didymus"), Gilbert's poem retells the Biblical tale of Sodom and Gomorrah from the point of view of Lot's wife, who was transformed into a pillar of salt when during her flight from the city she turned to look back at it. But by weaving passages into the poem from Frank W. Chinnock's *Nagasaki: The Forgotten Bomb* and Lifton's *History and Human Survival* she creates an ideogrammic effect that lends a mythic dimension to the plight of the *hibakusha*, who like the Sodomites were also "rained upon" by fire from the heavens. Adopting a woman's perspective on the hierarchic rule of men in the ancient cities, at first Gilbert's dramatic monologue focuses on the victimization of women (and children) by corrupt men: "There were violent gangs of men/ who raped men, and that seemed to many/ especially horrible," recounts Lot's wife (who, significantly, has no name of her own). "When women were raped/ that was wrong, they said,/ but there was no special horror to it" (67). Beyond this charge, though, she also expresses disgust at an honorable man, Lot himself, because when the henchmen come to the door of their house, he offers them his own daughters, rather than relinquishing the men for whom he has provided refuge: "The house of Lot was only Lot," she complains, "we were chattel and goods./ We women were his animals to breed./ Why didn't he offer himself to the men?" (69).

Nevertheless, the interjected passages in the poem about the atomic bombings are, pointedly, not as concerned with gender as with giving graphic proof of the emotional distance between the bombers and the bombed in order to convey, rather than just sexual difference, the difference between those with power and those without. The first quoted passage from Chinnock, for example, describes the pilot Sweeney as resembling "most bomber pilots who have formed a defensive armor about their particular role in war. Their function is to drop bombs on targets not on people" (66). Louise Kawada argues that this passage illustrates "how language can suppress the truth and deny connection between the doer and the deed" (117). But for Gilbert the frightening gap is not only within Sweeney's psyche; it is also between his power and the powerlessness of his victims, who are brutally ripped from their daily activities. The poem's collage form reinforces this contrast, for example, when it shifts abruptly from Lot's wife's voice to a passage from Lifton's book:

I knew my neighbors,
women like myself, going to the well,
weaving and spinning,
raising the family.
The little boys were noisy,
dirty, and quick,

the little girls, shy, quieter,
but sturdy.

". . . girls, very young girls, not only with their
clothes torn off but with their skin peeled off as well.
I thought should there be a hell this was it—the
Buddhist hell where we were taught people who could not
attain salvation always went." (66)

By poem's end, Lot's wife's grief for her lost children merges with our modern grief for those lost at Nagasaki. In fact, its final thirty-nine lines address the two tragedies as one, when as both Lot's wife and a *hibakusha* the poet asks, "For what were we saved?/ To turn our backs on slaughter/ and forget? To worship/ the power that spared our lives?" Acknowledging those decimated in the fire as "my other children," she equates Lot's escape from Sodom and Gommorah with America's emergent hegemony after World War II and asks the poem's central question:

How can I spit out
the bitter root I gnaw, foraged from the rubble,
more sour than the apple, the knowledge
of what power rules our lives,
the evil that knows but does not care,
that values men at nothing, and women less,
behemoth in love with death
and willing, to that end, to extinguish
even itself to celebrate its own spending? (70)

As in Ai's Oppenheimer poem, Gilbert's poem indicts not the bombing of Japanese civilians but, more broadly, the American postwar attempt to vindicate that act by developing ever more powerful weapons of extinction. Given the alternatives facing Lot's wife after her escape from the burning city—either to go forward and submit herself to an "evil that knows but does not care" and a "behemoth in love with death" or to "turn back,/ refusing to live God's lies" (71)—Gilbert offers a feminist revision of the tale from Genesis by having her persona, out of a heroic attachment to the powerless, *choose* her own fate, as she wills her body, "transfixed by grief,/ to rise in vigil/ over the ashen cities" of Sodom and Gomorrah, Hiroshima and Nagasaki. "Lot's Wife" rejects both nuclearism and the patriarchal ideology behind it, as Gilbert's dramatic retelling of history reminds us how brief has been the era of nuclear power.

As a fourth example of a longer psychohistorical poem, Turner's *The New World*, by following a Homeric epic form, appears initially to display an even grander missionary zeal than the others. In fact, though, Turner uses history for opposite reasons than Kaminsky does, namely, to propose *real* journeys with *imaginary* pushcarts in them, or to suggest a plausible *future* alternative to nuclear annihilation, thereby diminishing its power over our present imagination. As in his apocalyptic lyric "Early Warning," Turner is shy neither about his faith in the implicit power of poetry nor about the explicit ambition of *The New World*, which, he boldly asserts in his introduction, "is to demonstrate that a viable human future, a possible history, however imperfect, does lie beyond our present horizon of apparent cultural exhaustion and nuclear holocaust. Art has the world-saving function of imaginatively constructing other futures that do not involve the Götterdammerung of mass suicide; because if there is no other imaginative future, we will surely indeed *choose* destruction, being as we are creatures of imagination" (vii). The sweeping nature of his epic furnishes Turner with the broadest possible format in which to discuss history, science, economics, technology, politics, education, nature, even genealogy. His mythic landscape of the year 2376 is resplendent with details and a populace quite unlike our own yet unquestionably rooted in the twentieth century his poem critiques. While readers may take exception to particular assumptions rooted in parts of the poem, as a whole it attempts to create (and preserve) a body of ethical values for a society beyond this one.

What is peculiar, though, given Turner's announced intentions, is the manner in which he sidesteps the issue of potential nuclear annihilation by insinuating its historical insignificance. In part 2, he describes how the stand-off of the twentieth-century superpowers has come to result in "an empty travesty of government [lingering] in Washington," its bureaucratic and military forces "frozen forever in the great electronic deadlock/ of 2072" (39). Some pages later we learn that in "the late twentieth century/ the heavy machines of battle began to become/ so expensive that wars collapsed for lack of munitions" and

> the weapons of horror—gas, chemical, nuclear,
> biological—were practically useless, and beyond an exchange
> or two, which proved to the advantage of all interested
> parties except the combatants, were never used. (*New* 52)

The future Turner imagines (as in the novel *Warday*, the film *Testament* and much science fiction) includes a *limited* nuclear war, not the global holocaust or nuclear winter feared by writers like Schell and Carl Sagan. Indeed, he deliberately rejects "the image of war desired by the dream of the twentieth/ century," with its "towering mushroom cloud/ according to [our] most beautiful theory of cause" and its "explosion that effaces distinctions,/ reduces all wholes to their parts, and resolves the complexities/ embroidered in matter into a burst of radiant energy" (*New* 53). Such a notion, he explains, is "childish," the object of our "nightmare lust for cleanliness," and the result of a desire to "fall back on the comfort of despair" (53); he essentially dismisses our nuclear fears as untenable and, by doing so, deduces the continuity of humankind.

Throughout his epic, the weight of Turner's assertions ultimately rests on "the new world" he portends: Does his epic charm us sufficiently to abandon our post-Hiroshima sense of annihilation? And what of his tacit acceptance of the feasibility of a limited nuclear war? In a review, Mark Jarman argues that, for all its elaborate cultural and historical "machinery," *The New World* is nonetheless "quite a read, absorbing and atrocious, tasteless and tactless, bloodcurdling and inconsistent," not much different than a "fast-paced potboiler," but finally too "earnest" and "solemn" in tone to win us over entirely to Turner's prophesy (344). Turner's earnestness, though, is what actually saves his epic from being nothing but well-written schlock. By the end, it is not the *condoning* of warfare in *The New World*—albeit a warfare of knights using swords as well as "cheap, homegrown microprocessor[s]" (52)—as much as the poet's overriding optimism that humanity (unlike other species) can beat extinction, an optimism that permeates the very structure of the epic itself, that more profoundly troubles the reading of this otherwise yeoman effort to synthesize Eastern and Western philosophies, American family sagas, science fiction, medieval chansons de geste, and Augustan tropology.

In his second epic, *Genesis*, Turner again imagines an alternative future society that controls (or, in thinking of Williams's prescription, "contains") nuclear technology. This poem's dramatic center depicts a power struggle between an extreme but dominating environmentalist group, the Ecotheists, and a scientifically enlightened group, the Colonists, who eventually create a "biosphere" on Mars (which for Turner represents a utopian community, much within the pastoral tradition of his own British heritage). Here again, as is also characteristic of Turner's extensive theoretical writing, he attempts to reconcile contemporary ideas in mathematics and science with humanist thought—

in particular, to reconcile technological inventiveness with environmentalist skepticism. In style, form, and narrative, *Genesis* is subtler and more controlled than *The New World*, and the persona of the epic poet himself is more willing to admit to the uncertainty of his project. As Dick Allen has noted, a "slow reading" of the poem "deeply enriches readers' comprehension of Beauty and human purpose—Turner's obsessive concerns"—until "we find ourselves thinking of course poetry can communicate large concepts, of course it can wed the philosophic with the imagistic, of course its scientific and lyric passages can be one and the same" ("Storytellers" 321–22). But outside of his enthusiastic mingling of theories about computers, genetics, and physics and his array of mythic characters drawn from European, African, and Asian cultures (all composed in classical conceits in precisely 10,000 lines of blank verse), Turner seems frankly bored with the concept of nuclear annihilation, even when he raises it himself.

However, in this case, his failure to address it seems more clearly a strategy rather than an oversight. In Act I, scene v of *Genesis*, the poet explains why nuclear war is not a serious threat to the twenty-second century of his epic: The "last political idea" carried out before the Ecotheists came into power was to arrange the Olympic Games as the substitute arena for nuclear war, "so that we might not burn the world to dust/ And ourselves with it by our most-loved weapon —/ That white proof of reducibility/ Of all complexities of good to light" (66). As a "ritual whereby at the last/ Disputes of nations might be arbitrated," Olympic contests serve as a viable option to technological warfare in three ways. First, as a "trial by combat," they embody law or "superordinate authority" in the settling of international disputes, in the same way large-scale warfare has; second, if the Olympic rules are changed to allow for the death of the athletes, as was true in ancient Greece, each event becomes an authentic "War" game "where some who sought it might find trial in death/ And save the timid masses from their rage"; and third, since international terrorism constitutes "the one form of human conflict/ That [can] not be deterred by atom bombs," by "a triple paradox," the Olympics can provide the arena where terrorists exert their power on their enemies and on each other without endangering "the wise cowards of the billioned world" (66–67). "Let them, the scapegoats, do for us," the poet concludes, "what we,/ Our malice tamed by terror, cannot do" (67).

Surely, Turner does not seriously propose that the Olympics become a surrogate for nuclear war. Here again the poem implicitly seems to accept the inevitability of a nuclear deadlock, this time using the reasoning of deterrence theory. How, then, are we to understand his apparent dismissal of nuclearism itself? In an interview, Turner defends his rhetorical strategy in both *The New World* and *Genesis* by arguing for the need to resist the Romantic allure of an imagined postnuclear world. To imagine that world, he believes, "is then to imagine that whatever happens after the holocaust is going to be fraught with enormous dramatic significance. So the generation that wipes itself out with nuclear weapons is clearly going to be the most important generation that has ever existed" and therefore will "gain instant historical importance. Not only that, but we've managed the neat trick of making sure there can never be any revisionists" (Blanton 150). Such a pose, Turner believes, has "something too easy about it . . . because we get to decide how racist and sexist and bad generally, how backward and retrograde, all previous ages of history were, and nobody . . . gets to come along afterwards to make the same kind of judgment on us. We will have trumped the whole of history. And so, in that sense, nuclear war is a cheap thing to do" (Blanton 150). By imagining in poetry a method of containing the annihilatory extreme of nuclear war (no matter how infeasible), indeed, by deliberately trivializing it as he also does in "Early Warning," Turner hopes to fend off "the comfort of despair" and avoid creating what he calls "nuclear porn" in favor of a world that does not "have to buy the importance of certain kinds of actions by killing everybody off" (Blanton 151). In other words, only after we cease making grand assumptions about nuclearism as the central tenet of our times shall we overcome the stumbling block it imposes on postmodern thought.

Politically, the blind side of Turner's nuclear vision unequivocally separates his writing from the direct protest in Kaminsky's sequence and the understated pathos in Gilbert's collage. But as an example of a poet taking an imaginative leap, of breaking the bounds of how poetry can address ideological issues, and of questioning both the facts of nuclear technology and the "archivization" of how we understand them, his epic opens us to the breadth of possibilities for the nuclear future. As an epic poet, his Poundian desire for inclusiveness and multiculturalism, as well as his optimistic embrace of technology, at times may mask an irrefrangible Darwinism. But to discount his poetry because it refuses to place itself neatly on the political spectrum from left to right might be to close off its central premise—namely, as the character Beatrice expresses it in *Genesis*,

> That freedom is not choosing but creation,
> The making of a new alternative
> Where none before existed, and its rough
> Insertion in the bland ensemble of
> Existent futures lined up for our choice.
> Freedom is not a state but a volcano. (107)

Although Turner's epics, no more than Gilbert's "Lot's Wife" and Merrill's highly celebrated but even more idiosyncratic epic *The Changing Light at Sandover*, are unlikely in themselves to guide us from under the nuclear shadow, undoubtedly other psychohistorical poems of their ilk will follow them.[4] Once we engage their concepts of nuclear culture, we begin to experience a particularly imaginative way of nothingness that suggests what it really means to "change our modes of thinking" and to meet the deeper ideological challenges of our uncertain age.

The Ambiguous Paradise in James Merrill's *The Changing Light at Sandover*

No better evidence of the extent to which a nuclear awareness has permeated American letters exists than *The Changing Light at Sandover* (1982). James Merrill was long regarded among the most eclectic and effete of American poets. (Mark Strand once joked in conversation that when he first met Merrill he had the impression that the latter had spent his adult years locked in a boudoir being powdered by aging matrons.) Nor was Merrill ever tempted to follow fashion in poetry. Concerning his preference for ornate, or decorative, language, for example, he defended himself by asserting the vital role of "manners" in writing as "an artifice in the very bloodstream": "It's hard to imagine a work of literature that doesn't depend on manners, at least negatively. One of the points of a poem like Ginsberg's *Howl* is that it uses an impatience with manners very brilliantly; but if there had been no touchstone to strike that flint upon, where would Ginsberg be?" (*Recitative* 33). In a poetry richly allusive in both its literary and personal scopes, Merrill's politics (as much as can be discerned) were anything but revolutionary, dependent as his work is on the maintenance of a cultural elite to read, understand, and celebrate his art. Yet the explicit concern of Merrill's epic—the trilogy of *The Book of Ephraim, Mirabell's Books of Number,* and *Scripts for the Pageant,* concluding with *Coda: The Higher Keys*— is the threat of nuclear annihilation.[5] For a poet of Merrill's proclivities to have taken on such a mainstream (not to mention political) subject at the height of his career is not so surprising, however, once we discern three important aspects of *The Changing Light*'s conglomerative character—namely, the context of its composition, the Dantean tradition from which it is derived, and the dramatic structure of the poem, whose comic posture ingeniously performs Merrill's vision of the abiding ambiguity of nuclearism.

First of all, with its erudition, Merrill's voice is as different in sensibility from other psychohistorical poets as they are from each other. He was, in fact, as close an example as there has been in the United States in the late twentieth century of the gentleman of leisure and poet of privilege, having never *had* to earn a living (Labrie, *Merrill* 1). Even a poet as apparently comfortable and independent as he was, though, is still not exempt from nuclear war. (Indeed, those with the greatest material advantages may have the most to lose, if we accept that nuclear technology renders private defenses such as fallout shelters useless.) Nonetheless, because of his unique remove from the world and because, unlike Turner, he readily admitted that science and technology never held much interest for him, he was disassociated enough from that technology to look on it with skepticism and humor. He may have acknowledged its power, but he was not easily intimidated by it.

Second, concerning his form, Merrill's choice of the epic, rather than the lyric, gave him, like Turner, plenty of room to engage not only science, history, music, and other disciplines, but his own literary heritage as well. And because an epic inevitably involves an account of the creation and destruction of whatever world it imagines, its form also precipitates a poem that is inclusive, discursive, and social, even didactic in character (Spiegelman 192), rather than exclusive, expressive, and individuated. Instead of Homer and Virgil, however, Merrill's specific epic forebears were Dante, Milton, Blake, and Proust, writers concerned with exploring consciousness (or the spirit) as much as the origin of a nation or tribe. However, within *The Changing Light* itself, the predecessor who becomes its guiding presence is not Dante or Milton, but W. H. Auden, a poet of wit, irony, and social satire. As Lynn Keller has noted, through Auden's influence Merrill turned away from the "icy preciosity" and "tired Romanticism of his exaggerated claims for the imagination" sometimes evident in his earlier work in favor of "Auden's theatricality, his humor, and his conversational voice" as well as his "exuberant embodiment of intellectual curiosity" (*Re-making* 214–15). In addition, given that Auden was a poet whose work was openly engaged with the impact of modern science on consciousness, his presence in the poem prompts Merrill to respond to the major scientific developments of his own time, especially in atomic physics and molecular genetics.

Third, the structure of *The Changing Light*—namely, its staging of a series of conversations between mortals and spirits by way of a Ouija board—frees Merrill from having to make direct statements about political issues that might compromise his voice. His use of dialogue calls to mind the distancing techniques in Ai's Oppenheimer monologue, for instance, and Paul Zimmer's Imbellis and Zimmer characters, but Merrill creates a veritable choir of voices. Moreover the exotic setting of his poem is derived not only from cultural history but also from his personal experiences over a twenty-five-year period of using a Ouija board, a decidedly *non*-scientific contraption. The first book of the trilogy, *The Book of Ephraim* (divided into twenty-six sections, each beginning with a successive letter of the alphabet, as on the Ouija board itself) tells the story of the epic poem's conception under the otherworldly guidance of Ephraim, "Our Familiar Spirit," "a Greek Jew/ Born AD 8" who was later "throttled" by the Roman emperor Tiberius's imperial guard "for having LOVED/ THE MONSTERS NEPHEW (sic) CALIGULA" (8). Ephraim speaks his lines to both the poet, referred to as JM or the "Scribe," and his companion David Jackson, referred to as DJ or the "Hand," but only by way of the teacup that serves as the pointer for their Ouija board. Eventually, Merrill introduces a complex hierarchy of other otherworldly beings, including the spirits of Mirabell (known throughout by the number "741"), Auden, the scientist George Cotzias, the singer Maria Mitsotaki, the composer Robert Morse, the archangels Michael, Emmanuel, Raphael, and Gabriel, the twin gods God Biology and Mother Nature, and a host of others. Like Ephraim, all these characters communicate exclusively through the Ouija board, in front of which JM and DJ, the two mortals, sit like priests before an oracle. The closet-drama format of these discussions between spirits and mortals allows Merrill to stage a discussion of nuclear science while, at the same time, its very premise subverts the logical structures of most empirical science. But such an unusual form also complicates the poem's tone: Given the unpredictable, sometimes impenetrable array of shifting voices, just how are we to take these messages received from the spirits? Does the camp, sometimes burlesque quality of JM and DJ's parapsychic conversations ultimately undermine the poem's sometimes serious discourse on annihilation? Is Merrill's discussion of nuclear science truly interdisciplinary or merely parodic?

From Merrill's and Jackson's extratextual accounts of the poem's

composition,[6] it is clear that we are to accept the messages from the
spirit world (always presented in uppercase letters) as authentic, yet
Merrill is also to have revised and reshaped those messages into the poetry, so that, as Judith Moffett points out, Merrill's "role of Poet as distinct from his role of Scribe is a distinction readers should bear in mind.
Thinking of the two roles as Mind Conscious and Unconscious is one
very workable way of reading the poem—as if all of *The Changing Light
at Sandover* were an inexhaustibly elaborate dialogue between Merrill's
waking intelligence and its own unconscious sources of feeling, myth,
and dream, with David Jackson as essential catalyst (and supplemental
unconscious story-trove)" (128). Adopting this dual role grants Merrill
the psychohistorical advantage of being able to talk *around* nuclear issues while still involving himself in their implications. His double perspective also justifies the poem's approach to those issues, for two reasons: On the one hand, it explains why JM and DJ turn increasingly
toward the nuclear threat, because it is not the poet but the spirit of
Ephraim who urges them to do so; on the other hand, within the poem,
Merrill as poet continues to joke skeptically about the personal relevance of these global issues.

In Book II, *Mirabell's Books of Number*, for example, when the spirits instruct JM to compose "POEMS OF SCIENCE," his initial reaction is
one of comic resentment:

> Poems of *Science?* Ugh.
> The very thought. To squint through those steel-rimmed
> Glasses of the congenitally slug-
> Pale boy at school, with his precipitates,
> His fruit-flies and his slide rule? Science meant
> Obfuscation, boredom—; (*Changing* 109)

but upon reflection the Poet (or conscious mind unconsciously provoked by the spirit) begins to see poetic possibilities, even if in a mis-
guided fashion:

> once granted,
> Odd lights came and went inside my head.
> Not for nothing had the Impressionists
> Put subject-matter in its place, a mere
> Pretext for iridescent atmosphere.
> Why couldn't Science, in the long run, serve
> As well as one's uncleared lunch-table or
> *Mme X en Culotte de Matador?*

Man by nature was (I'm paraphrasing)
Ignorant. The man of science knew
Little, could therefore be enticed to learn.
Finally the few of more than common sense—
Who but they would be our audience!
This last bit put me in a mood to humor
Powers so naive about the world of men.
And what had I to lose? Misreading Ephraim's
Broken-off message above, I supposed vaguely
That inspiration from now on would come
Outright, with no recourse to the Board.
Would it have helped to know the truth? (109)

The subsequent interplay between the voices from the other world (in which the poet believes, even if his readers do not quite) and the voices of JM and DJ from this world establishes *The Changing Light's* narrative conflict. JM feels compelled to react responsibly to Ephraim's directions but initially expresses his own predilection for "the few of more than common sense," implying an elitism that rejects science in the guise of the "congenitally slug-/ Pale boy at school" as somehow uncultivated. Wrongly believing he might entice scientists to pay more attention to "the world of men," he goes confidently forward, but he obviously has a lot to learn for himself. Staging his self-consciousness about addressing scientific issues in this manner allows Merrill to explore his own thoughts without having to sacrifice his aestheticism. In other words, giving way neither to the proselytizing of those who take activist positions nor to the apathy of those who eschew any moral position, Merrill is tricked by Ephraim (or with him tricks his readers) into considering the cultural ramifications of atomic science in a way that, by the poem's dramatic format, potentially reconciles those ramifications with the Unconscious Mind.

Despite his having been coerced into writing "poems of science" by Ephraim, however, what eventually emerges as the key term in Merrill's response to the threat of annihilation is "resistance," a term he surprisingly shares with poets as different from him as Ginsberg and Levertov. But rather than voice that resistance as a protest, Merrill delves psychohistorically into the cultural ideology behind nuclearism. That is, by the way his cast of characters talk around, not against, annihilation, he ultimately expresses his resistance not to the weapons of annihilation but to the reductive tropes used to justify their existence.

As early as a third of the way into *The Book of Ephraim* (in section

"J"), the spirit Ephraim, a benevolent soul, reveals to JM and DJ his own deep-seated fear of the power of a nuclear-initiated metamorphosis; referring to a trip that DJ and he once took to Santa Fe, the poet explains how Ephraim "cannot think why we have gone out there/ That summer (1958)."[7] Then he quotes the spirit:

> THE AIR
> ABOVE LOS ALAMOS IS LIKE A BREATH
> SUCKED IN HORROR TOD MORT MUERTE DEATH
> —Meaning the nearby nuclear research
> Our instinct first is to deplore, and second
> To think no more of. (*Changing* 33)

Despite the radical nature of Ephraim's remark, JM and DJ do just what the poem suggests they will, that is, follow their instincts and avoid thinking about anything connected to "nuclear research" in favor of considering JM's novel-in-progress or their own domestic affairs. But six sections later, section "P" suddenly begins, "Powers of lightness, darkness, powers that be . . ." (54), establishing *The Changing Light*'s abiding thematic dichotomy of lightness (life, breath, creativity, music) and darkness (their opposites). Invoking the dangers of nuclear research a second time, Ephraim reiterates his fear of the danger of "power's worst abusers," to which JM replies, calmly:

> Here on Earth, we rather feel,
> Such wise arrangements fail. The drug-addicted
> Farms. Welkin the strangler. Plutonium waste
> Eking out in drowned steel rooms a half
> Life of how many million years? Enough
> To set the doomsday clock—its hands our own:
> The same rose ruts, the red-as-thorn crosshatchings—
> Minutes nearer midnight. On which stroke
> Powers at the heart of matter, powers
> We shall have hacked through thorns to kiss awake,
> Will open baleful, sweeping eyes, draw breath
> And speak new formulae of megadeath. (55)

As mortals, JM and DJ consider meddling with the atom or with matter's basic parts (such as DNA) to be an extension of the traditional powers of darkness taken to a polarizing extreme, but Ephraim sees such meddling as capable of upsetting the balance of the whole dichotomy and says: "NO SOULS CAME FROM HIROSHIMA U KNOW/ EARTH WORE A

STRANGE NEW ZONE OF ENERGY." "Caused by?" asks JM. "SMASHED ATOMS OF THE DEAD MY DEARS/ News that brought into play our deepest fears" (55). For Ephraim, to interfere with the atom threatens not only human existence but, through annihilation, spiritual existence as well. While the mortals may fear their own deaths in a nuclear war, they also begin to realize how it threatens the spirits—not with death but with destruction resulting in nothingness.

Later, in *Mirabell's Books of Number*, Part I.4, Ephraim returns to the idea of annihilation. Speaking from "WITHIN THE ATOM" (*Changing* 113), the spirit instructs JM and DJ in the ways of the universe by drawing a dichotomy between the power of the atom—a power that is responsible for "ADAM & LIFE & THE UNIVERSE" (118), is compared to the ancient and mystical power of the pyramid (126), and is later referred to as "A SPEARHEAD/ OF UNLIFE" (146)—and the power of "THE LIFE RAFT LANGUAGE" (119), a power that is described as "MANS TERMITE PALACE BEEHIVE ANTHILL PYRAMID" (118) and as belonging particularly to poets (who themselves can "STIR THE THINKERS & DETER THE REST" [118], thereby instructing humans to "SPARE THE GREENHOUSE" or earth [119]). In short, for both spirits and mortals, "THE SINGLE CONTEST IS THE ATOM" (119).

Always proliferating metaphors to aid the reader's understanding, while simultaneously (to use Derrida's terms) multiplying his "strategic maneuvers in order to assimilate that unassimilable wholly other" (28), Merrill further complicates matters. He draws a parallel between the atom and the DNA molecule, and then compares the "contest" of the atom to the story of Adam and Eve (in which human curiosity plays the role of the serpent) when he asks Ephraim, "Is DNA, that sinuous molecule,/ The serpent in your version of the myth?/ Asking, I feel a cool/ Forked flickering, as from my very mouth" (119). Ephraim's response is a qualifying and somewhat mystifying joke: "YES & NO THE ATOMS APPLE LEANS PERILOUSLY CLOSE/ . . . / THIS ATOM GLIMPSD IS A NEARLY FATAL CONSUMMATION" (119). Though poking fun at human anatomy and the Garden of Eden, this reply also at first seems a warning against cracking open nature's secrets. But Ephraim next extends this metaphor of temptation even further by defining the atom as consisting "OF INTENSE FISSIONABLE ENERGIES BLACK & WHITE/ WHICH EITHER JOIN & CREATE OR SEPARATE & DESTROY/ . . . /O IT IS SPERM EGG & CELL THE EARTH & PARADISE O" (119). Like genes that can both combine and separate, nuclear fusion and fission are considered both opposite and interdependent functions of physics. But whereas genes comprise the essence of life, fusion and fission comprise the interactions of all being, organic and inorganic, including the spirits.

Part I.5 of *Mirabell* follows with yet another approach to clarify Ephraim's concern for both human and spiritual existence. Again speaking allegorically, he describes annihilation as that which hangs in the balance in the contest between God's good and bad angels (with Ephraim, of course, belonging to the latter group):

> PUT SIMPLY THE ATOM IS L SIDED
> ITS POSITIVE SIDE GOOD   ITS NEGATIVE AH WHAT TO SAY
> A DISAPPEARANCE   AN ABSOLUTE VOID   ASTRONOMERS
> HAVE AT LAST SEEN OUR BENIGHTED WORK   THE BLACK HOLES
>   THEY GROW
> You caused them, the black holes, when you—
> THERE IS AN EVIL WE RELEASD   WE DID NOT CREATE IT
> CALL IT THE VOID   CALL IT IN MAN   A WILL TO NOTHINGNESS
> (119–20)

Although the spirits "RELEASD" them, Ephraim takes no responsibility for creating the black holes that annihilate existence. In other words, it is not an otherworldly force (or godlike power) that threatens us but the human "WILL TO NOTHINGNESS."

Much of the rest of *Mirabell* explores this "contest" of the atom, by debating physics, genetics, astronomy, and the history of science. Yet the way JM and DJ talk about these subjects with their otherworldly companions is nothing like the theoretical or scientific prose we're used to, and throughout his epic Merrill devotes at least as much time to such related subjects as music, literature, and philosophy. The level of discourse is the spontaneous one of drawing room conversations and interpersonal exchanges, not the controlled assertions of nuclear experts that Lawrence Freedman objects to. In fact, although the mortals seem to seek guidance for JM's task of writing "POEMS OF SCIENCE" that will help serve their world, on the whole the trilogy investigates a hierarchy of psychohistorical relationships between ideas and the dynamics behind them, between people and ideas, and between language and its metaphors. By its sheer length, *The Changing Light* insists on envisioning the threat of nuclearism as part of a larger cultural discussion. Whether for the sake of the truth or merely for amusement, Merrill explores the gamut of these relationships, making any attempt to paraphrase or explicate the whole poem a self-defeating, if not absurd, task. Nonetheless, by proliferating possible meanings, he avoids falling into a simplistic protest against the abuse of the atom, while he also resists making extremist predictions about the future.[8] Again, the resistance expressed is not to nuclear science but to reductive thinking.

In "The Last Lessons: 3" in the "NO" section of Book III, *Scripts for the Pageant*, the poem's underlying preoccupation with annihilation, about which JM remains mostly inquisitive while DJ begins to express his fear, finally takes center stage in the pageant itself. The section opens with Gabriel, the "Angel of Fire and Death," defining nothingness:

> OUR POET ASKED: THIS BLACK, BEYOND BLACK, IS IT A STOP TO
>   DREAM?
> POET, NO, FOR IT IS A DREAM.
> IS IT THE HOURGLASS DRAINED OF TIME?
> NO, FOR IT IS THE HOURGLASS IN WHICH S A N D R U N S U P!
> (*Changing* 448)

Gabriel imagines annihilation as a dream, not as an end to time but its reversal, time running backward. Without clarifying this image, the pageant next presents the spirit of Mohammed, "blackbrowed," who when commanded by Mother N(ature) to speak about blackness to the mortals recalls his own directive to "THIN OUT YOUR RACE AND KEEP IT THIN WITH BLOODSHED,/ FOR YOU SIT ON TIME MADE BLACK" (449). His speech alludes to an earlier passage in which the spirits suggest the necessity of thinning out the human population, an eventuality the poem does not entirely reject. Then Mohammed adds, about "THE BLACK":

> IT CALLS TO US 'COME BACK TO THE HEAVENS SPEEDING
> INTO O, COME TO THE LOST BLACK TREES, THE ANIMALS
> SINGING SONGS OF LOST IMMORTALITY, COME'
> THESE SUCK US DOWN   THE SAND RISES   WE GO
> TO MEET THAT BLACK (450)

Immediately after this passage he vanishes. JM interprets this process of "thinning" as the spirits "plundering Earth's resources," but Gabriel steps in to correct him. Mohammed is preparing for Earth's "LAST, HOLY WAR," during which "THE HOURGLASS," "CURVED LIKE A SWORD," will jab its point "INTO THE DESERT OF MAN'S FAITH" (450). Even if JM and DJ do not openly shudder at this apocalyptic image, its suggestion of a nothingness that supercedes death stirs a dread of Faustian proportions. Yet it still is not clear what the spirits mean, until RM (Robert Morse, the composer friend of the mortals) enters, also wearing black in this scene in the ballroom at Sandover, and offers to explain "TO MY FELLOW MORTALS/ THE SAD DISHARMONIES":

> THREE 'TIMES' OBTAIN:
> THIS FICTIVE SPACE WE HERE INHABIT IS
> THE STOP TO TIME. WHAT YOU, DEAR SCRIBE & HAND,
> NOW LIVE IN IS TIME'S FORWARD RUN. THE BLACK
> BEYOND BLACK IS OF TIME SET RUNNING BACK.
> THESE SOULS WERE CAUGHT IN THE FRICTION, STRIPPED LIKE GEARS,
> GIVEN VAST POWERS THAT COLLAPSING WERE
> SUCKED DRY OF EVERY HUMAN DENSITY.
> JUST AS CERTAIN STARS, SO CERTAIN SOULS. (451)

RM's image of the implosion of a black hole threatens both mortals and spirits, since "TIME SET RUNNING BACK" annihilates both existences. However, typical of Merrill's method, the angel Gabriel immediately steps in again to dismiss any moral implications in this threat. He reminds JM and DJ that, while worldly spirits such as RM and Auden "THINK THERE IS PUNISHMENT AND MERCY" and that "SIN EXISTS," in fact for the spirits, "THOSE MEASURES ARE BLANK. KNOWING NO TIME, WE DO NOT SENTENCE VAGRANT SOULS BUT SWEEP THEM/ (SHH SHH THERE IS NO HELL) UNDER THE (M)/ CARPET TO ETERNAL IDLENESS" (452). The spirits, being only after all "brains with wings," seem untroubled by their own precarious state, but not so this time the Scribe and Hand, who remain confused, asking once more, "Won't *someone* please explain the Black?" (452). Finally, it is the spirit of George Cotzias, the scientist, who clarifies the relationship between time and the negative power of the atom:

> NOT FORWARD TIME COMPRESSED (COMBUSTIBLE
> OILCAN OF 'THINNER') BUT ATOMIC BLACK
> COMPRESSED FROM TIME'S REVERSIBILITY,
> THAT IDEA OF DESTRUCTION WHICH RESIDES
> BOTH IN MAN & IN THE ACTINIDES.
> PART OF THE GREENHOUSE, FOR (THO MATTER HOLDS)
> THESE FORKED TONGUES FLICKER FROM ITS OILS & GOLDS. (452–53)

As DJ recognizes, such a "subtly interfused" energy, as in naturally occurring uranium, has always been present in the universe, but as the image of the forked tongues implies, we mortals must now assume responsibility for its future, so we must also be aware of its danger to mortals and spirits alike. Suddenly, all earlier metaphors associated with annihilation combine as JM begins to grasp his own role in this universal drama—expressed in this exchange with George's spirit:

THE CABLES SNAPPED. SNAPPER: THE MONITOR?
THUS MAKING SOURCES OF 1) NATURAL POWER
& 2) UNNATURAL. POWER TO SUCK THE EARTH
EGG TO AN O. But Matter *holds.* ITS BIRTH,
RESISTANCE   DON'T FORGET THAT FIRST THIN THIN
PASTE (453)

In response to this revelation JM asks, in amazement, "The Greenhouse from the start had been/ An act of resistance?" to which the scientist replies,

      JIMMY YES   A PLUS!
OR DISOBEDIENCE   GOD AS PROMETHEUS?
NOW THAT MAN TAPS THIS 2ND POWER, ONE WELL
TOO MANY & PUFF! Puff? THE WHOLE FRAIL EGGSHELL
SIMPLY IMPLODING AS THE MONITOR'S
BLACK FILLS THE VACUUM MOTHER N ABHORS (453)

So it is the mortals' function to help the "greenhouse" or the earth to hold, to resist, and to make certain the atoms "JOIN & CREATE," not just "SEPARATE & DESTROY" (119), to employ fusion, not just fission, in their activities. The gesture here toward human responsbility, though muted, echoes Denise Levertov's recognition of the human responsibility to "protect this perversely weak/ animal," the Lamb of God, in the last section of "Mass for the Day of St. Thomas Didymus" (*Candles* 114). And in the same way she couches her poem in a prayer, JM's staging of his own resistance to dichotomies in fact assists in the larger effort of matter to hold, not to give into "THE VACUUM" that would annihilate it. In other words, his method itself enacts the fusion the spirits implore.

Ultimately, then, Merrill returns to his own chief resource of resistance, "THE LIFE RAFT LANGUAGE," though not without also expressing his frustration with its limited ability to convey truth, as he concludes:

It all fits. But the ins and outs deplete us.
Minding the thread, losing the maze, we curse
Language's misleading apparatus.
For once I rather sympathize with Pound
Who "said it" with his Chinese characters —
Not that the one I need here could be found. (453)

In actuality, only by using language paradoxically, by fusing words yet signaling the undoing of the categories language uses to create meaning, can the poet JM accurately render the ambiguity of a world on the cusp between being and non-being. The power to hold is ironically wedded to "DISOBEDIENCE." Yet there remains an even deeper ambiguity, embedded in the poem that JM is prodded into writing at the end of "The Last Lessons: 3." No matter how inevitable it seems that language cannot express truth, that failure in itself promotes a further resistance: Language's imprecision prevents its users from reducing their understanding of things to an absolute, to that very "VOID" or "NOTHINGNESS" we have such a "WILL" to attain. The final paradox is that language and metaphor, which mean to reveal, inevitably resist the revelation they seek:

> My characters, this motley alphabet,
> Engagingly evade the cul-de-sac
> Of the Whole Point, dimensionless and black,
>
> While, deep in bulging notebooks, drawn by it,
> I skim lost heavens for that inky star. (454)

Through its encompassing approach to culture, The Changing Light engages the idea of resistance evident in other poetry about nuclearism, but it pursues that idea to its speculative roots. Through the magic of the spiritual world explored and dramatized within the poem, it tricks us into confronting the paradoxical manner by which we imagine annihilation and offers an alternative set of myths with nonreductive parameters.

Even if we accept this reading of Merrill's epic drama, though, we still need to consider its comic tone. Despite the density of The Changing Light, just how seriously can we take its concept of resistance for survival? The jury of critics has been deadlocked between those who circumscribe it as "a poem less of authority than of companionship" (von Hallberg, American 114) and those who praise its "grand heterocosm— a world elsewhere, a rival plenitude designed both to imitate and to preserve the totality of our world, now threatened by extinction" (Berger 285).[9] To reconcile this opposition, Williard Spiegelman stresses the importance of the "principle of duality" and "version of dichotomy with a didactic flourish" that lies at the heart of Merrill's method (228). Keller essentially agrees, when she identifies the poem's "postmodern perspective": "The reader's belief can be only momentary inspiration, not lasting credence—and Merrill would have it so, for all his show of didacticism. Belief here . . . is necessarily provisional and processive." To read the epic, she says, is to cultivate "tolerance of uncertainty as well as resistance to outmoded absolutes and firm boundaries" (*Re-making* 252). In explaining Merrill's difficult but camp humor as essential to that structural resistance, Walter Kalaidjian applies Mikhail Bakhtin's concept of the carnivalesque: "Like much poststructuralist writing," he observes, "Merrill's ludic textuality is designed to baffle and disperse the windy platitudes of the Western humanist tradition" (98). And Lee Zimmerman further argues that, as "the counterhegemonic fiction of the cosmic web," *The Changing Light* enacts a model of dialogue as the method by which we can best talk ourselves out of annihilation, locating its authority not in an absolutist view of the world but in the "interplay" between "self and other" (383).[10] As Merrill himself reminds us, the point is "to be always of two minds" (*Recitative* 51).

Because it refuses to take sides, then, *The Changing Light* is far from being a poem in protest of nuclear war, yet in cleaving to the idea that "MATTER HOLDS," it performs, rather than preaches, its resistance to nothingness. Is there a political directive to be gained from such a fluid play of language? Toward the end of *Scripts*, JM, exhausted from the elaborate descriptions of the spirit world, questions his own method when, in simple terms, he asks, "Resistance—Nature's gift to man —/ What form will it assume in Paradise?" (511). Nature herself replies by describing Paradise:

HOW WILL IT BE?
IT WILL HOLD A CREATURE MUCH LIKE DARLING MAN,
   YET PHYSICALLY MORE ADAPTABLE.
HIS IMMORTALITY WILL CONSIST OF PROLONGATION, IN THE
   BEGINNING PHASE, UNTIL HIS IDEAL IS REACHED IN NUMBER.
THEN TIME WILL STOP
AND LONG FRUITFUL SPACES BE GIVEN HIM TO LEARN THROUGH
   SONG AND POETRY
OF HIS OLD HELPLESS FEELINGS & WEARY PAST. (*Changing* 512)

The epic's postapocalyptic paradise will be neither that of mortal existence (where time runs forward) nor that of annihilation (where time runs backward), but that of the spirits, where (as described before) "TIME WILL STOP" (after the process of "thinning out" has been completed).[11] And as for the role of "resistance" in paradise,

THE RESISTANCE? NONE. HE WILL, YES, SWIM & GLIDE,
A SIMPLER, LESS WILFUL BEING. DULLER, TOO?

IF SO, IS THAT SHARP EDGE NOT WELL LOST
WHICH HAS SO VARIOUSLY CUT AND COST?
WE WILL WALK AMONG HIS KIND MADE NEW
(THE MASQUE CONCLUDED, WE & OURS
STEPPING FROM STAGE TO MIX WITH MORTAL POWERS)
SAYING, AS OUR WITTY POET CRIED
BACK TO YOUR SUNSET FACES: BONNE CHANCE!
AND AS MY OWN SWEET BRIGHTNESS ADDED: ON WITH THE DANCE!
FAREWELL (512)

Mother Nature's exit speech, as reassuring as Prospero's epilogue in *The Tempest*, proposes a paradise at once alluring and disconcerting in its languid simplicity. The myriad turns throughout *Scripts* allow us to revel for a moment in the pageantry that closes this book, but even here our comfort is tinged with a resilient uncertainty, down to the pun on the French idiom "BONNE CHANCE!" as Mother Nature's farewell.

With its sheer creative energy, *The Changing Light at Sandover* asks that we engage annihilation by giving in neither to reductive solutions nor to self-proliferating complications. Instead, like Miranda and Ferdinand in *The Tempest*, we are asked to be patient and to delight in its contrasts, always keeping in mind the paradoxical bounds of any inclination toward truth-telling. In the long run, as in other poems with psychohistorical breadth, the purpose of such art may be less to direct the way out of the nuclear predicament than to critique the self-enclosed modes of thinking that have allowed that predicament to arise and abide.

The ambiguity in *The Changing Light*, then—expressed even in the Ouija board's "YES & NO" that provide the structure of *Scripts*—vividly demonstrates a third way of nothingness in the poetry of the nuclear age. As a paradigm, it promotes the free play of mind needed to keep us from overestimating the power of nuclearism. While Merrill may not speak directly to our fear of annihilation with the same candor that Levertov does, and while his complex depiction of annihilation may fail to strike the poignant chord of dread that Wilbur does, his devotion to survival matches theirs. Moreover, with its ingenious staging and ambiguous tone, *The Changing Light* exercises an openness to change in cultural history that their poems, by virtue of their lyric premises, do not address—and therefore it makes its own critical contribution to the long-term rethinking of nuclear ideology.

FIVE

The Poetry of Destinerrance

"For an Untenable Situation": Nuclearism and Randomness

With its idiosyncratic voice, Merrill's *The Changing Light at Sandover* stands apart from nuclear protest and apocalyptic lyric poetry, primarily because it expresses neither overt opposition to nuclear proliferation nor a singularly meditative response to annihilation as much as it explores the mythic and ideological context of nuclearism. But it is the fundamental ambiguity of Merrill's vision, an ambiguity implicit in the nuclear referent, that relates it to my fourth way of nothingness, the way of poems that may or may not, in fact, employ the imagery and language of nuclear forces nor even acknowledge their cultural presence but instead engage the concept of annihilation itself as a phenomenon. These poems approach annihilation from *within* nothingness itself, rather than go against, through, or around it, as they envision the randomness of time and being in our era.

In my introduction I mentioned Lifton's diagnosis of "the absurdity of our double life" in an age on the verge of self-eradication: Lifton proposes that nuclear weapons have created an existential condition of absurdity on three levels of behavior. First, politically speaking, there is the "basic structural absurdity" of nation-states that are "poised to destroy virtually all of human civilization—destroy humankind—in the name of destroying one another." A second level of absurdity, viewed from a more psychosocial perspective, concerns our tendency to carry on with business as usual in the face of the nuclear threat "as though no such threat existed" (Lifton and Falk 4–5), that condition associated, as we have seen, with psychic numbing. But beyond these two levels lies yet another level of absurdity, entailing "the mind's relationship to the 'thing' ": "We simply cannot locate in our images anything like this 'nuclear holocaust,' " and this inability creates "the special absurdity of the mind, our struggle with our limited capacity to (in [Martin] Buber's phrase) 'imagine the real' " (Lifton and Falk 5). What concerns Lifton at this level is not the *process* of a nuclear holocaust (which we *can* imagine, with its mushroom clouds, fireballs, and scorched human skin—that imagery for instance that apocalyptic lyric poets often employ), but the *condition* of extinction itself, a condition that has seeped into contemporary consciousness. As he admits, "The image in question, really *imagery of extinction*, has never taken on sharp contours for me. Rather than experience the ready psychic flow associated with most lively images, I must struggle amorphously to encompass the *idea* of violently attained nothingness" (Lifton and Falk 58).

As Lifton argues, nuclear extinction has come to interfere with our awareness of the present, as well as of the future. It is this rupture that the poems in this fourth group address. Writing within the same political, social, and historical context in which protest poets assert moral authority, apocalyptic lyric poets connect the universality of the nuclear threat to personal fears, and the psychohistorical poets delve into nuclear culture, the poets in this final category concern themselves both substantively and stylistically with the implications of the *idea* of annihilation, as they replicate the psychic experience of nuclearity. What distinguishes this category of poems—including Thom Gunn's "The Annihilation of Nothing," Alan Dugan's "Winter: For an Untenable Situation," John Engels's "Moonwalk," C. K. Williams's "The Last Deaths," and John Ashbery's "The Absence of a Noble Presence"—is not how they treat the nuclear threat, but how they embody the same "way of nothingness" Lifton identified in the *hibakusha*, how they are informed with both *akirame* ("psychologically 'taking in' an experience, however extreme, and simultaneously reasserting one's sense of connection with the vast human and natural forces which extend beyond that experience" [*Death* 186]) and the abiding uncertainty of potential annihilation.

Of course, to create a category of nuclear annihilation poems in which the poems themselves may not explicitly address the subject at hand may beg the question, testing the limits of my critical method. Such a move poses the problem of arbitrarily including in this group any poem written since 1945. But it is precisely this risk of arbitrary meaning, of the meaninglessness created by the nuclear threat, that I want to invoke. Derrida takes up the idea of arbitary meaning in his essay on the nuclear referent when he speaks of that condition of literature he calls "destinerrance," or "a wandering that is its own end" (29). For Derrida, "randomness and incalculability" are "essential" elements of "destinerrance," not just factors of uncertainty that effect the "margin of indeterminacy" of a "calculable decision." Combining to form "an aleatory element that appears in a heterogeneous relation to every possible calculation and every possible decision," they best convey how in the nuclear age both missiles and language may "escape all control, all reassimilation or self-regulation of a system that they will have *precipitously* (too rapidly, in order to avert the worst) but irreversibly destroyed" (29). Insinuating (since he cannot more definitively articulate) a metaphysics for the nuclear referent, Derrida suggests that it is "the aleatory destinerrance of the *envoi*," or, to rephrase it, *the chance wandering of the sending forward of being itself*, that "allows us to think, if we may say so, the age of nuclear war" (29–30).

As I discussed in chapter 1, J. Fisher Solomon qualifies Derrida's deconstructive association of randomness with the nuclear referent by criticizing the way he privileges phenomenal over empirical conditions. "We cannot be certain of our destiny," concedes Solomon, "but we are not therefore abandoned to a chartless destinerrance," as he identifies "a factor within specific empirical situations that delimits the possible and defines the probable, the regular, the typical" (35). Solomon argues in favor of placing *some* modicum of value in *potential* realities or probabilities that can be hypothesized about or tested against "the background of reality, not discourse" (101). Applying Solomon's call for this kind of "potentialist discourse" to "post-nuclear holocaust fiction," William J. Scheick also qualifies the concept of destinerrance when he maintains that for a writer to compose in terms of randomness does not mean he or she must abandon reality or reason. To the contrary, because "the possibility of nuclear holocaust bears within itself real propensities for probable development . . . , the nuclear referent is not merely the fantastical product of our imaginations that requires a suspension of disbelief (as Derrida seems to contend), but it is also something extrinsic to us, something with *real* extra-conjectural, extra-interrelational, extra-linguistic dispositional potentialities" ("Post-nuclear" 80). Given this extrinsic power of nuclearism, to court disruption is more than mind-play. Since, as Scheick observes, the nuclear referent is in fact "something utterly *real* in its dispositional potentiality to kill the dreamer," to avert annihilation the dreamer must dream "into 'external' existence a 'fantastical reality' of alternative potentialities" (80). For the poet, then, to respond creatively to "randomness and incalculability" is to externalize the *idea* of annihilation in a manner other than the probably disastrous one of nuclear war.

While the poems in my first three categories explore our human responsibility for, intimacy with, and rationalizing of the nuclear present, the poems in this category—by touching on the subject obliquely at best yet still risking the "fantastical" and meaningless—renew in poetry the same question Derrida returns to: "Why is there something instead of nothing?" (30) Rather than openly oppose or reconfigure the power of the nuclear threat *per se*, they lend paradigmatic shape to that power, despite its potential to resist, elude, and ultimately destroy things human. Subsequently, the telling characteristics of these poems reside less in their subject matter than in their indirection, suspension of judgment, and stylistic depiction of "randomness and incalculability," as the embodiment of the paradoxes at the very heart of nuclearism. In defining what she calls "internal difference" as the appropriate political focus for contemporary literature, Barbara Eckstein, like Scheick and others,[1] defends the political efficacy of this kind of writing as a critique of postmodern ideology: "The most radical and humane possibilities for the antinuclear, or peace, movement are those which perceive and address paradox and uncertainty, those which try to present a social, psychological, historical, and rhetorical analysis of the whole condition, and those which propose action based on that analysis" (14–15). It is this

internal condition of postmodern nothingness which the poetry of destinerrance explores and exploits.

Admittedly, the poems I examine here rarely "propose action." In
fact, often they appear anarchistic or nihilistic. Yet if we recall Adorno's
characterization of post-Auschwitz art, the *appearance* of nihilism
might well be taken as an affirmation of meaning in the face of potential annihilation. "Art is semblance even at its highest peaks," writes
Adorno, "but its semblance, the irresistible part of it, is given to it by
what is not semblance. What art, notably the art decried as nihilistic,
says in refraining from judgments is that everything is not just nothing.
. . . Semblance is a promise of nonsemblance" (404–5). In the same way
that not to resist the proliferation of nuclear weapons is to abet their
material ascendancy, not to explore the paradox of nothingness within
the *idea* of annihilation is to assure its symbolic ascendancy, even
though the process of exploring it may appear "folly," to use Adorno's
term. By speaking from nothingness and risking meaninglessness, the
poems of destinerrance dwell within that paradox.

◇ To illustrate the distinctiveness of poems in this category, I want
first to contrast a post-Hiroshima poem on nothingness with an earlier
poem on the same topic. With the modernists, it would be pointless to
gauge the tenor of their work by nuclear history, but poets born in the
1920s and after have had to adjust to nuclear power as a constant, and
for many their art cannot help but reflect their awareness of potential
extinction. By focusing on the concept of nothingness in two poems,
then—Wallace Stevens's "The Snow Man" and Thom Gunn's "The Annihilation of Nothing"—I want to trace a fundamental difference in
their assumptions about the incalculability of presence and the vulnerability of consciousness. The difference between them reveals, I believe,
a paradigm of how ideas of nothingness have changed in the nuclear age:
While Stevens's poem is highly seductive in the way it imagines nothingness, Gunn's poem, despite its abstract language, provides a more realistically (or "extrinsically") grounded expression of nothingness, as
we have come to think of it since Hiroshima.

In "The Snow Man," which was originally published in 1921, Stevens
typically unleashes his imagination in an ingenious manner. But from
a post-nuclear perspective, ultimately his poem is a philosophic tour-
de-force that suspends the mind a little too comfortably. By its use of
simple diction and concrete imagery, the poem begins by lulling us

through several tercets, before turning toward its paradoxical closure about nothingness:

> One must have a mind of winter
> To regard the frost and the boughs
> Of the pine-trees crusted with snow;
>
> And have been cold a long time
> To behold the junipers shagged with ice,
> The spruces rough in the distant glitter
>
> Of the January sun; and not to think
> Of any misery in the sound of the wind,
> In the sound of a few leaves. . . . (9–10)

As an imagist might, Stevens captures a specific moment on a clear, cold January day after a snowstorm. The most complicated word he uses is "junipers," hardly a mind-stumper, and the imagery of the pine trees, junipers, and spruces firmly roots itself in the mind's eye. Furthermore, with its widely varied tetrameter line (Litz 100), stresses are determined by syntax more than syllables, creating a fluid, conversational rhythm. Indeed, syntax provides the key to its magic. All five stanzas comprise one sentence, which Stevens carefully strings through a series of infinitive phrases and subordinate clauses to tease us out of our present thoughts into his "mind of winter," that state of mind necessary to experience this landscape for itself. The main clause of the sentence uses the *im*personal pronoun "one," which suspends the identity of reader and writer alike, and the modal auxiliary verb "must," implying a prerequisite condition yet also suggesting that "one" may well *not* have the "mind of winter" needed to carry on through the poem. In this quickly established state of suspension, "one" adopts a "mind of winter"—either a brain made of snow like a snowman's (a virtual impossibility) or, more figuratively, the frame of mind one has during January in a cold climate.

Prompted by the clarity of the poem's first line, once we make the deceptively easy leap to a mind of winter we gain the power to perform three acts: "to regard" (an act both physical and cerebral), "to behold" (a physical act only), and "not to think" (an act most assuredly cerebral yet one that Stevens simultaneously negates). In a mind of winter, one can "regard" the scene before him or her, and if one has been "cold a long time" then he or she can look at that scene without thinking "of any misery" in its sights and sounds. Of course, not to attribute any emotional qualities to a landscape as a viewer perceives it is to be not a human but a "snow man," so what the poet asks of us is possible only within the imagination.

From this point, we drift through the series of phrases and subordinate clauses away from our inherently "human" minds into the very "mind of winter" Stevens has created until we come to the sound of the wind,

> Which is the sound of the land
> Full of the same wind
> That is blowing in the same bare place
>
> For the listener, who listens in the snow,
> And, nothing himself, beholds
> Nothing that is not there and the nothing that is. (10)

In these final six lines, Stevens includes no fewer than six subordinate clauses introduced by relative pronouns, each of which works to draw us further and further from our originally suspended state into his increasingly abstract landscape. Also, the imagery has become generalized: "The sound of the wind" and "the sound of a few leaves" have broadened to become "the sound of the land"; the vividly described trees in stanzas one and two have faded into "the same bare place"; even the snowman has become merely "the listener" who is "nothing himself" and whose only function is to listen. Despite the visual strokes of the poem's opening, Stevens has drawn us artfully through his subtle qualifiers and negative terms until, as Robert Pack has noted, "Gradually, almost imperceptibly, we are divested of whatever it is that distinguishes us from the snowman. We become the snowman, and we see winter through his eyes of coal, and we know the cold without the thoughts of human discomfort" (67). Yet as Walton Litz contends, the poem is neither "a poem of negation" nor a "critique of the man without imagination," but "an affirmation of primary reality" that "lays bare that irreducible reality upon which the poet builds his fictive structures, just as the lusher seasons build upon the frozen outlines of winter" (100).

Finally and most pointedly, what the listener actually "beholds" in the last line is "Nothing that is not there and the nothing that is." In other words, the snowman beholds two phenomena: (a) "nothing that is not there" and (b) "the nothing that is" there. The overt repetition of "nothing" lures us into construing an entirely barren scene, but rephrasing the line according to its parallel structure actually creates a choice:

Either the listener beholds the something that is there as well as the nothing that is not there, or, if we suspend the article "the" in the second clause, he beholds *nothing* that is not there and (yet) *some thing* that is not there. To say he beholds "nothing that is not there" implies that he beholds *only that which is there* and nothing else: such a listener perceives only what is before him. On the other hand, to say he beholds "the nothing that is" (or some thing that is *not* there) can only mean that he beholds *that which is not there,* namely, nothingness—an absence which, for Stevens, is an imaginary, not a real, state of being. As Michael Davidson explains it, these "double negatives literally produce a 'nothing' that is both full and empty at the same time" (149). No matter how we rephrase the line, the listener must admit to beholding these two phenomena of antipathetic natures—that which is only available to sense perception and that which is *not* available to sense perception but to the imagination.

To recall the poem's opening, for one with "a mind of winter," that "listener" who is "nothing himself," such a dichotomous, self-negating act of mind is possible with no disjunction of feeling. But for a human mind, that disjunction itself risks "misery," as the thought necessarily comes into conflict with our feeling about it. Consequently, to appreciate Stevens's expression of nothingness in this poem requires that we suspend our human part with its accompanying emotional baggage. In this way, as a modernist poem, "The Snow Man" stands as an evocative treatment of the mind in tension with its environment. As it follows the sentence's steady digressions, the mind alters its perspective on the winter landscape, while the landscape itself never changes. Instead, like Wordworth or Keats, Stevens draws us out of ourselves and sets us up for the paradox in the final line.

With imaginative lyricism, the poem approaches an almost ideal expression of nothingness, a landscape devoid of any human presence. As Edward Kessler has argued, "Stevens achieves what is probably the coldest, most naked poem in the language, a poem without hope or despair, good or evil—for all of these man-made ideas corrupt pure perception" (33). Stevens himself, in a 1944 letter, describes the poem as "an example of the necessity of identifying oneself with reality in order to understand and enjoy it" (Holly Stevens 464). But how "real" is the "reality" of nothingness imagined here? As delicate a balance as Stevens strikes, does not a conceptual problem arise if we reread the poem's rhetorical strategy from the perspective of the "potentialist discourse" of nuclear annihilation? Without dismissing the complex nature of "reality" throughout Stevens's oeuvre, might we not ask about this poem what it costs, in terms of human consciousness, to achieve that prerequisite "mind of winter" necessary "to understand and enjoy" reality?[2] The poem does, in fact, insinuate that death to the individual imagination would have to occur for one's mind to become the snowman's. But it does not take into consideration the erasure of the imagination beyond individual death. The point here is not to fault the poem or to detract from its light touch; rather, it is to draw attention to how Stevens concerns himself with an erasure of the imagination without feeling compelled also to consider that state of unimaginable nothingness beyond good and evil we call annihilation.

Written during the 1950s and published in *My Sad Captains* (1961), Gunn's "The Annihilation of Nothing," to my mind, begins where "The Snow Man" ends. Like Ted Hughes (a poet with whom he was often associated early on) and in the broad wake of *The Waste Land*, Gunn has consistently been attracted to the desolate and primeval, and this poem typifies his abiding preoccupation with Sartrean perceptions of experience. But despite the dark core of his vision, he also brings to his poetry a refined sense of language and a reliance on reason, so that, as an early reviewer remarked, his work encompasses "sharp disjunctions between controlling mind and chaotic matter" ("Separate" 439). Nevertheless, because of the historical context of Gunn's awareness of potential nothingness, "The Annihilation of Nothing" carries the fantastic, even pleasing conception of nothingness in Stevens to its logical, yet more terrifying, conclusion. In its assumption that a nuclear holocaust would eliminate human consciousness, Gunn's poem inevitably complicates speculation of the kind in which Stevens engages: In short, one is able *not* to think of any misery unless one is, a priori, capable of experiencing misery. But the nothingness Gunn imagines annihilates human experience altogether:

Nothing remained: Nothing, the wanton name
That nightly I rehearsed till led away
To a dark sleep, or sleep that held one dream.

In this a huge contagious absence lay,
More space than space, over the cloud and slime,
Defined but by the encroachments of its sway.

Stripped to indifference at the turns of time,
Whose end I knew, I woke without desire,
And welcomed zero as a paradigm.

But now it breaks—images burst with fire
Into the quiet sphere where I have bided,
Showing the landscape holding yet entire:

The power that I envisaged, that presided
Ultimate in its abstract devastations,
Is merely change, the atoms it divided

Complete, in ignorance, new combinations.
Only an infinite finitude I see
In those peculiar lovely variations.

It is despair that nothing cannot be
Flares in the mind and leaves a smoky mark
Of dread.
       Look upward. Neither firm nor free,

Purposeless matter hovers in the dark. (95)

Written in terza rima and strict iambic pentameter, the poem is more
formally controlled and less idiomatic than "The Snow Man." Instead
of one sentence across five stanzas, it has nine sentences in seven stanzas. Each of the first four stanzas contains a complete sentence, but after stanza four, the syntax begins to break apart, relatively, so that the
sentence in stanza five is enjambed, carrying over into stanza six, with
the final stanza dividing into three sentences, as well as visually dis-
persing on the page. The lines seem to decompose before our eyes, while
the self-perpetuating rhyme scheme of the terza rima, in which each
stanza plants a rhyme in the next, suggests its own "infinite finitude"—
in imitation of a Dantean descent into hell, perhaps, but also of a nuclear chain reaction multiplying itself, layer upon layer, and culminat-
ing in an atomic cloud. Like Stevens, Gunn also employs concrete
vocabulary, yet his appears to be more abstract: Words such as *dark
sleep, space, cloud, slime, encroachments, sway, sphere, landscape,
smoky mark,* and *matter* lack the visual distinctness of *junipers,
spruces,* and *glitter* because Gunn's is a metaphysical (or subatomic)
landscape, not a physical one. Furthermore, Gunn plays none of
Stevens's tricks with verbs. The first three stanzas use past indicative
verbs, while the last four switch to the present indicative, the only variation coming with the imperative "Look."

In this bleak landscape in which "nothing remained," the poet tells
how he "rehearsed" the "wanton name" of nothingness until he was

"led away" or drawn into a sleep "that held one dream" only. This dream itself, a dream of "absence" or nothingness, empties the poet of "desire"; but also, like the snow man with a "mind of winter," he loses his identity. Upon waking, however, he welcomes "zero as a paradigm," because so long as his state of nothingness is only *imagined*, he is able to suspend himself sufficiently to accept "the nothing that is" there.

At this point, though, the poem veers from Stevens's. In the fourth stanza, it is not the poet's *perception* of the landscape that changes but the landscape itself, when "it breaks" and "images burst with fire/ Into the quiet sphere where I have bided." Admittedly, by "holding yet entire," the landscape does not actually disintegrate, so the power that the poet has dreamt of as "ultimate in its abstract devastations" turns out to be not so ultimate as to cease being matter. What occurs is not the elimination of everything but "merely change," that is, merely the restructuring of atomic matter into "complete . . . new combinations." After the blast, something (not nothing) does exist, but, significantly, it exists "in ignorance," without a human knowledge of it. In other words, although "zero" might appropriately serve as the paradigm for the annihilation of matter, it cannot serve as well for the annihilation of consciousness, including, ironically, a consciousness of nothing. For Gunn, what matters more than what happens to matter is what happens to the mind that perceives it.

As the poem approaches its close, "Only an infinite finitude I see," writes Gunn, "in those peculiar lovely variations." Herein lies the poem's paradox, and from this point forward the poet depicts an almost imageless image of "purposeless matter" which, "neither firm nor free," "hovers in the dark." Being in the dark, it cannot be seen; being "neither firm nor free," it can be neither touched nor felt. Nor can it be heard, smelled, or tasted. Furthermore, with the elimination of a human presence, "nothing cannot be." To be sure, we might infer here some kind of consciousness that might "see" the variations as "lovely," that might experience a "despair" that "flares in the mind," and that might "look upward" as directed by the poet. In this sense, the "controlling mind" outside the poem contradicts the condition it portrays. Nevertheless, with convincing approximation, I think, the poem projects the utter depletion of nuclear annihilation, and Gunn's imageless image of "purposeless matter" hovering in the dark speaks to Lifton's notion of our incomprehension of "violently attained nothingness" in a manner that renders Stevens's rendering of nothingness fantastical by contrast. Although, like all of us, Gunn remains hopelessly strapped by the devices of consciousness he as a poet has to use—when, for instance, he imagines the setting devoid of consciousness while still relying on the pronoun "I" after line ten—does that limitation make his final image any less absent (short of poem and reader actually disappearing)?

If in "The Snow Man" Stevens draws us out of ourselves to "identify with reality" and "not to think of any misery," Gunn counters him by showing us what it means not to be ourselves, so we might more poignantly sense the despair or "smoky mark of dread" such an eventuality entails. Where Stevens willingly suspends a disbelief in human consciousness to give rise to the paradoxical conceit of a "mind of winter," Gunn concedes the limits of his art in order to articulate a central paradox in the age of mass death and potential annihilation, so that in Gunn's poem we discover "a universe in which matter has no purpose and can give no meaning to man. It ends by asserting a nihilistic position in which the individual must accept meaninglessness" (King 92).

Of course, by "asserting a nihilistic position," Gunn also insinuates opposition to it, in the way Adorno prescribes, and it is similarly this perspective of potential meaninglessness—not merely as abstract speculation but as the "semblance of nonsemblance"—that writers such as Lifton and Schell argue is inherent in the nuclear era. Schell notes how any mental attempt to picture extinction results in a "blankness, or emptiness": "[E]ven the words 'blankness' and 'emptiness' are too expressive—too laden with human response—because, inevitably, they connote the *experience* of blankness and emptiness, whereas extinction is the end of human experience. It thus seems to be in the nature of extinction to repel emotion and starve thought, and if the mind, brought face to face with extinction, descends into a kind of exhaustion and dejection it is surely in large part because we know that mankind cannot be a 'spectator' at its own funeral any more than an individual person can" (138–39). Reading "The Annihilation of Nothing" may leave us in the state of "exhaustion and dejection" Schell describes, because for better or worse Gunn invokes the "experience of blankness" that accompanies any thought of the experience of extinction. But the paradox here is that by imagining imminent annihilation, Gunn struggles so that we might not actually have to experience it. To the extent that any concept of the future functions integrally in present attitudes and behavior, nuclear annihilation now belongs to the present more than to the future (which, should we survive into it, will no doubt assign it to the past). It is this concept of *present* annihilation, one irrelevant to the context of "The Snow Man," that imbues "The Annihilation of Nothing" with destinerrance.

◇ Not all the poetry of destinerrance need be as abstract nor as somber as Gunn's. As with the other ways of nothingness, the voice in such poetry, in fact, can range from the comic to the compassionate, the determined to the delirious. But whatever its perspective, and whether it reflects on private experience, nature, or metaphysics, its progression follows a desultory route or "wandering that is its own end," and in its expression of uncertainty it often conveys the intensity, to use C. K. Williams's phrase, of "almost the rush to get something done before extinction" (Keller, "Interview" 174). In poems more colloquial than Gunn's (and less oblique than John Ashbery's), Alan Dugan, John Engels, and Williams—all of whom have written poems explicitly about the nuclear threat[3]—have also composed destinerrant works that speak out of nuclear uncertainty.

As apt an expression as any of the psychic tension created by the interference of potential annihilation in the present is "Winter: For an Untenable Situation," the final poem in Dugan's *Poems 2* (1963). In what at first seems an extended conceit about a married couple remaining together at any expense, the poem also offers an allegory for life in a time that seems willing to destroy itself for the sake of preserving its ideology, even when that ideology is self-consuming:

Outside it is cold. Inside,
although the fire has gone out
and all the furniture is burnt,
it is much warmer. Oh let
the white refrigerator car
of day go by in glacial thunder:
when it gets dark, and when
the branches of the tree outside
look wet because it is so dark,
oh we will burn the house itself
for warmth, the wet tree too,
you will burn me, I will burn you,
and when the last brick of the fireplace
has been cracked for its nut of warmth
and the last bone cracked for its coal
and the andirons themselves sucked cold,
we will move on!, remembering
the burning house, the burning tree,
the burning you, the burning me,

the ashes, the brick-dust, the bitter iron,
and the time when we were warm,
and say, "Those were the good old days." (*New* 130)

In relatively straightforward language satirizing bourgeois sentimen-
tality, Dugan uses the metaphor of winter's encroachment to depict the
immolation of American civilization—the burning of both house and
tree, both you and me—ostensibly out of self-interest. Yet he does more
than lament that self-destructive course, because he implicitly recognizes the vitality and industry with which Americans act according to
their values, even in the midst of collapse. The very style of the poem
embodies that vitality in its crisp language, energetic tetrameter and
trimeter rhythms, playful imagery, and enthusiastic, though self-depre-
catory, tone ("We will move on!"). In fact, characteristic of Dugan, the
final line here is one of surprising *celebration*, with its revelation that,
after all, *these* are "the good old days," regardless of their imminent
demise.

Despite the satire, though—and unlike Molly Peacock's "Don't
Think Governments End the World," for instance, which suggests a
psychoanalytic explanation for the horror of the nuclear dilemma—
Dugan's poem exposes how a sense of uncertainty about the world's future can plague even personal decisions, how when universal choices
have been undermined, individual choice is rendered meaningless. In
the first twelve lines he focuses on the threat of winter and its affects
on "our" current behavior ("oh we will burn the house itself/ for
warmth"). Then for the rest of the poem he imagines how "we" would
be likely to consider the present (that *does* exist) from the perspective
of a future that may or may not exist, after "the last brick of the fire-
place/ has been cracked for its nut of warmth." Throughout, Dugan employs mostly accessible imagery—"the white refrigerator car" of winter
contrasted by "the burning house, the burning tree,/ the burning you,
the burning me,/ the ashes, the brick-dust, the bitter iron"—and he
never explicitly addresses larger issues. But is not this poem ultimately
as much about annihilation as about the end of an affair or the depletion of winter fuel supplies? No matter how interpreted, it tangibly conveys the *idea* of extinction without having to imagine anything concrete about what extinction would actually entail; after all, the poem's
images derive from the present. As in Gunn's poem, what matters to
Dugan is not only impending annihilation but how the unknown otherness of it influences our thinking, as well as our self-destructive behavior.

For Engels, a poet who, like Paul Zimmer, witnessed a number of atomic bomb tests in the 1950s, the intrusion of images of annihilation into his poetry has a more poignantly experiential basis than for Gunn or Dugan. Stationed on Parry Island in the Eniwetok Atoll in the South Pacific in 1954, Engels served as a naval staff communications officer with Commander Task Group 7.3, the naval element of Joint Task Force 7, whose project was to explode a number of hydrogen and atomic devices in the Eniwetok-Bikini area. Assigned with other officers and crew to the USS *Curtis* (and later a jeep carrier) during the months that bombs were detonated some forty-five miles away, he was among the military personnel contaminated by radiation fallout, having "brushed white dust from our shoulders after the first Bikini shot, and watched it fall like a fine snow on the ship, for the wind had shifted unexpectedly, and brought the cloud over us and *The Lucky Dragon.*"[4] Although exposed to four times the level of radiation deemed safe for humans, so that years later he developed basal cell carcinoma on his head, face, and arms, Engels admits that at the time of the bomb tests he and his fellow crew members were not frightened of the fallout, because "we wore film badges, which were regularly checked, and no one in authority seemed to feel that we were in any special danger." Nonetheless, he adds, "the shots were, of course, spectacular and terrifying, and nuclear annihilation became a more *practical* possibility, or at least less speculative than it had been theretofore."

As with Gunn, this "practical possibility" of annihilation has contributed to the postnuclear sensibility of Engels's work, notably in poems he wrote in the 1960s and 1970s. Often, his poetry finds inspiration in nature—in sportfishing, for instance. Yet evidence of his exposure to atomic weapons has persistently found its way into his work. In particular, the last five poems of a section subtitled "Exorcisms" in his 1975 collection *Signals from the Safety Coffin,* including "The Fish Dream," "The Garden," "The Bedroom," "The Survivor" (recently revised as "The Survivors"), and "From the Source," make explicit reference to the bomb tests at Eniwetok-Bikini, especially to the clean-up operations the observers performed on themselves after having been exposed to the fallout. In "The Fish Dream," for example, Engels describes the crew being confined below the ship's deck while "topside// the flight deck blooms like Ol'/ Virginny with a thousand fountains." Afterward he lay "like a stain in my sodden bunk" while the blast and radiation

> made for dreams the umber-
> scaled and yellow-spotted fish with six-

inch needle teeth creeps out on fins like weed
stems over the red-hot deck and
gorged our heads while

we from the steaming
humus of our eyes
stare on

afraid to wake (63)

Engels's use of run-on sentences, disruptions in syntax, and distortions
in verb tense here help to convey the distorted image of the fish themselves. In "The Bedroom," these fish reappear in another dream, only
this time it has taken years for the poet to recall them. In the middle of
the night, he is abruptly awakened, rises from bed, and leaves his wife
and small son behind him, in order to write down notes

on a dream unaccountably remembered in which
I stare into the round mirror of a fish's mouth

and smear my face with black paint to the very
orbits of my eyes then roundly stare
back like a cat's in car light. (Signals 65)

He then juxtaposes this past dream against this night's dream:

I'd come to my house and the door
opens wide upon round rooms swirling
with fire burned clean scoured out

with flames the furniture
white ashes on the floors. (65)[5]

Though his current dream imagines the annihilation of his present life,
its imagery derives from his memory of the Eniwetok Atoll (the "round
rooms" like the fish's mouth, the white ashes like the fallout dust). Toward the end of the poem he returns to the bedroom, where his son and
he "stare into each other series// on series infinite and last night's fires/
feed on our bones," until dawn when, in a final allusion to the bomb's
blast, "the sun explodes." With its dominant imagery of eyes, the poem
suggests that although infinity may be internal to his gaze, externally it
is limited by the sun's incipient explosion.

Engels' stark imagery in his bomb test poems—depicting the fallout
dust, for example, as a "chalky rain" which he sticks out his tongue to
taste (66) or his own irradiated body as "frail arc of jaw and palate bone,/

outburst of iris lobes, wrenched/ diaphanous skull, faint// shades of bone" (*Signals* 67).[6]—makes them compelling apocalyptic lyrics. But it is more evident in his poems ostensibly on other subjects, particularly in "Moonwalk" and "*Terribilis est locus iste,*" that a destinerrant random-ness prevails. In the context of his bomb-test experience, it is at first tempting to think of the subject of the former poem—namely, Neil Arm-strong's first walk on the moon—as an extended conceit for the world af-ter a nuclear blast. But in fact the poem uses the imagery of both the bomb tests and Armstrong's walk to evoke the overarching idea of annihilation itself, portrayed in the poem as a shadow behind us we may never turn around to examine. For an astronaut, Engels has pointed out, "to look into a shadow on the moon, onto the shape you make when you stop light, would be to go blind."[7] "Moonwalk" depicts Armstrong's shadow as a "whole blackness" in which "he will be able to see/ nothing" and then describes the danger of his being blinded by "the coronal glare about the black/ total hole of his head shape" on the moon's surface (*Signals* 27). This figure of the moonwalker, who "routinely vigilant looks only// sun-ward or at the oblique," is identified with the poet, who has also "played/ that game myself before" and dreamt of being "careful not to look back,// the skull bursting outward and the eyes/ brief flares like supernovae/ or bombs" (28), but he also represents all of us in the nuclear age, who dare not look into the blankness we trail behind us.

So "how/ about courage then," the poet asks, "how about it,"

when the brain crumbles,
clicking as it cools,
and the teeth blackly
powder, and the tongue

drains backwards down
into the belly's open pits? (28)

The grim image of the body's decomposition here recalls the landscape at the end of "The Annihilation of Nothing." Engels equates going blind with self-decay after death. Ironically, to act with courage in this situa-tion is reversed from the norm, from staring boldly at the source of the threat to looking away from it. Yet from the poet's earthbound per-spective, not only the moonwalker but all of us cast a dangerous shadow. "It is all in shadow," he writes, so the moonwalker stares "sun-ward" instead, because "the walker/ must not look/ back, for all time the/ walker must not/ look" (*Signals* 28–29). Even the sky beyond the moonscape is described as "the memory/ of no light," and though Engels never quite expresses the "smoky mark/ Of dread" left by the "despair that nothing cannot be" in "The Annihilation of Nothing," nor does he pretend to resolve the paradox of the moonwalker's predicament. Rather, he closes the poem by acknowledging that "the black deep/ of the center" is "drawing near." As an image of impending annihilation, the moonwalker's shadow is, in fact, "man-shaped" yet "total": To turn and look at ourselves is to lose our sight forever, and the self-imposed blindness we are left with becomes our signifying emptiness.

The obliquity and abrupt, often ungrammatical shifting found in Engels's poetry also characterize C. K. Williams's work, especially his first two collections, *Lies* (1969) and *I Am the Bitter Name* (1971). The difficult, often obscure poetry in these books, expressed in a "sometimes thunderous but colloquial voice" (Keller, "Interview" 157), manifests what Williams labels the "disjunctive consciousness" by which "our minds swoop and hover and move in what are surely three directions at once" (Hirsch 155). Despite this technique, he has also written his share of political protest poems, especially in response to the war in Vietnam, the economic conservatism of the 1980s, and the nuclear threat. Oddly, while poems in his more recent collections have become increasingly accessible, more openly narrative, and less abstract, their political content has become more diffuse, less intensely focused.

When asked in the mid-eighties whether he still considers himself a political poet, Williams responded, "Yes—but not enough of one, never enough of one. If the poems don't break apart with rage as much as they used to, it might be because I'm trying to put more of everything else into them, but my rage and frustration is much greater now than it was then" (Hirsch 154). What Williams implies here about the thematic change in his poetry (a change accompanied by his technique of writing almost exlusively in long, proselike lines, instead of in the cryptic lines of his earliest work) is that the *appropriate* poetic response to extreme political concerns is not an equally extreme distortedness or rage, but an absorption of the horrors the poet sees into his own consciousness. In other words, although his midcareer poems are more comprehensive and less obscure than earlier ones, as with other poets of destinerrance, he now deliberately gambles with what he calls "the outrageous jump between the irrational and our social structures which try to act so 'sanely' in their blind madness" (Hirsch 156) so that his poetry might embody the incalculability that lies at the heart of contemporary experience. What results from his obeying, while still seeking a shape for, the leaps of his subconscious mind—at least in a poem such as "The Last Deaths"—is that he finds reconciliation not in uncovering truth, but in accepting his own limits and frailties.

The "outrageous jump" that occurs in "The Last Deaths" binds the poet's awareness of annihilation with his love for his child, in the midst of a commonplace yet disconcerting moment of crisis. The poem divides into five stanzas of eight, sixteen, eight, six, and twelve lines. Though the thematic turn it takes at the end may be unforeseen, its overall structure is in fact as organized as Gunn's "The Annihilation of Nothing" or even Coleridge's "Frost at Midnight," to compare it to another poem that addresses the poet's child: The first stanza succinctly narrates the moment of crisis, the second provides its exposition, the third identifies the problem, and the fourth and fifth express the poet's reply both to and for his daughter, in his attempt to justify the world she may inherit from him. Unlike in Engels's poems, the abrupt shifts occur not in the poem's diction and syntax but in the world it portrays.

The crisis concerns his daughter Jessie's discovery of death. While father and daughter read a book together "about a boy who makes a zoo out of junk he finds in a lot" (a seemingly arbitrary detail that establishes a context of arbitrariness), the ubiquitous television in the room with them shows an image of "the most recent bombings," involving a woman whose entire family has been murdered and who in desperation throws herself against the legs of the soldiers responsible. Suddenly, "Jessie looked up and said, 'What's the matter with her? Why's she crying?' " (*Poems* 142). Before citing his response, in the second stanza the poet reveals that, presumably due to a divorce, he has not lived with his daughter for a year and therefore does not know "what I can say to her,/ what I can solve for her without introducing more confusions than there were in the first place" (142). He recalls how when some time earlier she had first quizzed him about death he had avoided explaining it fully, comparing it to sleep, so when several days later she asks him again about the woman on the news—now transformed in Jessie's dreams into "that girl" (143) whose house had been knocked down—he again sidesteps the brutal truth about war.

In the third stanza, though, he confronts this conflict by jumping "between the irrational and our social structures":

These times. The endless wars. The hatreds. The vengefulness.
Everyone I know getting out of their marriage. Old friends
   distrustful.

> The politicians using us until you can't think about it anymore
>   because you can't tell anymore
> which reality affects which and how do you escape from it
>   without everything battering you back again?
> How many times will I lie to Jessie about things that have no
>   meaning for either of us? (143)

Instead of diffusing his focus, the wide-ranging associations here organize the poet's thinking process, even as they leave him in despair about
his ability to protect his daughter from "the same ridiculous illusions"
he has. "There'll be peace soon," he says at the end of the stanza,
"They'll fling it down like sick meat we're supposed to lick up and be
thankful for and what then?" A momentary calm, he realizes, does not
mean the deeper uncertainties of imminent violence have been allevi-
ated. Despite his pained ignorance and impotence, however, the fourth
stanza addresses itself directly to Jessie, even as it seems to flounder in
what Williams reluctantly acknowledges is an "absence" or "dread"
that will inevitably "flame" between daughter and father "like an enormous, palpable word that wasn't spoken." Led by his own thoughts into
questioning the fundamental nature of being, he asks her, "Do we only
love because we're weak and murderous?/ Are we commended to each
other to alleviate our terror of solitude and annihilation and that's all?"
(144). Without warning, at the very moment the poet wants most to offer consolation, to Jessie if not to himself, he instead finds himself with
nothing, bereft even of love itself.

But the poem is not finished. Continuing his mental leaps, he offers
to exchange his own previous night's dream of annihilation (a "calm and
abstract" one) with Jessie's in which she was "trading deaths" with the
woman on television:

> I was dreaming about the universe. The whole universe was
>   happening in one day, like a blossom,
> and during that day people's voices kept going out to it, crying,
>   "Stop! Stop!"
> The universe didn't mind, though. It knew we were only cursing
>   love again
> because we didn't know how to love, not even for a day,
> but our little love days were just seeds it blew out on parachutes
>   into the summer wind. (144)

In the same way William Carlos Williams discovers the power of annihilation in the beauty of an asphodel, C. K. Williams finds it revealed in

his dream of an apocalyptic blossom spreading its seeds. The cry of voices for the blossom to stop is not just a cry against loss, nor a cry for life, but a cry for understanding what it is we are about to lose, what exactly it is we want so much to preserve. In other words, not to understand what annihilation means is not to understand being either, and it is our being to which we must attend, if we hope to avert its extinction.

The poem takes one more turn, back toward love, as Williams concludes his account of his dream:

Then you and I were there. We shouted "Stop!" too. We kept
   wanting the universe to explode,
we kept wishing it would go back into its root, but the universe
   understood.
We were its children. It let us cry into its petals, it let its stems
   bend against us,
then it fed and covered us and we looked up sleepily—it was time
   to sleep—
and whatever our lives were, our love, this once, was enough.
   (144)

Seeing himself as both parent and child, the poet adopts a tone of reassurance while admitting to his vulnerability. Though his desire for certainty, for clarity, may reduce him to wanting the universe either "to explode" or "go back into its root" in a return to prelapsarian nothingness, short of those alternatives he is left to himself (a godless self) to continue in his sleeping state of ignorance and devise his own myths. Despite this ignorance, though, the dream and the poem conclude on a note of calm: "Whatever our lives were, our love, this once, was enough." As a poem of destinerrance, "The Last Deaths" hovers incalculably between despair and consolation, annihilation and the present, yet by questioning love, though it may limit love's power to direct the will or shape the world, it newly reasserts love's presence (if only temporarily) in human relations. Without the prospect of love, of course, annihilation would be of no consequence.[8]

Regardless of the varying styles of these poems of destinerrance, what they accomplish by interacting with randomness is to create room in the language for the continuing presence as well as for the potential absence of everything we know. This fourth way of nothingness comes closest to acquiescing to the end of the world. For this reason, it is also the furthest removed from directions for political action, as these poems express little open resistance to the seemingly inevitable. However, by engaging the "randomness and incalculability" imposed on us by the untenable facts of nuclearism, they also remain open to the arbitrary possibility of *other* experiences as well. While there is no assurance that other experiences will exempt us from rupture or annihilation, these poems' destinerrant gestures can refresh our sense of love or grief, fear or delight, and construct a context in which those ancient emotions might be felt, unrepressed by our awareness of their impending disappearance.

En Route to Annihilation: John Ashbery's Shadow Train

More than with any poet I discuss, randomness and uncertainty characterize John Ashbery's poetics. The combined intensity and imperturbability of his work replicate the intensity and imperturbability of living in the nuclear age. In the sea of critics debating Ashbery—whose poems have been accused of having no subject other than themselves— one of his staunchest proclaimers, Helen Vendler, places him prominently within the "Western lyric tradition." "He comes from Wordsworth, Keats, Tennyson, Stevens, Eliot," she has argued, "His poems are about love, or time, or age" (120). But Robert Richman disagrees: "Ashbery's poetry of non-production—involving endless linguistic copulation with no creation—threatens to destroy the enterprise of art altogether. Like the surrealists, who frightened even Sartre for this reason, Ashbery's radicalism is purely negative. Self-referentiality breaks down the vital link between the object and the world; the idea that the mind is a conduit breaks down the attachment between object and thought" (68).[9] Between these extremes of praise and attack can be found more measured comments—that Ashbery's is "a poetry of brilliant surfaces, where the verbal gestures . . . are often poses for stylistic fun rather than purposive parts of some coherent whole" (Young 4), that "ideas in Ashbery are like the melodies in some jazz improvisation where the musicians have left out the original tune to avoid paying royalties," resulting in "wild variations on a missing theme with only the original chord changes as a clue" (Gioia, "Poetry" 588), and, in a more laudatory vein, that the obscure in Ashbery is part of his "procedure," of finding "a 'disparate account' rather than a unified and referential one, even at the risk of discovering an essential incoherence" (Jackson, "Elegies" 858).

Despite these diverse opinions about the subject of Ashbery's work, several critics have provided useful foundations for arriving at his "ideas." In arguing that Ashbery "is much concerned with a true solicitude for the bitter impressions of meaninglessness" (29), for instance,

David Shapiro defends Ashbery's relevance by cataloguing the ways his poetry systematically undermines each type of meaning, as meaning itself is outlined by I. A. Richards and C. K. Ogden in *The Meaning of Meaning*, and he praises Ashbery's "confidence in a new threshold for incoherence and randomness, leading to affirmations of freedom" (30–32). It is precisely his "tolerance for negativity," concludes Shapiro, that earns Ashbery his authority. But why should a "tolerance for negativity" and a talent to be charmingly impenetrable have any appeal? Given his modernist predecessors in experimental verse, ranging from Stevens to Stein, Laura Riding to W. H. Auden (all important influences on Ashbery), why this late in the century should his brand of randomness gain such regard? Is it that his "structured dysfunctioning of bourgeois discourse" (Cohen 147) is "an integral part of a very serious attack, through language, on basic assumptions, institutions, and modes of thought in contemporary America" (Cohen 128)? Or in opposite fashion, might it be that "the difficulty with Ashbery is that his poetry is *so* public, so accurately a picture of the world we live in, that it scarcely resembles anything we have ever known" (Crase 30)? Are his poems determinedly polemical, or do they herald a world of understanding yet to come?

Whether anticipating annihilation or prophesying renewal, Ashbery's poems are propelled by a courting of absence. As a poetry of destinerrance, his work risks wandering from, circumventing, and deconstructing not only the subjects it addresses, not only the world it inhabits and observes, but itself. While not particularly *about* anything[10]—and therefore not clearly about creation or annihilation either—as a poetry of "the experience of experience" (Poulin 245), it nevertheless participates in Derrida's "aleatory destinerrance of the *envoi*," both as a record of the poet's internal receiving of himself and as an expression of or "sending" of being. It is concerned less with the *what* than with the *how* and *why*. As Charles Altieri argues the case, the impulse or "motive" behind Ashbery's verse "is not to represent confusion but to dramatize qualities of mind, shifts of emotional levels, and possible structures of coherence among dispersed particulars and interpretive codes" (138). Subsequently, the appearance of nihilism, the absence of didacticism, and the "promise of nonsemblance" (to use Adorno's term), while undermining even the remote chance of offering political solutions to nuclear dilemmas, do provide in his work a creative encounter with potential annihilation. While his speculations on such an encounter may provide no clear direction or hope for his readers or himself, they do open possible ways to proceed from nothingness toward the construction of alternative modes of thinking about survival. As Peter Schwenger reasons in applying Lacanian ideas about language and the unconscious to alternative literatures in the nuclear age, "the 'truth' of the unconscious is not a stable one, nor is the unconscious 'as such' even attainable"; therefore, in its latent manifestations, language "mirrors the subject, a subject in continual motion," serving not as " 'representation,' but a more vague and ongoing 'indicating' . . . [of] the subject's *search* for the true in the unconscious" (149). In language's embodiment and expression of this motion, concludes Schwenger, "the very sliding of signs, the radical instability of language, can be a principle of hope" (149). While an important operating word here is "can" (as opposed to "must"), it is this same "radical instability" in Ashbery's poetry that displays his way of nothingness.

Although much of it is unintelligible, an awareness of annihilation is evident in Ashbery's earliest work, poems interested in experimentation and dadaist play more than in ordinary meaning. "A Last World" in *The Tennis Court Oath* (1962), for example, regardless of its abrupt shifts and comic tone, is reminiscent of Byron's "Darkness," for in both the speaker recounts some unearthly legend about an apocalyptic landscape. Ashbery's speaker begins by recalling that "wonderful things/ Were planted on the surface of a round mind that was to become our present time," but to "somebody" who "was wise," he adds, "the whole of things might be different/ From what it was thought to be in the beginning, before an angel bandaged the field glasses" (*Selected* 42). To imagine this difference in the past, "one could say nothing hear nothing/ Of what the great time spoke to its divisors," but "now all is different without having changed/ As though one were to pass through the same street at different times." Somehow, this poem says, we find ourselves in a different state without knowing how we arrived here, yet despite the "wonderful things" that have survived, "Still it is not too late for these things to die" (42).

Asserting this awareness of possible immolation, the poem's first strophe ends with a sigh: "And the truth is cold, as a giant's knee/ Will seem cold." The six strophes that follow tell a Raymond Roussel–like tale of one who "wished to go far away from himself" (42), as the poem imagines a landscape heretofore unimagined—including in it a woman who "is completely out of this world" (43), a "happy old man" whom the poet addresses directly, a flower, another woman "who thought herself good only for bearing children" and who is "decked out in the lace of fire" (44), naked men who "pray the ground and chew it with their hands," other scant figures, and a pervasive fire whose "silver blaze calms the darkness," all leading to this apocalyptic scene:

> We thought the sky would melt to see us
> But to tell the truth the air turned to smoke,
> We were forced back onto a foul pillow that was another place.
> Or were lost by our comrades
> Somewhere between heaven and no place, and were growing
>   smaller.
> In another place a mysterious mist shot up like a wall, down
>   which trickled the tears of our loved ones.
> Bananas rotten with their ripeness hung from the leaves, and
>   cakes and jewels covered the sand. (45)

This litany of unrelated images builds (or falters?) toward a kind of inverse climax in the last eight lines, where "a last world moves on the figures" (whatever that means) and finally "everything is being blown away" by the poet himself, including language. Then, suddenly, "a little horse trots up with a letter in its mouth, which is read with eagerness/ As we gallop into the flame" (45). What "A Last World" closes with is less an image of the end of the world than an enactment of an end to meaning, as the letter, its contents, and its language are consumed, along with the speaker.[11] Although the poem is drenched in the imagery of apocalypse, its real subject ultimately emerges as the role of language in constructing memory, where the only "methods" of survival involve recalling the "moments of the others/ Seen through indifference" (45).

Though almost uninterpretable, "A Last World" starts to address the subject of annihilation. Usually with Ashbery, though, annihilation hovers around the borders of his poems, instead of being their subject, creating what Herman Rapaport identifies as Ashbery's "apocalyptic tone" (394). It is crucial to remember, though, that this pervasive sense of annihilation does not undermine the poet's voice. Rather, like for those "moments of the others/ Seen through indifference," it stirs, on the one hand, a qualified sense of caution, while it produces, on the other, a "sigh" or shrug from the poet. Ashbery "does not recoil at the foreseeable majesty of a holocaust: for with the recognition of a difficult freedom an indifferent tone emerges, one that is unfrightened," as well as "neutralized, sopped up, forgotten, muffled, understated" (396).[12] In contrast to the assertive tone of Stevens, as Lynn Keller demonstrates,

Ashbery's understated expression of acceptance reflects a major rhetorical shift in American verse after modernism. This deference to uncertainty in his "flagrantly unsystematic poetry" suggests not a dismissal of the reader nor a fundamental despair, as Ashbery's critics sometimes conclude, but *akirame,* an acceptance of the limits of what remains accessible: "Since life's moments of meaning or happiness occur randomly, one cannot anticipate them; one can only strive to be there in the present to receive them if they should appear" (*Re-making* 77).[13]

In *Houseboat Days* (1977), Ashbery's incorporation of uncertainty, of the ubiquity of annihilatory thinking, finds particular lyric poignance. Even the volume's title conveys a sense of everyday life in a floating or unstable environment. One poem, the "Ice-Cream Wars," a poem like so many of Ashbery's from this period that are ostensibly about the difficulty of making art, or about poetry itself, begins with this qualification: "Although I mean it, and project the meaning/ As hard as I can into its brushed-metal surface,/ It cannot, in this deteriorating climate, pick up/ Where I leave off" (*Houseboat* 60). Not only does the poem raise a philosophic question about the gap between intention and meaning, but it attributes something of this gap to the interference of "this deteriorating climate," clearly a cultural more than a meteorological disruption. The poem proceeds to cite several examples of how art misapprehends the present, until its speaker finally gives way to the "few black smudges/ On the outer boulevards, like squashed midges" that continue breaking up the integrity of the mind's focus, at which point

> the truth becomes a hole, something one has always known,
> A heaviness in the trees, and no one can say
> Where it comes from, or how long it will stay—
>
> A randomness, a darkness of one's own. (60–61)

The *distraction* of blankness, the fragmentation imposed by the uncertainty of what the poet means to say in the first place, becomes his project here, as though it were the "heaviness in the trees" found in a more traditional nature poem, since ultimately he can claim ownership not of enlightenment but only of darkness.

Even more preoccupied with its own wandering than "The Ice-Cream Wars," "Blue Sonata" specifically sets out to explore time and how we understand the present from other temporal viewpoints. Composed in formal imitation of the sonata, it begins by looking at the present from the perspective of the past, in order that we might recall how we used to look at the future with its contingent uncertainties and with the understanding that "*that* now" (the present that was once the future) "is our destiny/ No matter what else may happen to us" (*Houseboat* 66). In short, we are both the subjects of time's fancy and an integral part of the present, that "part of the day [which] comes every day." And as long as "we not give up that inch," that "breath/ Of becoming before becoming may be seen," we can believe ourselves to be both present and in the flux of time. But in the second strophe, the poet explains how, in coming to know something we did not know in the past, something new about ourselves, there inevitably comes with it "a grain of curiosity/ . . . that unrolls/ Its question mark like a new wave on the shore," and "we have . . . gained or been gained/ By what was passing through" (66–67); that is, in the same moment that we look backward to gain new insight into the present, we create for ourselves the uncertainty of our future, and as a consequence, "We live in the sigh of our present."

For Ashbery, if all we needed to understand the future was to study the past, "we could re-imagine the other half, deducing it/ From the shape of what is seen, thus/ Being inserted into its idea of how we/ Ought to proceed" (67). But such a complete parallel would be "tragic," he says, "For progress occurs through re-inventing/ These words from a dim recollection of them." To extrapolate here, in thinking about nuclear annihilation, together with the applicability of this poem to a concept of time, we must remember that the *true* uncertainty of the future implies that, despite the seeming inevitability of holocaust, it may after all *not* occur, and it would be "tragic" for us to *assume* that it will, "to fit/ Into the space created by our not having arrived yet." It is at least partially up to us to decide how to "re-invent" words for "violating" the "space" of the future "in such a way as/ To leave it intact." In other words, given this critical role of ours in "the sigh of our present,"

> we do after all
> Belong here, and have moved a considerable
> Distance; our passing is a facade.
> But our understanding of it is justified. (67)

As a poem of the nuclear age, read not for its political, social, or historical comment but its metaphysical vision, "Blue Sonata" articulates precisely that combination of *akirame* and self-consciousness Lifton discovered among the *hibakusha*, but it also displays the predominant uncertainty of "our present" about which we must readjust our thinking if we hope to avoid catastrophe. As a statement without pretensions beyond what its own paradoxical circumstance allows, Ashbery's elusive technique is not only appropriate, but essential to the difficulty of his subject. As Douglas Crase observes, "The present is indeed a world none of us has ever known, because the words to describe it can be put together only after the fact. When the poet [like Ashbery] does put them together the combination comes as a shock" (30).

◇ In the case of *Shadow Train* (1981), Ashbery's elusiveness takes on a further complicating dimension, in that the collection stands either as a sequence of fifty discrete poems (each self-contained, if any Ashbery poem is, in four four-line stanzas), or as a single long poem. Mimicking minimalist artists such as Donald Judd, the book's structure, as Ashbery himself describes it, employs an "antiform" that "lacks the 'meaning-fulness' of the sonnet" and imposes "an asymmetry, a coldness, an al-teration" on its subject matter by its "almost brutal arbitrariness" (Jackson, *Acts* 75–76). Also, as a paradigm of the whole of Ashbery's work, the book's resonance often comes from its allusions to earlier (or even later) poems, in that words, phrases, and images tend to generate meaning, as motifs, internal to his vision. Given this intertextuality, to select one poem to represent the concerns of the whole sequence is undoubtedly to misread its form.

Nevertheless, rather than range indiscriminately through *Shadow Train* and pick stanzas or phrases that gesture at annihilation, I prefer to focus on its conception of nothingness in a single poem, "The Absence of a Noble Presence," as an indication of how to read the rest. Explicating the poem, however, requires constantly turning to other relevant passages that illuminate Ashbery's multiple perspectives on the "ideas" evoked in the poem. In process, an idea in one line of any Ashbery poem has a tendency to fade as quickly as the mind becomes absorbed in the next. Yet it is precisely this experience of the fading and recalling, the grasping and letting go, that simulates the thinking of the nuclear age. "So many/ Patterns to choose from," Ashbery sighs in "Farm Film" (*Shadow* 17), and earlier he echoes, "It is still too many ideas for a landscape" in "The Prophet Bird" (12), as his fragments of meaning orbit around each other like subatomic particles in a nucleus. Still, like a physicist devising theories based on the false but working assumption that those particles can be isolated and named, a reader is free to unravel one idea of Ashbery's vision by artificially isolating it from others.

As the eleventh poem in *Shadow Train*, "The Absence of a Noble Presence" follows "At the Inn," a poem roughly concerned with the death of an individual, and precedes "The Prophet Bird," one of the sequence's more optimistic pieces. In its title we encounter Ashbery's notion of absence, associated throughout his work not just with nothingness, as we have seen, but with loss—"love's lost paradise, *deus absconditas*, the absence of law, the loss of childhood, loss of memory" (Shapiro 105). For the mind, of course, absence has no conceptual meaning other than of some lost presence (in this case, a "noble" one), which can be either remembered or imagined. Herein lies one working dichotomy for Ashbery, who has remarked that for him the sense of absence is "no more important in my poetry than the sense of presence" (Poulin 253). Yet given the balance as expressed in "Blue Sonata," the reverse notion must also hold true—that *presence* of whatever kind cannot be assumed, is no more of a given, than absence. Both are equally vulnerable. Nonetheless, though weighted against each other in a manner that helps to define each, both absence and presence also pose a significant difference in our perception of the other: Whereas "presence" is perpetually subject to uncertainty, change, or loss, "absence," as a kind of death or nothingess, suggests a certainty *not* subject to change. A few pages later in *Shadow Train*, in "Of the Islands," Ashbery writes, "Only to be an absentee frees from the want of speculation" (16). That is to say, to be present is to be changing yet to be uncertain of what that change will entail, but the loss of a "noble presence" frees the mind to define nothingness beyond any further transformation.[14]

Given this twofold understanding of the title—where we must think of "absence" and "presence" both as interdependent, dichotomous terms and as fundamentally not so—the poem opens with another uncertainty:

If it was treason it was so well handled that it
Became unimaginable. No, it was ambrosia
In the alley under the stars and not this undiagnosable
Turning, a shadow in the plant of all things

That makes us aware of certain moments,
That the end is not far off since it will occur
In the present and this is the present. (*Shadow* 11)

As Stephen Yenser has noted, Ashbery is a master of the fluid or "protean" pronoun; words such as *it, you, this, that, they,* and *we* often shift from one implied antecedent to another ("Recent" 118), so we learn to distrust any apparent associations we want to make with them. In this case, the shifting pronoun is "it" in line one: Does "it" refer to "ab-sence" or "presence"? Or neither? Might it refer to both? Furthermore, isn't the opening conditional clause (*"If* it was treason") insinuating that the loss of the noble presence (of some love, law, or god) might *not* have been an act of treason? Such an alternative reading of absence may be possible, the poet seems to imply, but he opts for this one. Still, if that loss came by false or treacherous means, "it was so well handled" that it somehow transcended, or at least avoided, any notice on the part of the loser. True absence, in other words, is not suffered, once it has ex-tricated itself from presence, because the speculation by which we ex-perience loss is possible only for one who is present, the survivor of loss. That which is lost is itself beyond imagination.

"No," continues the poem, "it was ambrosia/ In the alley under the stars." The word "no" certainly suggests that it (the absence, most likely, not the presence) was *not* in fact treason after all but "ambrosia," the stuff of dreams and immortality. Here the idea of loss is balanced against a feeling of immortality "in the alley under the stars." In other *Shadow Train* poems, city streets and alleys are usually associated with play or pleasure, as in the last line of "The Ivory Tower": "And you find the right order after all: play, the streets, shopping, time flying" (5). Stars are associated with light—in opposition to the pervasive shadow im-agery. Whatever the poet is recalling by saying, "it *was* ambrosia," his being "in the alley under the stars" has provided him with a sense of transcendence, and as he adds in "Oh, Nothing" several pages later, "To be amused this way/ Is to be immortal, as water rushes down the sides of the globe" (15).

Not to rest on this moment, though, after saying that "it was am-brosia," Ashbery shifts back again to say what "it" was *not*—"not this undiagnosable/ Turning," not this speculative yet finally indiscernible process of experiencing absence by experiencing loss. Absence is not the process (to cite Yenser) of "transforming, changing, versing" ("Recent" 118), nor is it "a shadow in the plant of all things// That makes us aware of certain moments." It may be that true absence, when it occurs, is "unimaginable." But the *threat* of change, of annihilation, is entirely imaginable, albeit frightening, and that threat forces itself into con-sciousness, like those "few black smudges" in "The Ice-Cream Wars," making us painfully aware of those other moments when we do not feel the "turning" or the shadow—that is, when we are free from a crippling self-consciousness of ordinary death.

Broadly speaking, the shadow imagery woven through *Shadow Train* usually looms as the threat of a darkness overpowering light. For example, in the opening poem, "The Pursuit of Happiness," a poem ostensibly about lost dreams in America, the shadow first appears as "one/ Who all unseen came creeping at this scale of visions/ Like the gigantic specter of a cat towering over tiny mice" (1). It is a huge and menacing threat,

> An incisive shadow, too perfect in its outrageous
> Regularity to be called to stand trial again,
> That every blistered tongue welcomed as the first
> Drops scattered by the west wind. (1)

In this poem, the overwhelming power of the shadow cannot be questioned; indeed, it is "welcomed" by "every blistered tongue" because of its certainty, even though, as the poem continues in the fourth stanza, "knowing// That it would always ever afterwards be this way/ Caused the eyes to faint, the ears to ignore warnings" (1). Feared as much as welcomed, the shadow's inevitable presence, once the poet acknowledges it, necessarily dulls the senses and numbs the self—which cannot vitally accept this omnipresent threat of absence.[15]

Is the striking parallel between Ashbery's image of the shadow and the specter of nuclear annihilation merely coincidental? What exactly is the shadow train itself? The first question, though a legitimate one, allows only a speculative response, since Ashbery resists identifying the subject matter of any of his poetry.[16] Surely, though, he is not only imagining the shadow as ordinary death but as the absence of an awareness of death, a blindness like that in Engels's "Moonwalk," an extinction. To address the second question requires looking at the book's title poem, "Shadow Train," where "the 'Violence' of 'history' " and " 'one's private guignol,' " are joined together "in some huge, shady, shape-shifting undertaking" (Yenser, "Recent" 118). The threat of the shadow train—which admittedly offers the certainty of eventual absence—is both a personal and a public, both a private and a universal, menace. "Shadow Train" poem begins:

> Violence, how smoothly it came
> And smoothly took you with it
> To wanting what you nonetheless did not want.
> It's all over if we don't see the truth inside that meaning. (48)

If we consider the "train" not just as a locomotive but also (like a wedding train) as something that trails behind us, following us through the

entire sequence, then the certainty of the shadow (with its inevitable presence), the certainty of the violence, and the intrusion of the
shadow's threat on our quotidian lives mean that the train *takes us* as
much as we *take it*. Given this power, it transforms us into wanting it,
even though we do *not* want its actual arrival. We are attracted to the
certainty of the shadow train, but not to the vehicle itself. How tempting it is to transliterate these lines into a statement about nuclearism:
Its threat trails us everywhere, the knowledge of how to manufacture
weapons of extinction is ours for good (in that we cannot unlearn that
knowledge, though we might wish to), and our awareness of it has ush-
ered in an era in which we embrace nuclear power as "a new 'fundamental,' as a source of 'salvation' and a way of restoring our lost sense
of immortality" (Lifton and Falk 87). However, despite our tendency to
deify the shadow, the power behind it, a power that can bring about
"unimaginable" absence, remains a real, not an imagined, potential.
"It's all over if we don't see the truth inside that meaning," writes Ashbery; we must admit to our "want" without giving ourselves over to it:

> To want is to be better than before. To desire what is
> Forbidden is permitted. But to desire it
> And not want it is to chew its name like a rag. (48)

Because of the cleaving effect of the line break here, "to desire what is"
is equated to desiring what is forbidden. Both desires are "permitted," so
long as we do not attempt to deny our wanting "it" (the shadow train's
certainty). If we do not admit to our human longing after irritable fact and
reason, "it's all over," and we will "chew" and sully the name of the
shadow "like a rag." But the shadow train will never absent itself, and as
Ashbery notes in "The Desperado," "I am the shadowed" (41).

With this intertextual definition of the shadow train, we can return
to "The Absence of a Noble Presence" with a better sense of the
shadow's symbolic potential. Absence itself, we remember, "was ambrosia," not the "turning," not the pervasive "shadow" of that absence
"that makes us aware of certain moments" in the present, those moments in which we realize "That the end is not far off since it will oc-
cur/ In the present and this is the present." In other words, those moments when we are conscious of absence, though they themselves may
not be the experience of absence but only its shadowing, nonetheless
have the power to distract and divorce us from the present, much like
the "grain of curiosity" in "Blue Sonata" that "unrolls/ Its question
mark like a new wave on the shore."

But here we need to pause again in reading the poem, in order to re-view Ashbery's treatment of time and futurelessness. Through the idio-syncratic use of verb tenses that fluidly, almost unnoticeably shift, as well as through a series of direct statements, he conceives of a past that flows into the present almost identically to the future flowing into the present. Yet conspicuously missing are any assertions about an an-ticipated, or even a desired, future. Allusions to the future in *Shadow Train* frequently collapse into comments on the present, as in "Joe Leviathan": "I have seen and know/ Bad endings lumped with the good. They are in the future/ And therefore cannot be far off" (19). Or in "Hard Times":

In the future it will filter down through all the proceedings

But by then it will be too late, the festive ambience
Will linger on but it won't matter. More or less
Succinctly they will tell you what we've all known for years:
That the power of this climate is only to conserve itself. (37)

Or in "The Desperado": "Is there a future? It seems that all we'd planned/To find in it is rolling around now, spending itself" (41).

The past, too, is always collapsing into the present, so there is no refuge there either, as in "The Leasing of September," when Ashbery writes, "To him/ The love was a solid object, like a partly unpacked trunk,/ As it was then, which is different now when remembered" (32). Even dreams of the future have no value except as their own processes: "My personality fades away// As dreams evaporate by day, which stays, with the dream/ Materials in solution, cast out in a fiery precipitate" (*"Moi, je suis la tulipe . . . ,"* *Shadow* 38). In "Shadow Train," he writes that only "the violence dreams," whereas "history" "merely stretches today into one's private guignol" (48); the past has meaning only when played out in the present on one's own private stage of dreams, as a kind of puppet show from memory.[17]

Throughout the sequence, the only time is "the time it takes for noth-ing to happen" ("The Prophet Bird," *Shadow* 12), namely, "the present and this is the present." In the present, we are "rooted in twilight, dreaming, a piece of traffic" ("We Hesitate," *Shadow* 40), in a time con-stantly threatened by annihilation yet a time during which we can be "surprised, somewhat, but sure" (*"Moi, je suis la tulipe . . . ,"* *Shadow* 38). It is also a time about which we can tell stories. Remember, though, that in "The Absence of a Noble Presence" all these definitions of "it" *seem* to be of what "it" is, when they are not: "it was ambrosia." These other conceptions of absence, as close as they may come to "it" as part of some process, are not "it." "It" remains "unimaginable" and finally unnamable:

No it was something not very subtle then and yet again

You've got to remember we don't see that much.
We see a portion of eaves dripping in the pastel book
And are aware that everything doesn't count equally —
There is dreaminess and infection in the sum. (11)

Again, in the first line here, in trying to say what "it" is (rather than what "it" is not), Ashbery slips back into the past tense, while at the same time he reminds us that his subject is not elusive; it is simply beyond speculation, beyond anything we see. All we see is "a portion of eaves dripping in the pastel book." This metaphor and the line that follows can be understood in two ways: (1) "We" (that is, "you" in line nine and "I," or a more generalized "we," meaning "one") operate in two parallel fashions, as readers of the pastel book *and* as thinkers on the nature of equality; (2) *Because* we see only "a portion of eaves," we may become "aware that everything doesn't count equally." Both these readings, however, strike a delicate balance between what we can perceive, which is limited, and how we understand what we perceive.

In other words, for Ashbery, absence and presence do indeed balance each other, but because one is unimaginable and the other filled with uncertainty, "we" have come to see them as irreconcilable. Although the present and a future that will bring an end to the present are clearly distinct from each other, we cannot experience that distinction without losing our grasp on the present; we can only speculate on its meaning, while we experience it both as a shadow (which threatens annihilation) and as a light (which offers possibility). In the midst of this double vision we remain "rooted in twilight."

Combining this partial perception of absence and our Protean, unsettling awareness of presence, the poem next unfolds into yet another dichotomy, after the dash: "There is dreaminess and infection in the sum." What on the one hand provides us with the "source of our energy" (Perloff 67) is on the other hand inseparable from what is infectious.[18] Though still four lines from the end of the poem, this statement seems conclusive, wisely summarizing the interdependence, yet opposition, between certain absence and uncertain presence—until we complete the final stanza:

And since this too is of our everydays
It matters only to the one you are next to
This time, giving you a ride to the station.
It foretells itself, not the hiccup you both notice.

"This" in line thirteen may refer to the "sum" of "dreaminess and infection," though it may also refer to everything the poem has expressed
to this point. But what Ashbery insinuates is that the absence he is describing and the presence he believes we experience are both part of "our
everydays." To be sure, the offhand manner of his colloquialisms reinforces his oscillation between the intellectual and the mundane, the
ethereal and the profane. In fact, his insouciant tone suggests that the
presence of all these ideas under the threat to their existence is not a
condition that merits special attention: It is merely how things are, so
that "it matters only to the one you are next to/ This time." If we take
"it" as still referring to "absence" here, the poem bifurcates into "absence" as loss (the one "you" will depart from when "you" arrive at the
station) and "absence" as death (in that death, even extinction, can only
be experienced locally, not globally). The "station" may likewise be understood as, literally, the train station from which "you" will depart, or
as, figuratively, the fixed place toward which the shadow train is head-
ing, that place where the anticipated annihilation will become manifest, that place where no one in an Ashbery poem ever quite arrives,
"though many are traveling" toward it (Lehman, "Shield" 119).[19] Because of the persistent ambiguity here, the personal and the universal
remain inextricably intertwined.

The last line of "The Absence of a Noble Presence" provides one more
twist. Still in the present tense, the poem ends (beyond its conclusion,
we might say): "It foretells itself, not the hiccup you both notice." What
foretells itself? Absence? Annihilation? The "sum" of half-knowledge
and uncertainty? As with the first two stanzas, this last line concerns
what is *not* foretold, namely, the hiccup during the ride to the station.
As nothing but a guttural noise, the hiccup suddenly upsets the language and tone of the whole poem, and typically Ashberian, it comically
undercuts the lofty ideas preceding it.[20] What jump to mind are the last
two lines of Eliot's "The Hollow Men," "*This is the way the world
ends/ Not with a bang but a whimper*" (82), which Ashbery is parody-
ing. This hiccup at the end dissolves the poem's earlier divisions of
meaning and returns us to "our everydays." Yet in fact it ends *not* with
"the hiccup you both notice" but the shadow: Whatever the "unimag-

inable," ambrosial, "not very subtle" nature of nothingness may be, "it foretells itself." It cannot be foretold by any other means and has no paradigm.

To place "The Absence of a Noble Presence" within the rest of the sequence, finally, it is important to acknowledge its energy of renewal, of surprise, of play, and of telling stories, an energy that perpetually springs from these poems that perpetually deconstruct themselves. As Lifton reminds us, "Ultimately, genuine transformation requires that we 'experience' our annihilation in order to prevent it, that we confront and conceptualize both our immediate crises and our long-range possibilities for renewal" (*Life* 149). What binds the pages of *Shadow Train* is its ritualizing of annihilation as part of a potential process of rebirth. In an interview, Ashbery says, "I have a feeling that everything is slipping away from me as I'm trying to talk about it—a feeling I have most of the time, in fact." But this consciousness of loss, whether by death or annihilation, abides in his poetry "not because of any intrinsic importance the feeling might have, but because I feel that somebody should call attention to this. Maybe once it's called attention to we can think about something else, which is what I'd like to do" (Poulin 245). Drawing attention to absence in the guise of the shadow train creates the "long-range possibilities for renewal" Lifton prescribes, even if it does not provide assurances about their character.

In its encounter with nothingness, *Shadow Train* discovers neither truth nor wisdom, particularly, but beginnings, new stories, and even legends that "always come around to seeming legendary" ("The Vegetarians," *Shadow* 50). By imagining the experience of annihilation (or at least the experience of the experience of annihilation), Ashbery does not offer a cure for it, nor does he suggest that a cure is necessary. He forgoes even a gesture of protest against the practices and ideology that have fostered the growth of nuclearism. Left to itself his poetry is not likely to inspire political action as Levertov's does, challenge our conception of nature's infinitude as Wilbur's does, or expand our perspective on nuclear culture as Merrill's does. Rather, as a way of nothingness, *Shadow Train* takes us as far as American poetry has traveled in its speculations on the traces of the "unthinkable" as both a material potential and a psychic disruption. The odd comfort it provides comes in its articulation of a daily sense of uncertainty, its visceral expression of nothingness, its imagining the real. In the late twentieth century, "There is no freedom, and no freedom from freedom./ The only possible act is to pick up the book, caress it/ And open it in my face. You knew that" ("Everyman's Library," *Shadow* 47). Or to cite "Frontispiece," which with characteristic Ashberian irony appears "toward the end" of *Shadow Train*,

Sometimes toward the end
A look of longing broke, taut, from those eyes
Meeting yours in final understanding, late,

And often, too, the beginnings went unnoticed
As though the story could advance its pawns
More discreetly thus, overstepping
The confines of ordinary health and reason

To introduce in another way
Its fact into the picture. It registered,
It must be there. And so we turn the page over
To think of starting. This is all there is. (46)

Speaking out of the uncertain middle of nothingness, Ashbery's poems are liable to fade as quickly as they flare in the mind. But is not fading in and out in the nature of our ordinary thinking about annihilation? As a species and as individuals, we fail again and again to hold fast to ideas of ourselves long enough to assure our survival beyond a shadow of a doubt. Yet paradoxically, in those same moments, where occasionally unnoticed alternatives may be glimpsed, it may also occur to us "to think of starting" and to move on to the next page.

A LAST WORD

On annihilation, there can be no final word. Because the issue of survival in a time of human-made mass death touches every aspect of being—from the material to the symbolic, the political to the metaphysical, the inanimate to the sacred, and the quotidian to the sublime—it necessarily engages each of us. No one is safely beyond the reach of its influence and potential, whether we choose to respond actively to it or not. For this reason, I have taken the liberty throughout this book of using the pronoun "we"—not because I presume a homogeneous community of readers, but because of the ubiquitous nature of nuclearism and its attendant technologies. By taking up ways of nothingness, the

poets I have discussed, with varying degrees of emphasis, not only affirm life but assert that poetry in fact *does* matter and *does* contribute
to authentic cultural changes. Its impact may be neither readily felt, nor
easily measured, yet by cracking open "our modes of thinking," reconfiguring our language and scrutinizing how we imagine ourselves in the
nuclear era, in the long run its importance may well rival that of international diplomacy for the reduction of nuclear arms or scientific discoveries that render radioactivity less menacing.

By organizing this study and categorizing poets according to their formal techniques and stylistic approaches to nuclearism, I want to affirm
that political positions in and of themselves do not determine the quality or scope of poetry. On the other hand, only those poets who have
confronted both their private demons and the larger ideological forces
of their time are likely to achieve the breadth and depth of the poets here
whose work I have examined most closely. Not only is it clear that nuclear issues fall within the American poet's purview, but a poet has little choice not to confront the relationship of nuclearism to the intimate
concerns of art.

My intention has been to arrange these poems from the most focused
way of nothingness to the most wide open—that is, from those poems
that demonstrate an alert politics to those informed by the metaphysics
of nuclear uncertainty. As the first group, nuclear protest poems draw
direct attention to the crisis of nuclearism by speaking out about the
need for citizen and state action to keep the forces of nuclear technology in check. Often, however, in their vigilance and desire for political
change, they structurally polarize the political interests behind nuclearism and can obscure our need to acknowledge our own complicity
in endangering the world. Taking a less activist position in finding
metaphors for the nuclear threat, apocalyptic lyric poems are less resolute in considering it only as unthinkable and, therefore, create an
opening for us to reevaluate its impact on the self. In most instances,
these poems also voice a protest, though a more muted one, yet their inherent celebration of individual experience may tend to diminish their
political efficacy and understate the integral connection between social
ideals and subjective meaning. Psychohistorical poems concern themselves more directly with those social ideals, especially in relation to
history and myth, thereby placing less emphasis on private experience
than on the cultural constructions that dictate the quality of that experience. Because these poems express the impact of nuclearism on ideological values more than on the political present, they are even further

removed from immediate events than apocalyptic lyric poems, but they do enhance our understanding of the implications of nuclearism and keep us from isolating it as the exclusive concern of technologists, scientists, miltary officials, protestors, and politicians. Finally, the most speculative approach to nothingness, expressed in poems of destin-errance, is also the most remote from political engagement, and on their own these poems have little practical application to policy. But ideologically speaking, because of their immersion in randomness and potential meaninglessness, they do provide the most cogent model of suspension from which genuine changes in thinking may arise, even as their openness anticipates or even courts the kind of catastrophe that nuclear protest poems cry out vehemently against.

As a paradigm of crosscultural responses to the nuclearism, then, this chorus of voices provides more than communal opposition to weapons of mass destruction. It also enacts in poetry the range of responses we all may have, and together these poems go the ways of nothingness the nuclear age has opened before us. Through their art, American poets have made major strides in bringing forth and displaying those conditions we now must accept in order to imagine a world not held hostage by its own self-destructive impulses.

Of course, should annihilation occur, all poetry, indeed all language, will disappear. Strange as it may seem, such a disappearance continues within the realm of possibility. While the warming of relations between the two major nuclear powers, the United States and the former Soviet Union, holds out the promise of a significantly reduced number of weapons by the start of the next century, even in the most optimistic scenario there will remain for the foreseeable future enough warheads in their arsenals to initiate Armageddon. Furthermore, as we have witnessed before, it takes little time to develop and deploy new or additional weapons of mass destruction, if those in power are so disposed, and no treaty between particular nations will guarantee disarmament or halts in weapons production by other nations or groups. In the meantime, poets like Denise Levertov who have expressed a sense of the "unremitting political urgency" of the present are liable to lose patience with those who think in only long-term ways about nuclearism or who avoid thinking about it at all, just as poets like James Merrill may disdain the nuclear protest poets' preoccupation with the ephemeralities of political maneuvering. But given the strength of their art—and I am convinced of, if nothing else, the intensity and beauty of the American poetry produced in the last fifty years—these poets' words will shimmer "even in the eyes of all posterity/ That wear this world out to the ending doom." As radical changes in cultural consciousness occur, undoubtedly the critical means for reading and understanding poetry will also change, so that the struggle for freedom from the specter of annihilation will need to be redefined. But because that specter, whether by nuclear or other technological means, persists into the uncertain present, we need both the vision of poets and the imagination to fathom what they suppose, as each word grants us another.

◇

NOTES

Introduction: The Way of Nothingness

1. Lifton defines "psychic numbing" as that state of mind "characterized by various degrees of inability to feel and by gaps between knowledge and feeling. Its subjective experience need not be only that of apathy or 'deadening,' but can take the form of anger or rage . . . or even guilt or shame. . . . Psychic numbing, as the central impairment within the formative process, can occur in association with the entire gamut of survivor experience, including that of everyday life" (*Life* 79). See also Lifton and Falk 103–5.

2. In *Knowing Nukes: The Politics and Culture of the Atom*, William Chaloupka provides a similiar definition of "nuclearism" as "the position taken by managers and leaders of nuclear states, even if they seldom identify this as an identifiable political stance. Nuclear technology encompasses the artifacts of nuclearism, including bombs and electrical generating facilities" (xv–xvi).

3. See also Theodore B. Taylor and Lev P. Feoktistov, "Verified Elimination of Nuclear Warheads and Disposition of Contained Nuclear Materials"

(Calogero 45–66), and Boyle et al. 4. Lest the break-up of the Union of Soviet Socialist Republics and the end of the Cold War suggest that the stockpiling of nuclear weapons is a thing of the past, we only need to recall that in 1976, for example, in the midst of the Cold War, it was estimated that the number of nuclear weapons in the world totaled 12,358, approximately one-fifth of the total existing only fifteen years later and still less than half the number remaining after recent agreements (Gompert 348–49). Furthermore, despite the visibility of weapons treaties between the United States and the former Soviet Union, scientists and military personnel still face problems with the verification of the dismantling of weapons, the safe disposal of uranium, plutonium, and weapons-grade materials, and the high costs of disarmament. See Joseph Rotblat and Vitali I. Goldanskii, "The Elimination of Nuclear Arsenals: Is It Desirable? Is It Feasible?" (Calogero 205–23), as well as Sivard 16–17.

4. For a full overview of the worldwide distribution of nuclear weapons in the 1980s, see Leonard S. Spector (with Jacqueline R. Smith), *Nuclear Ambitions: The Spread of Nuclear Weapons, 1989–90* (Boulder, Colo.: Westview Press, 1990). For a dramatic account of the post–Cold War methods by which nuclear technology and weaponry are still spreading, see William E. Burrows and Robert Windrem, *Critical Mass: The Dangerous Race for Superweapons in a Fragmenting World* (New York: Simon and Schuster, 1994).

5. To cite one extreme, in *The Abolition*, while arguing for a method of eliminating nuclear weapons worldwide, Jonathan Schell writes, "Abolition would not give us a world from which nuclear weapons had been eradicated forever, which is to say that it would not return us to the pre-nuclear world. Nothing can do that" (155). Schell then characterizes deterrence theory with the analogy of a roundhouse and a group of railroad engineers, each of whom could destroy the roundhouse as a way of controlling the routes of all other trains: By their agreeing to back their trains as far away from the roundhouse as possible, the engineers decrease the chance of a sudden, mad collision at the center and "the whole business of crashing into each other [might] gradually become fantastic and unreal—a nightmare from a barbaric and insane past" (156). Even in this scenario, the knowledge to bring about annihilation would not be eliminated, only distanced.

6. In arguing to outlaw nuclear weapons under international law, amid the easing of East-West tensions, Boyle et al. remark on the instability of the superpowers as well: "The Soviet Union . . . faces a world history that demonstrates little support for the propositions that collapsing empires fade quietly. And in our increasingly high-tech world, with military research and development (R & D) fast at work on atomic guns, particle-beam cannons, and other space-age deviltries that divert attention from the perils of nuclear proliferation, dozens of regimes in Western Asia and elsewhere have been

acquiring nuclear and other weapons of mass destruction—and the means to deliver them to almost anywhere on earth—with frightening ease and speed. Not to be overlooked either is the unabated intensity with which the United States and to a lesser extent the Soviet Union pursue the modernization of their strategic arsenals and the ease with which during the Persian Gulf war, commentators were able to recommend the use of nuclear weapons, eroding the taboo against them" (4–5).

7. For an array of similarly expressed ideas about the shift in war authorities, by authors otherwise widely differing in their nuclear concerns, see Robert C. Aldridge, *Nuclear Empire* (Vancouver: New Star Books, 1989), 142–47; Caldicott 215–80; Lifton and Falk 256–65; Robert Scheer, *With Enough Shovels: Reagan, Bush & Nuclear War* (New York: Random House, 1982), 120–25; Schell, *The Fate of the Earth* 186–88; and Zuckerman, *Scientists and War* 43–51. I discuss Edith Wyschogrod's philosophical analysis of the effect of this shift in "war" from a military to a technological mode of death in chapter 1.

8. Examples of works with varying focuses that provide such a history or overview include, but are not limited to, Brians; Philip L. Cantelon, Richard G. Hewlett, and Robert C. Williams, eds., *The American Atom: A Documentary History of Nuclear Policies from the Discovery of Fission to the Present*, 2d ed. (Philadelphia: University of Pennsylvania Press, 1991); Jane Caputi, *Gossips, Gorgons and Crones: Female Power and the Nuclear Age* (forthcoming); the film *The Atomic Cafe* (dir. Kevin Rafferty, Jayne Loader and Pierce Rafferty, 1982); and Spenser Weart, *Nuclear Fear: A History of Images*.

9. David Dowling identifies five techniques among fiction writers' treatment of nuclear apocalypse: (1) the use of "indirection, by skirting round the perimeter of the gaping chasm of disaster"; (2) the treatment of "nuclear disaster . . . as a concept to be satirised"; (3) the framing of the disaster "usually from a longer perspective of future time and through some pre-existing documentation"; (4) "the internalising of the nuclear crisis" by treating "the premonition of disaster, the living through and the survival afterwards [as] all matters of psychic stress which often seem simply a more extreme form of the continuing modern *angst*"; and (5) "post-modernist techniques of reflexivity" which "attempt to locate the experience of nuclear disaster by surrounding the inexpressible with verbal strategies" (5–14). Having succinctly described these categories, however, Dowling proceeds to organize his own analysis thematically instead of stylistically. Since the range of poems I discuss includes narrative and lyric, concrete and abstract, and overt and oblique expressions of annihilation, I prefer to arrange my chapters according to technique.

Chapter One: Poetry and Annihilation

1. "Annihilation" has had theological meanings but not exclusively so. The *Oxford English Dictionary* indicates that the word "annihilation" was

not included in Randle Cotgrave's *A Dictionarie of the French and English Tongues* (1611), although the words, "An adnihilating, *annichilation, annullation,*" were. The *OED*'s first citation of the use of the word is from Joseph Mede's *Works* (1638) in his *Paraphrase* of 2 Peter *iii.7:* "A destruction of the whole creature it self by utter annihilation" (which so far as I can discern is translated as the phrase, "perdition of ungodly men" in the King James version). Another word often associated with the nuclear threat is "holocaust," a sacrifice by fire: While the word aptly describes the nature of nuclear war, it applies more to the occurrence of war than to its final consequences. Also, with its heavily theological overtones (especially in relation to the genocide of whole races or ethnic groups), the word resembles "apocalypse" and "eschatology."

2. Jonathan Schell takes Lifton's logic here a step farther, when he reasons that ignoring the threat of nuclear war is a potential cause of its execution: "Our failure to acknowledge the magnitude and significance of the peril is a necessary condition for doing the deed. We can do it only if we don't quite know what we're doing. If we did acknowledge the full dimensions of the peril, admitting clearly and without reservation that any use of nuclear arms is likely to touch off a holocaust in which the continuance of all human life would be put at risk, extinction would at that moment become not only 'unthinkable' but also undoable" (*Fate* 186).

3. Lifton observes a comparable sense of guilt among the *hibakusha* in Hiroshima. See *Death* 489–99.

4. Adorno's line of thought here recalls the lines from W. B. Yeats's "The Second Coming": "The best lack all conviction, while the worst/ Are full of passionate intensity" (187).

5. Adorno further explains in the same paragraph, "By 'believing in nothingness' we can mean scarcely more than by nothingness itself; by virtue of its own meaning, the 'something' which, legitimately or not, we mean by the word 'believing' is not nothing. Faith in nothingness would be as insipid as would faith in Being. It would be the palliative of a mind proudly content to see through the whole swindle" (379).

6. Wyschogrod identifies three "characteristic expressions" of manmade mass death to fall under the term "death event": (1) recent wars that have deployed weapons of maximum destruction, (2) the annihilation of persons "*after* the aims of war have been achieved or without reference to war," and (3) "the creation of death-worlds, a new and unique form of social existence in which vast populations are subjected to conditions of life simulating imagined conditions of death, conferring upon their inhabitants the status of the living dead" (15).

7. Wyschogrod explains this reliance of technological society in terms of Zeno's paradoxes of the unity of all being. Zeno argued against the Pythagoreans "that the conclusions which follow from the idea that everything that is, is multiple, are even more absurd than . . . that being is one."

But what interests Wyschogrod here is that "the idea of infinite divisibility which lies behind Zeno's paradoxes presupposes an infinite supply of parts." When combined with "the myths of totalitarian societies, which themselves are born from the ashes of technological society" (36), it does not require much thought to see how Zeno's idea is misapplied: "The only imaginative leap required is that we picture a demographic unit, a people, as a spatial continuum. On analogy with Zeno's idea of the whole, such a unit, however reduced in size, will always provide an infinite supply of parts [for instance, the Nazi working assumption that there will always be a supply of Jews to fill the gas chambers]. What is 'forgotten' in the death event is that a group of people is a *collection* which is exhaustible. Its individual members are not 'parts' which can be subdivided over and over again. This existential application of Zeno's argument in the death event points up a category mistake that unconsciously dominates totalitarian discourse" (38). To presume that the *spatial* continuum of things and people in the lifeworld is ineradicable, "that the world's supply of people is unlimited," Wyschogrod adds elsewhere, allows technological society to continue to function, making possible the existence of "nonbeing"; "the death event expresses this structure in the form of radical annihilation" (63).

8. A political example that comes to mind here is President Ronald Reagan's enthusiastic promotion of the Strategic Defense Initiative in the 1980s as a technological answer to the terror imposed on the United States population by its own and the Soviet Union's nuclear arsenals. For a discussion of how the fantasy of technological solutions are played out in popular films, especially in *Night of the Living Dead* (dir. George Romero, 1968) and *Return of the Living Dead* (dir. Dan O'Bannon, 1985), see Caputi 60–65.

9. Two examples of other concerns for Wyschogrod, as to how the lack of a mythic foundation for technological society has shaped consciousness, are the way the "nuclear void" reconfigures the sense of spatial and temporal continuity (29) and Heidegger's concept of technology's effort to stockpile "what nature yields" as a " 'standing reserve' (*Bestand*) of energy destined for future use" (179).

10. Solomon defines the "nuclear referent" as a *"potential* reality" or "actual situational configuration of political and technological conditions that bear within themselves their own concrete potentialities for future development" and are "bound to the present not only by a tie of logical possibility but by one of empirical potentiality as well" (28).

11. To be clear, I am not suggesting here that Adorno denies the value of poetry, but that Wyschogrod embraces a fairly positivist notion of poetry as a vehicle for changing language, whereas Adorno favors a poetry like Samuel Beckett's, which rejects the possibility of discrete meaning, as well as the possibility of overcoming evil.

12. Wyschogrod arrives at this distinction between Heidegger's preoccupation with "things" as Being, rather than with persons, through her dis-

cussion of Heidegger's account of Rainer Maria Rilke in "What Are Poets For?" "To be sure," she writes in agreement with Heidegger, "there is an aspect of Rilke's work which belongs squarely within the Augustinian tradition of introspective consciousness and which culminates in the modern stress on the subject. But another side of Rilke's thought also comes to fruition here. Just as Heidegger believes mortals must prepare an abode for the god, Rilke thinks we must prepare an abode for the dead: Rilke's world is one in which not only things but also the beloved pass away" (194). Then even more explicitly, Wyschogrod faults Heidegger for his "striking omission of a key theme in Rilke's work—thwarted love, the theme of the lover whose beloved dies or rejects the lover or the lover who renounces the beloved but continues to cling to love. Such love exists in an altogether different space from that of sensible experience, from the possibility of active fulfillment" (194). Wyschogrod's emphasis on the realm of spiritual love is critical, it seems to me, in any argument for the efficacy of a poetry in what she calls "the death-world," a world of whatever kind threatened by annihilation.

13. Dowling's opposition to Schell's idea is further underscored, in fact, by the reproduction in his own book of eight of Albrecht Dürer's woodcuts from his Apocalypse series.

14. In a more indirect manner, Alan Williamson defends "subjectivism" in contemporary poetry against the critical or political charge of narcissism by arguing, "The energy of original vision, at least in the arts, comes from within more than from objective perception. . . . Thus, I see no need to apologize for regarding the self as one of the great human and poetic subjects; always acknowledging that the most adequate poetry of the self is likely to be the most aware of its paradoxes" (Introspection 6). Yet Williamson never raises the Foucaldian question of whether "objective perception" is actually possible. As others argue, nuclear annihilation dismantles the subjectivity/objectivity dichotomy altogether as a frame of reference for the self. What is required, it seems to me, is neither an assertion of the importance of subjectivism nor a dismissal of it, but a suspension of both.

15. For a thorough summary, explication, and critique of Derrida's essay, see Solomon 18–33.

16. Solomon does not use the word "noise" in this context and is, in fact, primarily thinking of empirical science, not artistic expression. But his argument for "potentialist" meaning strikes me as akin to Frank Kermode's comment on the potential of the avant-garde in art: "Novelty in the arts is either communication or noise. If it is noise there is no more to say about it. If it is communication it is inescapably related to something older than itself" (102). In the nuclear age, as I hope to suggest, it is possible for a poem to be both noise and communication.

17. In The Language of Fiction in a World of Pain, Barbara Eckstein compiles a list of those who warn against the danger of "infinite regression

within the practice of what is called deconstruction," while at the same time she applauds deconstructionism's "resistance to totalitarian assignments of meaning" (25–26).

18. Another term I could use here, in distinguishing this function of poetry from deconstructionism as defined by both Schwenger and Solomon, is Charles Altieri's term "decreation" as he distinguishes it from deconstructionism in a note in *Self and Sensibility in Contemporary American Poetry:* "Decreation I take to be a deliberate poetic act intending to disclose possible forms of relatedness, and consequently other possible grounds for identity and value, sharply different from the host forms or conventional expectations that the decreation parasitically restructures. Decreation, in essence, is a means for working within the seams and expectations of dominant modes of discourse by disclosing fresh ways of making sense. . . . Deconstruction, on the other hand, invokes the spirit of skeptical lucidity without a lyric counterpressure" (229). While Altieri specifically has the parodic function of poetry such as John Ashbery's in mind here, his use of "decreation" could apply more generally to any poems self-consciously addressing nothingness, in the world as well as in themselves.

19. For an account of various apocalyptic movements throughout history, from the earliest known versions of the Great Flood to the nuclear holocaust of World War III, see Otto Friedrich, *The End of the World: A History* (New York: Coward, McCann, and Geoghegan, 1982). Also for early Western renditions of the apocalypse from the Antichrist to the voyages of Columbus, see Bernard McGinn, *Visions of the End of the World: Apocalyptic Traditions in the Middle Ages* (New York: Columbia University Press, 1979).

For obvious reasons in limiting this study, I do not treat poetry of annihilation in English or in other languages from outside the United States, though there is clearly a wealth of such poetry. Similarly, among American poets I have chosen not to discuss several poets whom other readers may consider important voices—including, for example, W. S. Merwin, Robert Bly, George Oppen, and LANGUAGE poets such as Bob Perelman and Charles Bernstein. Though he is more concerned with the lack of "mystical contact" than with the political implications of nuclear annihilation in particular, Anthony Libby writes extensively about both Merwin and Bly in his book *Mythologies of Nothing: Mystical Death in American Poetry, 1940–70;* Robert von Hallberg briefly discusses poems written in response to nuclear proliferation in the late 1950s and early 1960s in *American Poetry and Culture, 1945–1980* (129–33); Rob Wilson discusses Perelman (235–37ff.).

20. Kermode returns to "Notes Toward a Supreme Fiction" (1947) throughout *The Sense of an Ending,* while Rob Wilson mentions both "Man on the Dump" (1938) and "Esthetique du Mal" (1944) as anticipating post-Hiroshima poems about annihilation in *American Sublime* (238–39).

21. The only other writing about the atomic bomb by Stein (who died in

1946) is in her short novel *Brewsie and Willie*, developed as a series of conversations among U.S. servicemen and women in Europe after World War II. Several phrases used in "Reflection on the Atomic Bomb" can be traced to this novel. For instance, when a character named Janet challenges the central character Willie about military personnel's prospects for work once they return to the United States, she argues for the value of rebuilding a society by saying, "When you have got a lot to do you are kind of happy and pioneering" (83). But Willie objects to this concept of progress, answering her with a rhetorical question: "What do you want, do you want us to drop our atomic bombs on ourselves, is that what you want, so we can go out and pioneer, is that the idea" (83). There is a yoking here of atomic bombs and nothingness as a new American wilderness. But in the next chapter, Willie makes the same point Stein does in "Reflection on the Atomic Bomb" when she says that, unless the bomb annihilates everyone, "there are always lots left on this earth." Speaking of the devastation caused by the war in Europe, Willie tells his friend Brewsie, "Somehow everybody just does keep on living, look at everybody over here, by rights they ought all to be all dead, all of them over and over again dead, all of them and they aint Brewsie, they aint at all dead" (86). And again a page later Willie insists that annihilation, whether by the Nazis or the Americans, simply cannot be accepted: "No matter what does happen everybody somehow goes on living, and there always seem to be lots more of them lots more than anybody needs but they all go on living. . . . they just do go on living, you cant kill them off. Dont you make any mistake about that atom bombs or potato bugs or concentration camps or religion or poverty or no jobs or education, it does not make it go any other way, they just go on living, they dont disappear" (87).

22. The irony noted here is the same as in Wyschogrod's account of how Nazi death camp guards would have had to assume an endless supply of Jews to kill, in order to keep the mechanism of mass death going and themselves employed and fed. See Wyschogrod 31, 37–39.

23. For a comparable use of the word "scared," see again Stein's *Brewsie and Willie*, where the servicemen and women debate their various postwar prospects in America, "our own dear beautiful rich country," which the character Pauline fears "will go down like England did." When Willie answers, "Not on your life," "Yeah, said Pauline, that's easy, be the strong white man, who never can be brought down, that's all right if you had never left home, but you have left home, you're scared, you're thinking about everything and way back deep down you're scared, scared. I know I am scared too, here I am scared, said Willie, sure you're scared, said Pauline, and he's got to tell us what to do. But, said Brewsie, you got me scared, how can I tell you what to do, I can tell you what's wrong, I can kind of tell you what's going to happen, and it will, said Jane, yes it will. All right, said Willie, it will. I know, said Brewsie, logic is logic, facts are facts" (69).

24. After characterizing Williams in this way, Paul Mariani, his biogra-

pher, goes on to discuss how the poet's "politics" cost him the position of Poetry Consultant to the Library of Congress in 1952, as well as contributed to his physical and psychological breakdown (651–78).

Chapter Two: Nuclear Protest Poetry

1. The notoriety of the poems, in fact, may stem as much from the notoriety of the activism of the poets themselves as from their poems. For example, Robert Bly founded "American Writers against the Vietnam War" in 1966 and used the opportunity of receiving the National Book Award in 1968 to criticize his own publisher for supporting the war, as well as to donate his income from the award to the Draft Resisters' League. Robert Lowell became the first American to decline an invitation to Lyndon Johnson's White House, because of his opposition to U.S. policy in Vietnam; and Denise Levertov and Adrienne Rich, among others, marched in antiwar demonstrations.

2. For a defense of using the term "nuke," see Chaloupka xvi; for a criticism of it, see Lifton and Falk 106 (also quoted in chapter 3). Regarding special collections of antinuclear literature, Brians lists three that "emphasize poetry more than fiction" (99): *Warnings: An Anthology on the Nuclear Peril, Northwest Review* 22.1–2 (1984); Schley; and Sklar. Other anthologies include Jan Barry, ed., *Peace Is Our Profession: Poems and Passages of War Protest* (Montclair, N.J.: East River Anthology, 1981); Herman Berlandt and Neeli Cherkovski, eds., *Peace or Perish: A Crisis Anthology* (San Francisco: Poets for Peace, 1988); Robert J. Lifton and Nicholas Humphrey, eds., *In a Dark Time: Images for Survival* (Cambridge: Harvard University Press, 1984); and Betty Shipley and Nina Langley, eds., *Meltdown: Poems from the Core*. Also, John Bradley has edited an anthology to commemorate the fiftieth anniversary of the bombings of Hiroshima and Nagasaki, *Atomic Ghost: Poets Respond to the Nuclear Age* (Minneapolis: Coffee House Press, 1995). For Barry's account of assembling his anthology, see Barry 86–92.

3. A 1987 issue of *Critical Inquiry* devoted entirely to poetry and politics includes essays on poets, ranging historically from Pindar to the LANGUAGE poets. See von Hallberg, *Politics and Poetic Value*.

4. For salient essays addressing these issues, see especially Robert Bly's "Leaping Up into Political Poetry" (Jones 129–37, reprinted from *Forty Poems Touching on Recent American History* [New York: Harper and Row, 1970]), and Adrienne Rich's "When We Dead Awaken: Writing as Re-Vision" (Jones 138–55, reprinted from *On Lies, Secrets, and Silence: Selected Prose 1966–1978* [New York: W. W. Norton and Co., 1970]), which discuss the conflict between the personal and the political. For the relationship between poetic language and politics, see Robert Pinsky, "Responsibilities of the Poet" (von Hallberg, *Politics* 7–19) and Jerome J. McGann, "Contemporary Poetry, Alternate Routes" (von Hallberg, *Politics* 253–76), as well as Richard Jones's "Introduction: The Imprisoned Imagination"

(Jones 9–16). For a discussion of spirituality and politics in poetry, see Denise Levertov, "On the Edge of Darkness: What Is Political Poetry?" (Jones 162–74, reprinted from *Light*), and her more recent essay "Poetry and Peace: Some Broader Dimensions" (*New and Selected Essays* [New York: New Directions Books, 1992], 154–71).

5. In his introduction to *Politics and Poetic Value*, Robert von Hallberg argues that, while there is "clearly a rhetorical danger" for poets to assume political authority—in that it may lead to "grandiosity"—and while poets are only "figuratively" in the role of political visionaries, nevertheless "a case can be made for poets in democratic societies invoking only the authority of citizens participating in the social and cultural institutions we speak of as the state" (4). In this role, they are as likely to influence public policy as are other citizens with other talents. Von Hallberg's position is the one I argue here.

6. For part of this reading of "Dirty Words" I am indebted to William J. Scheick, in correspondence.

7. A poem such as Minnie Bruce Pratt's "Strange Flesh," in which the central figure (a woman) chooses to walk away triumphantly from the "predictable despair" of an antinuclear die-in, may argue against the effectiveness of particular actions taken by antinuclear activists, but the poem also gives every indication of opposing the actual production of nuclear weapons. See Kawada 121–23.

8. For Charles Altieri's evolving views on Snyder's political vision, see both his 1970 essay, "Gary Snyder's Lyric Poetry: Dialectic as Ecology" (Patrick D. Murphy 48–58) and "Gary Snyder's *Turtle Island:* The Problem of Reconciling the Roles of Seer and Prophet" (*boundary 2* 6.3 [1976]: 761–77). For another endorsement of Snyder, see Thomas J. Lyon, "The Ecological Vision of Gary Snyder" and "Twenty Years Later—A Coda" (Patrick D. Murphy 35–48).

9. Jody Norton argues that "not a consistent poetic form, but a ruled play of absences . . . has allowed Snyder to cause the most conditional of conditional realities—language—to signify that for which no words are adequate. The very absoluteness of this inequivalence has led Snyder to level the usual structural hierarchy of poetic texts, so that his poems take place as much within their lacunae as within their language" (185).

10. Levertov herself apparently thinks differently. In an interview she remarks, "It's certainly harder for American poets, or any English-speaking poets, to write engaged poetry than it is for Hispanic poets, for the simple reason that there isn't an accepted tradition. If you look for it in the past, you can't find it" (Smith, "Interview" 599). She then goes on to trace what tradition there is in English, at least as far back as the Romantic poets.

11. For the framework for her thesis, Smith refers to Paul Lacey, "Poetry of Political Anguish," *Sagetrieb* 4:1 (Spring 1985): 61–71 ("Songs" 163, 172n). Lacey's essay is reprinted in Wagner-Martin 187–96.

12. For Levertov's own account of what the term *gods* means to her, see Smith, "Interview" 602.

13. In her account of "Mass," Smith reinforces the idea of the successful merging of private and public voices in the poem: "The solemn procession of liturgical sections works emotionally as an actual mass does to save the poem from ponderousness. . . . As in a mass, private emotions find release in communal ritual and, as in so many of Levertov's later political poems, the lyric voice is a collective 'we' rather than a singular 'I' " ("Songs" 168).

Chapter Three: The Apocalyptic Lyric

1. Caldicott is a pediatrician, not a psychologist, so it is not surprising that her assessment is expressed in dramatic terms. In fairness to her, though, her earlier book, *Nuclear Madness: What You Can Do!* (Brookline, Mass.: Autumn Press, 1978), while providing alarming details about the growing danger of the nuclear threat, provides a more circumspect analysis of the motivations of military, technological, and political personnel. A more subtle and detailed gender analysis of the scientists and military leaders of the nuclear age is Brian Easlea's *Fathering the Unthinkable: Masculinity, Scientists and the Nuclear Arms Race.* After a feminist psychoanalytic critique of what he calls "compulsive masculinity" in scientists from the time of Francis Bacon to Los Alamos, Easlea reaches the conclusion, among others, "that the principal driving force of the nuclear arms race is not the brute fact of scarce material resources, important though it is, but masculine motivation—in essence, the compulsive desire to lord it over other people and nonhuman nature, and then manfully to confront a dangerous world. . . . [I]t is the perpetually increasing risk of nuclear war and of the prospect of nuclear disaster that give to these masculine participants [in nuclear policymaking] a very special thrill and sense of ultimate power, importance and meaning" (165–66). Writing in 1983, he even went so far as to predict that if "the economy of the Soviet Union [were] to collapse . . . , then no doubt after a period of masculine exultation American promoters of the arms race would weep over the body of their erstwhile antagonist as the monster wept over Dr. Frankenstein's. A great deal of purpose, meaning and excitement would have gone from their lives" (166). Also, in recent research, Jane Caputi has been examining the increasingly violent and misogynist masculinity of the nuclear imagery in popular magazines and films.

2. Here, as well as later, Wilson examines poems by LANGUAGE poet Bob Perelman as examples of how the nuclear sublime might deconstruct "American Rapturism" within the tradition of the American sublime, in order to undo the "ideology of nation-state power that would attempt to localize this vastness of space or energy as a national property," adding that "acts of ideological critique are called for to rupture the romantic sacralization of power and force" (253–54). What he has in mind here, I believe, corresponds to what I call "the poetry of destinerrance" in chapter 5.

3. In his essay on James Merrill's *The Changing Light at Sandover,* Lee Zimmerman identifies this same risk in contemporary poetry dealing with apocalyptic concerns and attributes the idea to Christopher Lasch in *The Minimal Self,* where Lasch writes, "A language of extremity, the only language appropriate to extreme situations, soon loses its force through repetition and inflation. It facilitates what it needs to prevent, the normalization of atrocity" (101). Zimmerman contends that one way of dealing with this problem is through "indirection," citing Emily Dickinson's famous line, "Tell all the Truth but tell it slant" (373), which is, of course, another way of describing how metaphors work.

4. Although in chapter 1 I state my preference for the term "annihilation," I have opted to use "apocalypse" here in the manner that Joseph Dewey uses it when he defines "the apocalyptic temper," as that which "resists the crisis of change by inculcating change into its very vocabulary"; it also "speaks most eloquently and most directly to a community of the frightened, the despairing, the uncertain and assures it that the apparent disorder of history will finally affirm order, will finally give heart" (11). Like Dewey's "apocalyptic temper," these poems also resist "the fantasy of simple optimism," resolving instead "to face squarely the staggering implications of history gone suddenly awry by suggesting that the present can be understood compassionately only by imagining the end itself" (11).

5. Paul Zimmer made these comments to me in an interview conducted in Iowa City on 14 April 1992. For a photograph of Zimmer standing at Camp Desert Rock with an atomic bomb cloud rising in the distance behind him, see Susina 15. For corroborating accounts (though not always so discerning as Zimmer's) from other eyewitnesses at Camp Desert Rock and other Nevada test sites, see Carole Gallagher, *American Ground Zero: The Secret Nuclear War* (Cambridge: MIT Press, 1993).

6. In an interview with Michael Pettit, Zimmer explains the genesis of Imbellis this way: "I think about cruelty—my own and other people's—and I've always been appalled by it. I want to regard that in poems. When the Viet Nam war was going on, I was so shaken by it, I was unable to write about it. My way of writing about it was to make the Imbellis sequence. To try and understand. My God, it was astonishing, the ultimate cruelty that was going on, and we were responsible for it! Imbellis becomes a cruel person, and he reappears in other work of mine" (Pettit 57).

7. Another recent poem by Zimmer, "Imitations of Fatherhood, Operation Desert Rock, 1955," recreates this contrast between the omnipotence of nuclear bombs and the fragile splendor of the life they threaten, when Zimmer again recalls the imagery of the fireball and the blinded rabbits. This time, however, the poem takes an even larger leap away than "The Sweet Night Bleeds from Zimmer" and "But Bird" do from the scene portrayed in *Earthbound Zimmer,* in order to purge the scene of its previous horror. The rabbit appears here as a baby jackrabbit, "blinded and matted

with blood" (*Big Blue* 29). But instead of kicking the rabbit or helplessly watching it die, as he does in earlier poems, there is a dramatic difference: Addressing himself in the second person, as the one whose boot the rabbit runs into, he writes, "you undo/ a pocket and gently slip/ the rabbit child into the warmth/ then fasten the button again," as he hurries to catch the others, "bearing" his "secret toward the fire" (*Big Blue* 29). While the poem insinuates that both the rabbit and its surrogate father will be decimated by the fire they approach, it also conveys a tenderness toward the threatened world with a grace not achieved in "Poem Ending with an Old Cliché." Without pretending to be able to prevent annihilation, the reconstructed self in "Imitations" acts out of love and guardianship for life, regardless of whether that love will prevail or not.

When I interviewed Zimmer, I asked him whether he thought there was any justification for the bomb tests and the damage they wreaked on the troops and on nature. He replied, "No, there was no justification for that, no . . . , and you're right, we were all scarred by that experience and carried it with us, at least mentally and some physically, for the rest of our lives. There was no justification; there was no justification for knocking off at least 100,000 Iraqis either [in the Persian Gulf war]. There's no justification for a lot of things and that's the despair."

8. In Rich's 1983–85 sequence of poems, "Contradictions: Tracking Poems," she again returns to nuclear imagery, but this time metonymically rather than metaphorically, in poem 22's image of a woman wandering through "the radioactive desert" of a test site, which is clearly killing her. "Shall we accuse her of denial/ first of the self then of the mixed virtue/ of the purest science" Rich asks, "Shall we praise her shall we let her wander/ the atomic desert in peace?" (*Your Native* 104). These questions at first recall Rich's 1974 poem "Power" about physicist Marie Curie whose "wounds came from the same source as her power" (*Fact* 225), but in the three poems that follow, she turns to American history—"My country wedged fast in history/ stuck in the ice" (*Your Native* 105)—and, interestingly, to the Jewish holocaust as appropriate precedents for the sense of loss that the concept of nuclear annihilation stirs in us (*Your Native* 107).

9. For other poems (notably, by women) that blend a keen consciousness of everyday existence with that of annihilation see, among others, Maxine Cassin, "Anniversary: Hiroshima" (45); Celia Gilbert, "Nature" (54–55); Maxine Kumin, "Lines Written in the Library of Congress After the Cleanth Brooks Lecture" (*Our Ground* 36–42) and "How to Survive Nuclear War" (*Long* 51–54); and Honor Moore, "Spuyten Duyvil" (626–33). I should also mention Denise Levertov's "During a Son's Dangerous Illness" (*Breathing* 35) and "The Batterers" (*Evening* 71), poems I discuss in chapter 2, although most of Levertov's poems concerning annihilation more openly protest nu-

clearism than do apocalyptic lyrics. For a discussion of women poets' responses to the nuclear threat, see Kawada.

10. See, for example, Theodore Holmes's 1962 review of *Advice to a Prophet* (72–75); see also Charles R. Woodward's summary and rebuttal of such criticism, "Richard Wilbur's Critical Condition" (221–31).

11. Earlier in this same essay Wilbur makes a similar point about the independent and resilient nature of the world when he writes, "It is the province of poems to make some order in the world, but poets can't afford to forget that there is a reality of things which survives all orders great and small. Things *are.* The cow is there. No poetry can have any strength unless it continually bashes itself against the reality of things" (217).

12. This generalization is derived, in part, from Derrida's discussion of the nuclear referent, including his idea of the inherent opposition of existence and meaning (or language as meaning). Derrida argues that that which imagines its own annihilation (or absence), which he calls "literature," at the same time creates the possibility of being seen in its own "totality," thereby providing a frame of reference for meaning while simultaneously inferring the fictionality of that frame of reference (27).

13. Hill even notes that audiences have been moved to tears when hearing Wilbur read "Advice to a Prophet" aloud (136).

14. Wilbur here anticipates Lifton's discussion (which I detail in chapter 5) of the mind's incapacity to imagine the "imagery of extinction" (Lifton and Falk 5, 58).

15. Robert F. Sayre remarks that Wilbur stresses the word "own" in this line when he reads it aloud, further emphasizing the difference between *this* physical world and some other world of abstraction (155).

16. Ejner J. Jensen explains how "trued" "recalls the final line of '0,' where particular objects ('hawk or history') are called to the speaker's aid ('to true my run') when abstractions will not suffice" (248). The idea is a provocative one, and Jensen goes on to support my reading of the undermining of faith in particulars in "In the Field." But even within this context, "trued" must still be taken ironically.

Chapter Four: Psychohistorical Poetry in the Nuclear Age

1. For models of the first method of psychohistorical research (psychobiography), see, for instance, Robert Jay Lifton, Shuichi Kato, and Michael Reich, *Six Lives/Six Deaths: Portraits from Modern Japan* (New Haven: Yale University Press, 1979), and Philip Pomper, *The Structure of Mind in History: Five Major Figures in Psychohistory* (New York: Columbia University Press, 1985); predecessors of such works include Freud's psychobiographical studies of Leonardo da Vinci and Woodrow Wilson and Erik Erikson's of Luther, Hitler, and Gandhi. The second method (the psychodynamic reading of groups) is explained by Bruce Mazlish in "What Is Psycho-History?":

202 Notes to Pages 117–36

"What are the consequences for psycho-history? In the first place, it means that instead of working from an individual, a great man, out to the psychological history of a period, we move the other way, and go from the general mood, or *Geist*, back to ordinary individuals. In the second place, though building on the theories of individual psychology and life-history, as well as family history, we need to bring these into correspondence with newly developed theories of collective psychology and group history" (29). For a theoretical explanation of both "psychobiography" and the "psychohistory of collective phenemona," see Saul Friedlander, *History and Psychoanalysis: An Inquiry into the Possibilities and Limits of Psychohistory* (New York: Holmes & Meier Publishing Co., 1978).

2. Other poems regarding nuclear weapons within a broader mythic context include Honor Moore's "Spuyten Duyvil," which combines mythic imagery of the Dutch along the Hudson River in New York with imagery from everyday life, and two of Ray A. Young Bear's poems, "A Drive to Lone Ranger" and "Race of the Kingfishers: In the Nuclear Winter" in *The Invisible Musician*, where Young Bear refers to nuclear annihilation in terms of the Mesquakie prophesy that "when the Northern Lights reach across the skies and touch the southern horizon, a great world war will ensue, causing an end to all life" (97). In the first poem, Young Bear describes the Northern Lights as "celestial messengers in green atomic oxygen,/ highlighted by red—the color of our impending/ nuclear demise" (34), and in the second he describes women dancers of the Kingfisher race enacting those same messengers in a colorful dance (44–45). As far as I know, Young Bear has yet to write a poem whose central concern is nuclear annihilation.

3. Quoted with permission from a letter I received from Dick Allen, dated 20 January 1992.

4. Other titles I have in mind here include Richard Kenney, *The Invention of Zero* (New York: Alfred A. Knopf, 1993); James Sherry, *Our Nuclear Heritage* (Los Angeles: Sun and Moon Press, 1991); Juliana Spahr, *Nuclear* (Buffalo: Leave Books, n.d. [1993]); and Bill Witherup, *Men at Work* (Boise, Idaho: Ahsahta Press, 1990).

5. In a 1967 interview with Donald Sheehan, Merrill confesses, "We all have our limits. I draw the line at politics and hippies" (*Recitative* 32), but Moffett, when identifying the "overt theme" of all three books of *The Changing Light*, comments, "All were originally undertaken as a warning against nuclear disaster" (154), and Harold Bloom refers to the poem as "an apocalyptic epic whose true starting-point is Hiroshima" (7). Stephen Yenser characterizes its "central question" as "whether humanity can save itself from destruction" (*Consuming* 288).

6. See, for example, Helen Vendler, "James Merrill's Myth: An Interview," *New York Review of Books* 26 (3 May 1979): 12–13 (rpt. in Merrill, *Recitative* 49–52), and J. D. McClatchy, "DJ: A Conversation with David Jackson," *Shenandoah* 30.4 (1979): 23–44.

7. Citing Merrill's Audenesque travel essay about Japan, "The Beaten Path" (*Recitative* 143–51), Zimmerman dates the earliest recorded evidence of Merrill's thinking about annihilation and Paradise from 1950 (374), but the essay itself dates his first trip to Hiroshima in 1956. He spent three months in New Mexico two years later.

8. As Yenser explains Merrill's method, "What the trilogy gives us in the end is not a belief but rather a dialectical process, the process of thought and imagination—a process such that it will not tolerate any single belief, or even species of belief, whether monistic or dualistic, materialistic or idealistic. Unity in duality (or in multiplicity, since dualism propagates) constitutes the poem's fundamental principle, metaphysical and aesthetic alike" ("Names" 275).

9. Peter Sacks praises Merrill by writing, "The poem gathers a great moral urgency in its almost Miltonic plea for a submissive rather than pridefully exploitative attitude toward the sources of human and natural power" (Lehman and Berger 172). A more skeptical Bloom admits that, although *The Book of Ephraim* is "almost continuously superb," *Mirabell's Books of Number* "can numb one, in between bouts of sublimity," while *Scripts for the Pageant* "all too frequently compels me to believe I may be an uninivited guest at a post-Wildean tea-party, where I wander lost among the cucumber sandwiches and hashish fudge, plaintively mewing for something closer to my usual healthy diet" (6). Charles Altieri is even more critical, complaining that Merrill's poems in general are "so self-conscious of his own position that they offer only attitudes to strike, not significant things to say, with regards to topics flowing through his mind" (165). Finally, in remaining unconvinced by Merrill's multiple manuevers, Vernon Shetley criticizes "not the particular ethical content" of *The Changing Light* but "the failure of skepticism that takes place around it. The reader comes to be in an odd position; the more the reader shares the values the poem embodies, the more tempted he or she will be to literalize its cosmic framework, which is precisely, Merrill indicates, what an ideal reader would not do" (100).

10. Zimmerman adds, "As opposed to the narcisstic denial of the Other basic to absolutist world views, in conversation one voice depends upon its counterpart; the interplay requires both self and other—and *Sandover* locates authority or truth precisely *in* this interplay" (384).

11. Merrill's concept of the "thinning out" of populations smacks of elitism, countering the egalitarianism of most nuclear protest poets, as well as a Whitmanian poet like John Ashbery. Concerning this "thinning out," Shetley argues that it is not "the belief itself" that is "problematic, though I don't happen to share it, but rather its being posited as a given rather than as something that has to be earned through the discipline of skeptical questioning in which Merrill's lyric poetry is so rich" (101). But again, if we accept the epic's ambiguous tone, its sometimes self-derogatory characteriza-

204 Notes to Pages 145–61

tion of JM, and the lack of resolution of most conversations in it, they structurally provide a check against an endorsement of this questionable position. In other words, despite what the spirits say, the comic atmosphere of
the pageant disrupts both elitist and egalitarian views.

Chapter Five: The Poetry of Destinerrance

1. Martha Bartter makes a similar claim in her study of postnuclear science fiction: "If we are to change our sociopolitical behavior, we need to
know the assumptions it rests upon, not what we 'believe' to be true but
what we actually do when we are not looking. . . . As we have encoded the
current assumptions in fiction, so we need to encode new ones, to try them
out as thought experiments, to make them 'real' in our imagination, and
then to adopt or reject them. This is not a call for 'uplifting' or 'moral' fiction, for self-conscious mythmaking, but for creative exploration of new
possibilities in human relations" (11).

2. In examining the impact of modern physics on Stevens, Lisa Steinman
discusses Stevens's own uncertainty about the material premises implicit
in his poems that "celebrate the invigorating exchange between self and
world" (155). "Even when Stevens sounded most at home with unending,
provisional encounters with the world [as in "The Snow Man" and "The
Man on the Dump"], he voiced anxiety about how the importance of such
activity, exhilarating as it might be, could be defended," observes Steinman.
"In particular, Stevens's statements from the 1930s suggest his worry that
the motions he celebrated and the uncertainty he courted never adequately
presented the *central* of self or world" (156).

3. For Dugan, who has written explicitly about nuclear issues less often
than Engels and Williams, see "Takeoff on Armageddon" (*Poems Six* 11), a
bitterly satiric piece on the Reagan arms build-up of the 1980s; I read it as
mocking not only Reagan's military posturing but also his ethic. Some of
Engels's other poems I discuss in the text. Williams's most celebrated poem
on the nuclear threat, "Tar," an apocalyptic lyric on the near meltdown of
the Three Mile Island nuclear power plant in 1979, uses the extended
metaphor of roofers and the "dark, Dantean broth" (*Poems* 218) of the tar
they are spreading over the poet's apartment building as a nuclear metaphor.
In my view, however, "Tar" deals less satisfactorily with the implications
of extinction than Williams's earlier poems "What Is and Is Not" (*Poems*
16) and "Giving It Up" (*Poems* 31). For a more recent poem on annihilation,
also an apocalyptic lyric, see "The Dream" (*Flesh* 50).

4. This background information and Engels's comments throughout this
paragraph are used with permission from a letter I received from him, dated
24 November 1991. *The Lucky Dragon* is the Japanese civilian fishing ship
that strayed into the atomic testing area and suffered serious contamina-
tion, resulting in the death of its crew.

5. Engels's later manuscript revision of "The Bedroom," which he kindly provided me, makes the contrast of these two dreams more explicit: "I am leaving// to write this down, notes/ on a dream unaccountably remembered/ in which I stare into a fish's mouth// and then last night the dream in which/ I come to my house and the door/ opens wide on rooms// aswirl with fire, scoured clean/ with fire, the furniture/ white ashes on the floors." For a similarly revised version of "The Fish Dream," see *Walking* 42.

6. In his letter to me cited in note 4, Engels adds that the imagery of the body in the poem where these lines appear ("From the Source") is partly "influenced by a film made by a Swedish medical photographer of a fetus *in utero*. This fire and light-burst has sustained itself in various forms in my work ever since."

7. Quoted with permission from Engels's letter cited in notes 4 and 6. For a revised version of *"Terribilis est locus iste,"* see *Walking* 35–36.

8. Williams's expression of love at the end of this poem, with its sense of interpersonal loss, recalls Edith Wyschogrod's critique of Heidegger on Rilke, where she asserts the importance of intersubjectivity, love, and language as "the naming inherent in kinship structure" in the age of man-made mass death (194–200).

9. Curiously, Richman's litany of Ashbery's faults echoes Schell's prescription for the role of art in the nuclear age (which I discussed in chapter 1), when he writes that "if it wishes to truthfully reflect the reality of its period, whose leading feature is the jeopardy of the human future, art will have to go out of existence" (*Fate* 165). Yet by being "purely negative" (as Richman claims) and dismantling "the attachment between the object and thought," Ashbery's poetry, one might contend, does in fact "go out of existence" in the way we have heretofore understood it as art.

10. In one interview, Ashbery confesses that the subject of his poetry is time, adding that it is "what I have been writing about all these years during which I thought I wasn't writing about anything" (Labrie 29).

11. The mythic or fabulous qualities of Ashbery's "last world," consisting of the breakdown of language more than imagery, strike a vivid contrast to MacLeish's "The End of the World" and Weldon Kees's "To the North" (which I discuss in chapter 1), which both focus on the imagery at the end of the world, rather than what is being thought of in that last moment.

12. Rapaport argues that Ashbery "participates in the writing of texts like those of Derrida and [Maurice] Blanchot which do not make cataclysm or disaster climactic or apocalyptic in the sense we usually have of the word. He takes catastrophe as something pervasive and banal, so ubiquitous and monotonous, that we live this end of man to the end of each day, exist against the backdrop of a deathwork or *thanatopraxie* whose style we have become" (390). Then he goes on to distinguish two kinds of "holocausts" in Ashbery's verse: "The one is foreseeable, recognizable, plain, and political;

the other is fantastic, imagined, visceral, but also extremely remote like something hard to remember. The historical is a kind of inaccessible reality or otherness which we know but cannot conceive outside of objectified facts which, like things, resist penetration. The 'other tradition' is what is achieved by a difficult liberty, what goes on inside one without one's having to do anything about it. The latter, not unlike the hiccup, threatens the coherence of the system" (396).

13. In comparing Ashbery to Stevens, Keller writes, "Sweeping statements, even proclamations of fundamental uncertainty, are tempered by ironic awareness of human limitation. The flux that Stevens sought to render Ashbery sees as swirling tumult, and the process of mind he sought to capture is for Ashbery a disjunctive series of confrontations in a tortuous maze" (Re-making 76).

14. While analyzing "The Skaters" in Rivers and Mountains (1966), Shapiro connects Werner Heisenberg's "Uncertainty Principle" in quantum physics to Ashbery's portrait of understanding as being falsely static, while uncertainty itself remains fluid (105). Later, he adds, "The only certainty, says Ashbery, is perpetual uncertainty and the root uncertainty is that of certain death" (119). While I think he overstates the fixed place of uncertainty in Ashbery, Shapiro's reading affirms the qualitiative difference (rather than the complementary opposition) between certainty and uncertainty, just as there is between absence and presence.

To define presence (as I do) to be "changing" yet also "uncertain of what that change will entail" relates the term, psychosocially, to Lifton's concept of "Proteanism." For Lifton, the Protean mode of behavior entails continuously trying to change one's conditions, even oneself, because of a "dialectical relationship between continuity and re-creation so that, formatively speaking, everything connects with what has gone before, and nothing stays exactly the same. What we call stability may well depend precisely upon degrees of change, just as transformation may depend upon continuity with the past" (Life 77–78). This Proteanism is a marked characteristic of Ashbery's elusive form and diction. It also parallels Schwenger's postnuclear "principle of motion" of the "letter bomb" which he argues "becomes also a principle of preservation" (22).

15. This numbed self recalls Lifton's idea of "psychic numbing," which Ashbery invokes again in "Breezy Stories": "There are still others whom we know nothing about/ And who are growing, it seems, at a rate far in excess/ Of the legislated norm, for whom the 'psychological consequences'// Of the forest primeval of our inconsistency, nay, our lives/ If you prefer, and you can quote me, could be 'numbing' " (Shadow 14).

16. As Ashbery says in the Poulin interview, "What I am trying to get at is a general, all-purpose experience—like those stretch socks that fit all sizes. Something which a reader could dip into and maybe get something out of without knowing anything about me, my history, or sex life, or what-

ever. . . . I'm hoping that maybe someday people will see it this way, as try-ing to become the openest possible form, something in which anybody can see reflected his own private experiences without them having to be defined or set up for him" (251). While this statement may discourage attempts to name the subject of an Ashbery poem, it also means that thinking about the poem in any terms, however speculative, is not unwarranted.

17. Marjorie Perloff aptly sums up the meaning of dreams and reveries in Ashbery's work: "Dream is . . . regarded as the source of our energy, our élan, of life itself; and yet that life remains curiously 'unknowable.' This paradox is at the heart of Ashbery's poetry and accounts for his preoccupation with dream structure rather than dream content. Not *what* one dreams but *how*—this is the domain of Ashbery" (67).

18. In "Tide Music" a similar "sum" of parts accumulates from "patterns of distress settling into rings/ Of warm self-satisfaction and disbelief" (*Shadow* 34). In this case, the gratification of one's "dreaminess" is matched with "disbelief," or the self's unwillingness to accept the shadow's threat.

19. Lehman believes that "no one ever gets anywhere in an Ashbery poem, though many are traveling; if Keats perenially froze his characters . . . , Ashbery's fictional *selves* and *others* seem sometimes jolted out of time al-together. . . . More often than not, the journeys these characters embark on are incomplete; they are interrupted before they get off the ground" ("Shield" 119–20).

20. In his analysis of *Three Poems*, Rapaport alludes to the hiccup in the light of Derrida's reflections on the syllable *gl* in *Glas*, as a "spasm" that "neutralizes, makes impossible any text which would accede to be some-thing particular, nullifies the attempt to write within a particular genre or type of writing," and therein bluntly impedes "the production of a classical or systematic text" (389). For a discussion of the leveling effect of humor for Ashbery, see "T. A. Fink, "Comic Thrust of Ashbery's Poetry," *Twentieth Century Literature* 30 (1984): 1–14.

Adorno, Theodor. *Negative Dialectics.* Trans. E. B. Ashton. New York: Seabury Press, 1973.

Ai. *Sin.* Boston: Houghton Mifflin Co., 1986.

Aiken, William. "Denise Levertov, Robert Duncan, and Allen Ginsberg: Modes of the Self in Projective Poetry." In Wagner-Martin, q.v., 132–47.

Allen, Dick. *Anon and Various Time Machine Poems.* New York: Dell Publishing Co., 1971.

———. "Storytellers & Mystics." *Hudson Review* 42.2 (1989): 321–29.

Altieri, Charles. *Self and Sensibility in Contemporaray American Poetry.* New York: Cambridge University Press, 1984.

Anisfield, Nancy, ed. *The Nightmare Considered: Critical Essays on Nuclear War Literature.* Bowling Green, Ohio: Bowling Green State University Popular Press, 1991.

Ashbery, John. *Houseboat Days.* New York: Viking Press, 1977.

———. *Selected Poems.* New York: Viking Press, 1985.

———. *Shadow Train.* New York: Viking Press, 1981.

Auden, W. H. "The Poet & the City." In Jones, q.v., 36–51.

Barry, Jan. "The End of Art: Poetry and Nuclear War." In Anisfield, q.v., 85–94.

Bartter, Martha A. *The Way to Ground Zero: The Atomic Bomb in American Science Fiction.* New York: Greenwood Press, 1988.

Benoit, Raymond. "From 'The New American Poetry.' " In Salinger, q.v., 162–68.

Berger, Charles, "Merrill and Pynchon: Our Apocalyptic Scribes." In Lehman and Berger, q.v., 282–97.

Bixler, Frances. "Richard Wilbur: 'Hard as Nails.' " *Publications of the Arkansas Philological Association* 11.2 (1985): 1–13.

Blanton, Mackie J. V., and John Gery. "A Conversation with Frederick Turner." *Epiphany* 3.2 (1992): 133–56.

Bloom, Harold, ed. *James Merrill.* New York: Chelsea House Publishers, 1985.

Bottoms, David. *Under the Vulture-tree.* New York: William Morrow and Co., 1987.

Boyle, Francis A., et al. *In Re: More Than 50,000 Nuclear Weapons: Analyses of the Illegality of Nuclear Weapons Under International Law.* Northampton, Mass.: Aletheia Press, 1991.

Breslin, James E. B. *From Modern to Contemporary: American Poetry, 1945–1965.* Chicago: University of Chicago Press, 1984.

Breslin, Paul. *The Psycho-Political Muse: American Poetry since the Fifties.* Chicago: University of Chicago Press, 1987.

Brians, Paul. *Nuclear Holocausts: Atomic War in Fiction, 1895–1984.* Kent, Ohio: Kent State University Press, 1987.

Burkard, Michael. *Ruby for Grief.* Pittsburgh: University of Pittsburgh Press, 1981.

Caldicott, Helen. *Missile Envy: The Arms Race and Nuclear War.* New York: Bantam Books, 1984.

Calogero, Francesco, et al., eds. *Verification: Monitoring Disarmament.* Boulder, Colo.: Westview Press, 1991.

Caputi, Jane. "Psychic Numbing, Radical Futurelessness, and Sexual Violence in the Nuclear Film." In Anisfield, q.v., 58–70.

Carter, Jared. *Millenial Harbinger.* Philadelphia: Slash and Burn Press, 1986.

Cassin, Maxine. "Anniversary: Hiroshima." *Maple Leaf Rag: 15th Anniversary Anthology.* New Orleans: Portals Press, 1994. 45.

Chaloupka, William. *Knowing Nukes: The Politics and the Culture of the Atom.* Minneapolis: University of Minnesota Press, 1992.

Chernus, Ira. *Dr. Strangegod: On the Symbolic Meaning of Nuclear Weapons.* Columbia: University of South Carolina Press, 1986.

Cohen, Keith. "Ashbery's Dismantling of Bourgeois Discourse." In Lehman, *Beyond Amazement*, q.v., 128–49.

Cole, Richard. "The Last Days of Heaven." *New Yorker,* 27 August 1984, 36.

Crase, Douglas. "The Prophetic Ashbery." In Lehman, *Beyond Amazement*, q.v., 30–65.

Cummins, Paul F. *Richard Wilbur: A Critical Essay*. Grand Rapids, Mich.: William B. Eerdmans Publishing Co., 1971.

Daniels, Kate. "Interview with Galway Kinnell." In Jones, q.v., 293–99.

Davidson, Michael. "Notes Beyond the *Notes:* Wallace Stevens and Contemporary Poetics." In *Wallace Stevens: The Poetics of Modernism*. Ed. Albert Gelpi, 141–60. New York: Cambridge University Press, 1985.

Derricotte, Toi. *Captivity*. Pittsburgh: University of Pittsburgh Press, 1989.

Derrida, Jacques. "No Apocalypse, Not Now (full speed ahead, seven missiles, seven missives)." Trans. Catherine Porter and Philip Lewis. *Diacritics: A Review of Contemporary Criticism* 14.2 (1984): 20–31.

Des Pres, Terence. "Self/Landscape/Grid." *New England Review and Bread Loaf Quarterly* 5.4 (1983): 449.

Dewey, Joseph. *In a Dark Time: The Apocalyptic Temper in the American Novel of the Nuclear Age*. West Lafayette, Ind.: Purdue University Press, 1990.

Disch, Tom. *Yes, Let's*. Baltimore: Johns Hopkins University Press, 1989.

Dowling, David. *Fictions of Nuclear Disaster*. Iowa City: University of Iowa Press, 1986.

Driscoll, Kelly. "A Sense of Unremitting Emergency: Politics in the Early Works of Denise Levertov." In Wagner-Martin, q.v., 148–56.

Dugan, Alan. *New Collected Poems, 1961–1983*. New York: Ecco Press, 1983.

——. *Poems Six*. New York: Ecco Press, 1989.

Dunn, Stephen. "The Cocked Finger." *New England Review and Bread Loaf Quarterly* 5.4 (1983): 460–61.

Easlea, Brian. *Fathering the Unthinkable: Masculinity, Scientists and the Nuclear Arms Race*. London: Pluto Press, 1983.

Eckstein, Barbara. *The Language of Fiction in a World of Pain: Reading Politics as Paradox*. Philadelphia: University of Pennsylvania Press, 1990.

Eliot, T. S. *The Complete Poems and Plays*. New York: Harcourt, Brace and World, 1963.

Engels, John. *Signals from the Safety Coffin*. Pittsburgh: University of Pittsburgh Press, 1975.

——. *Walking to Cootehill: New and Selected Poems, 1958–1992*. Hanover, N.H.: Middlebury College Press/University Press of New England, 1993.

Freedman, Lawrence. *The Evolution of Nuclear Strategy*. New York: St. Martin's Press, 1983.

Gery, John. Interview with Denise Levertov. WWNO-FM Radio (National Public Radio). New Orleans, 27 April 1990.

Gilbert, Celia. *Bonfire*. Cambridge, Mass.: Alice James Books, 1983.

Gilbert, Sandra M. "Revolutionary Love: Denise Levertov and the Poetics of Politics." *Denise Levertov: Selected Criticism.* Ed. Albert Gelpi, 201–17. Ann Arbor: University of Michigan Press, 1993.

Ginsberg, Allen. *Plutonian Ode and Other Poems, 1977–1980.* San Francisco: City Lights Books, 1982.

Gioia, Dana. *Daily Horoscope.* St. Paul, Minn.: Graywolf Press, 1986.

———. "Poetry Chronicle." *Hudson Review* 34.4 (1981–82): 579–94.

Gompert, David C., et al. *Nuclear Weapons and World Politics: Alternatives for the Future.* New York: McGraw-Hill Book Co., 1977.

Grossman, Allen. *The Woman on the Bridge over the Chicago River.* New York: New Directions Books, 1979.

Gunn, Thom. *Collected Poems.* New York: Farrar, Straus and Giroux, 1994.

Heidegger, Martin. *Introduction to Metaphysics.* Trans. Ralph Manheim. New Haven: Yale University Press, 1959.

Hill, Donald L. *Richard Wilbur.* New York: Twayne Publishers Inc., 1967.

Hirsch, Ed. "A Written Interview with C. K. Williams." *Missouri Review* 9.1 (1985–86): 151–62.

Holmes, Theodore. "A Prophet Without a Prophecy." In Salinger, q.v., 72–75.

Jackson, Richard. *Acts of Mind: Conversations with Contemporary Poets.* University: University of Alabama Press, 1983.

———. "The Elegies of Style." *Georgia Review* 42.4 (1988): 856–60.

Jarman, Mark. "Singers and Storytellers." *Hudson Review* 39.2 (1986): 334–47.

Jarrell, Randall. *Poetry and the Age.* New York: Vintage Books, 1953.

Jellema, Rod. "The Klutz as Emerging Prophet in the Zimmer Poems." In Susina, q.v., 67–77.

Jensen, Ejner J. "Encounters with Experience: *The Poems of Richard Wilbur.*" In Salinger, q.v., 243–64.

Jones, Richard, ed. *Poetry and Politics: An Anthology of Essays.* New York: William Morrow and Co., 1985.

Kalaidjian, Walter. *Languages of Liberation: The Social Text in Contemporary American Poetry.* New York: Columbia University Press, 1989.

Kaminsky, Marc. *The Road to Hiroshima.* New York: Simon and Schuster, 1984.

Kawada, Louise Myers. "Enemies of Despair: American Women Poets Confront the Threat of Nuclear Destruction." *Papers on Language and Literature* 26 (1990): 112–33.

Kees, Weldon. *Collected Poems of Weldon Kees.* Rev. ed. Ed. Donald Justice. Lincoln: University of Nebraska Press, 1975.

Keller, Lynn. "An Interview with C. K. Williams." *Contemporary Literature* 29.2 (1988): 157–76.

———. *Re-making It New: Contemporary American Poetry and the Modernist Tradition.* New York: Cambridge University Press, 1987.

Kermode, Frank. *The Sense of an Ending: Studies in the Theory of Fiction.* New York: Oxford University Press, 1967.

Kessler, Edward. *Images of Wallace Stevens.* New Brunswick, N.J.: Rutgers University Press, 1972.

King, P. R. *Nine Contemporary Poets.* New York: Methuen and Co., 1979.

Kinnell, Galway, et al. "Poets against the End of the World." In Jones, q.v., 300–316.

Kooser, Ted. *One World at a Time.* Pittsburgh: University of Pittsburgh Press, 1985.

———. *Sure Signs: New and Selected Poems.* Pittsburgh: University of Pittsburgh Press, 1980.

Kumin, Maxine. *The Long Approach.* New York: Viking Press, 1985.

———. *Our Ground Time Here Will Be Brief.* New York: Viking Press, 1982.

Labrie, Ross. *James Merrill.* Boston: Twayne Publishers, 1982.

———. "John Ashbery: An Interview by Ross Labrie." *American Poetry Review* 13.3 (May–June 1984): 29–33.

Lasch, Christopher. *The Minimal Self: Psychic Survival in Troubled Times.* New York: W. W. Norton & Co., 1984.

Lehman, David. "The Shield of a Greeting: The Function of Irony in John Ashbery's Poetry." In Lehman, *Beyond Amazement*, q.v., 101–27.

Lehman, David, ed. *Beyond Amazement: New Essays on John Ashbery.* Ithaca: Cornell University Press, 1980.

Lehman, David, and Charles Berger, eds. *James Merrill: Essays in Criticism.* Ithaca: Cornell University Press, 1983.

Levertov, Denise. *Breathing the Water.* New York: New Directions Books, 1987.

———. *Candles in Babylon.* New York: New Directions Books, 1982.

———. *Evening Train.* New York: New Directions Books, 1992.

———. *Light Up the Cave.* New York: New Directions Books, 1981.

———. *Oblique Prayers.* New York: New Directions Books, 1984.

———. *Poems, 1960–1967.* New York: New Directions Books, 1983.

Levine, Philip. *Selected Poems.* New York: Atheneum, 1986.

Libby, Anthony. *Mythologies of Nothing: Mystical Death in American Poetry, 1940–70.* Urbana: University of Illinois Press, 1984.

Lifton, Robert Jay. *Death in Life: Survivors of Hiroshima.* New York: Basic Books, 1967.

———. *The Future of Immortality and Other Essays for a Nuclear Age.* New York: Basic Books, 1987.

———. *The Life of the Self: Toward a New Psychology.* New York: Basic Books, 1976.

Lifton, Robert Jay, and Richard Falk. *Indefensible Weapons: The Political and Psychological Case against Nuclearism.* New York: Basic Books, 1982.

Lifton, Robert Jay, and Eric Olson, eds. *Explorations in Psychohistory: The Wellfleet Papers.* New York: Simon and Schuster, 1974.

Litz, A. Walton. *Introspective Voyager: The Poetic Development of Wallace Stevens.* New York: Oxford University Press, 1972.

Loeb, Paul. *Nuclear Culture: Living and Working in the World's Largest Atomic Complex.* New York: Coward, McCann, and Geoghegan, 1982.

Loewenberg, Peter. *Decoding the Past: The Psychohistorical Approach.* New York: Alfred A. Knopf, 1983.

Lowell, Robert. *Collected Prose.* Ed. Robert Giroux. New York: Farrar, Straus and Giroux, 1987.

———. *Life Studies* and *For the Union Dead.* New York: Farrar, Straus, and Giroux, 1964.

Lynch, Denise. "Levertov's 'An English Field in the Nuclear Age.' " *The Explicator* 46.4 (1988): 40–41.

Mariani, Paul. *William Carlos Williams: A New World Naked.* New York: McGraw-Hill Book Co., 1981.

Marten, Harry. *Understanding Denise Levertov.* Columbia: University of South Carolina Press, 1988.

Mazlish, Bruce. *The Leader, the Led, and the Psyche: Essays in Psychohistory.* Hanover, N.H.: Wesleyan University Press, 1990.

———. "What Is Psycho-History?" In *Varieties of Psychohistory.* Ed. George M. Kren and Leon H. Rappoport. New York: Springer Publishing Co., 1976.

Meinke, Peter. *Night Watch on the Chesapeake.* Pittsburgh: University of Pittsburgh Press, 1987.

Merrill, James. *The Changing Light at Sandover.* New York: Alfred A. Knopf, 1982.

———. *Recitative: Prose by James Merrill.* Ed. J. D. McClatchy. San Francisco: North Point Press, 1986.

Michelson, Bruce. *Wilbur's Poetry: Music in a Scattering Time.* Amherst: University of Massachusetts Press, 1991.

Moffett, Judith. *James Merrill: An Introduction to the Poetry.* New York: Columbia University Press, 1984.

Molesworth, Charles. *Gary Snyder's Vision: Poetry and the Real Work.* Columbia: University of Missouri Press, 1983.

Moore, Honor. "Spuyten Duyvil." *New England Review and Bread Loaf Quarterly* 5.4 (1983): 626–33.

Murphy, Kay. *The Autopsy.* Peoria, Ill.: Spoon River Poetry Press, 1985.

Murphy, Patrick D., ed. *Critical Essays on Gary Snyder.* Boston: G.K. Hall and Co., 1991.

Nathan, Otto, and Heinz Norden, eds. *Einstein on Peace.* New York: Simon and Schuster, 1980.

Norton, Jody. "The Importance of Nothing: Absence and Its Origins in the Poetry of Gary Snyder." In P. Murphy, q.v., 166–87.

Olds, Sharon. *The Gold Cell.* New York: Alfred A. Knopf, 1987.

Olsen, William. "Fireworks." *Iowa Review* 21.2 (1991): 147–48.

Pack, Robert. *Wallace Stevens: An Approach to His Poetry and Thought.* New Brunswick, N.J.: Rutgers University Press, 1958.

Pape, Greg. *Border Crossings.* Pittsburgh: University of Pittsburgh Press, 1978.

Peacock, Molly. *Take Heart.* New York: Random House, 1990.

Perloff, Marjorie. " 'Fragments of a Buried Life': John Ashbery's Dream Songs." In Lehman, *Beyond Amazement,* q.v., 66–86.

Pettit, Michael. "With Zimmer: A Conversation with Paul Zimmer." In Susina, q.v., 51–66.

Poulin, A., Jr. "The Experience of Experience: A Conversation with John Ashbery." *Michigan Quarterly Review* 20.3 (1981): 241–55.

Powell, Jim. *It Was Fever Made the World.* Chicago: University of Chicago Press, 1989.

Rapaport, Herman. "Deconstructing Apocalyptic Rhetoric: Ashbery, Derrida, Blanchot." *Criticism* 27.4 (1985): 387–400.

Reibetanz, John. "What Love Sees: Poetry and Vision in Richard Wilbur." *Modern Poetry Studies* 11.1 and 11.2 (1982): 60–86.

Rich, Adrienne. *The Fact of a Doorframe: Poems Selected and New, 1950– 1984.* New York: W.W. Norton & Co., 1984.

———. *Your Native Land, Your Life.* New York: W.W. Norton & Co., 1986.

Richman, Robert. "Our 'Most Important' Living Poet." *Commentary* 74:1 (1982): 62–68.

Rodgers, Audrey T. *Denise Levertov: The Poetry of Engagement.* Rutherford, N.J.: Fairleigh Dickinson University Press, 1993.

Salinger, Wendy, ed. *Richard Wilbur's Creation.* Ann Arbor: University of Michigan Press, 1983.

Sanchez, Sonia. *Homegirls & Handgrenades.* New York: Thunder's Mouth Press, 1984.

Santos, Sherod. "Near the Desert Test Sites." *New Yorker,* 20 January 1986, 77.

Sayre, Robert F. "A Case for Richard Wilbur as Nature Poet." In Salinger, q.v., 153–61.

Scheick, William J. "Nuclear Criticism: An Introduction." *Papers on Language and Literature* 26 (1990): 1–11.

———. "Post-Nuclear Holocaust Re-Minding." In Anisfield, q.v., 71–84.

Scheick, William J., and Catherine Rainwater. "Brambly Hope on Stoney Ground." A Review of Peter Schwenger, *Letter Bomb: Nuclear Holocaust and the Exploding Word. Papers in Language and Literature* 29.3 (1993): 351–56.

Schell, Jonathan. *The Abolition.* New York: Alfred A. Knopf, 1984.

———. *The Fate of the Earth.* New York: Avon Books, 1982.

Schley, Jim, ed. *Writing in a Nuclear Age.* Hanover, N.H.: University Press of New England, 1984. Reprint of *New England Review and Breadloaf Quarterly* 5 (1983).

Schwenger, Peter. *Letter Bomb: Nuclear Holocaust and the Exploding Word.* Baltimore: Johns Hopkins University Press, 1992.

Scully, James. *Line Break: Poetry as Social Practice.* Seattle: Bay Press, 1988.

"Separate But the Same." *Times Literary Supplement* 16 April 1971, 439.

Shapiro, David. *John Ashbery: An Introduction to the Poetry.* New York: Columbia University Press, 1979.

Shetley, Vernon. *After the Death of Poetry: Poet and Audience in Contemporary America.* Durham, N.C.: Duke University Press, 1993.

Shipley, Betty, and Nina Langley, eds. *Meltdown: Poems from the Core.* Edmond, Okla.: Full Count Press, 1980.

Sivard, Ruth Leger. *World Military and Social Expenditures,* 15th ed. Washington: World Priorities, 1993.

Sklar, Morty, ed. *Nuke-Rebuke: Writers and Artists against Nuclear Energy and Weapons.* Iowa City: The Spirit That Moves Us Press, 1984.

Smith, Lorrie. "An Interview with Denise Levertov." *Michigan Quarterly Review* 24.4 (1985): 596–604.

———. "Songs of Experience: Denise Levertov's Political Poetry." In Wagner-Martin, q.v., 156–72.

Snyder, Gary. *Left Out in the Rain: New Poems, 1947–1985.* San Francisco: North Point Press, 1986.

———. *Turtle Island.* New York: New Directions Books, 1974.

Solomon, J. Fisher. *Discourse and Reference in the Nuclear Age.* Norman: University of Oklahoma Press, 1988.

Spiegelman, Willard. *The Didactic Muse: Scenes of Instruction in Contemporary Poetry.* Princeton: Princeton University Press, 1989.

Spires, Elizabeth. *Annonciade.* New York: Viking Press, 1989.

Stafford, William. *Stories That Could Be True: New and Collected Poems.* New York: Harper and Row, 1977.

Stein, Gertrude. *Brewsie and Willie.* New York: Random House, 1946.

———. *Reflections on the Atomic Bomb: Volume I of the Previously Uncollected Writings of Gertrude Stein.* Ed. Robert Bartlett Haas. Los Angeles: Black Sparrow Press, 1973.

Steinman, Lisa M. *Made in America: Science, Technology and American Modernist Poets.* New Haven: Yale University Press, 1987.

Stevens, Holly, ed. *Letters of Wallace Stevens.* New York: Alfred A. Knopf, 1966.

Stevens, Wallace. *Collected Poems.* New York: Alfred A. Knopf, 1954.

Strand, Mark. *Selected Poems.* New York: Atheneum, 1984.

Susina, Jan, ed. *Poet as Zimmer, Zimmer as Poet: On the Poetry of Paul Zimmer.* Houston: Ford Brown Publishers, 1986.

Taylor, Henry. "Two Worlds Taken as They Come: Richard Wilbur's *Walking to Sleep*." In Salinger, q.v., 88–100.

Turner, Frederick. *April Wind*. Charlottesville: University Press of Virginia, 1991.

———. *Genesis: An Epic Poem*. Dallas: Saybrook Publishing Co., 1988.

———. *The New World: An Epic Poem*. Princeton: Princeton University Press, 1985.

van Creveld, Martin. *Nuclear Proliferation and the Future of Conflict*. New York: The Free Press, 1993.

Vendler, Helen. "Understanding Ashbery." *New Yorker* 16 March 1981, 108–36.

von Hallberg, Robert. *American Poetry and Culture, 1945–1980*. Cambridge: Harvard University Press, 1985.

———, ed. *Politics and Poetic Value*. Chicago: University of Chicago Press, 1987.

Wagner-Martin, Linda, ed. *Critical Essays on Denise Levertov*. Boston: G.K. Hall and Co., 1991.

Weart, Spencer. *Nuclear Fear: A History of Images*. Cambridge: Harvard University Press, 1988.

Wilbur, Richard. *New and Collected Poems*. New York: Harcourt Brace Jovanovich, 1988.

———. *Responses: Prose Pieces, 1953–1976*. New York: Harcourt Brace Jovanovich, 1963.

Williams, C. K. *Flesh and Blood*. New York: Farrar, Straus, and Giroux, 1987.

———. *Poems, 1963–1983*. New York: Farrar, Straus, and Giroux, 1988.

Williams, William Carlos. *The Collected Poems of William Carlos Williams: Volume II, 1939–1962*. Ed. Christopher MacGowan. New York: New Directions Books, 1988.

Williamson, Alan. *Introspection and Contemporary Poetry*. Cambridge: Harvard University Press, 1984.

———. *The Muse of Distance*. New York: Alfred A. Knopf, 1988.

Wilner, Eleanor. *Sarah's Choice*. Chicago: University of Chicago Press, 1989.

Wilson, Rob. *American Sublime: The Genealogy of a Poetic Genre*. Madison: University of Wisconsin Press, 1991.

Wood, David. "A More Frightening Nuclear Age Emerges." *New Orleans Times-Picayune*, 5 June 1994, A-12.

Woodward, Charles R. "Richard Wilbur's Critical Condition." In Salinger, q.v., 221–31.

Wormser, Baron. *Good Trembling*. Boston: Houghton Mifflin Co., 1985.

Wyschogrod, Edith. *Spirit in Ashes: Hegel, Heidegger, and Man-Made Mass Death*. New Haven: Yale University Press, 1985.

Yamazoto, Katsunori. "How to Be in This Crisis: Gary Snyder's Cross-Cultural Vision in *Turtle Island*." In Patrick D. Murphy, q.v., 230–47.

Yeats, W. B. *The Collected Poems of W. B. Yeats*. Ed. Richard J. Finneran. New York: Macmillan Co., 1989.

Yenser, Stephen. *The Consuming Myth: The Work of James Merrill*. Cambridge: Harvard University Press, 1987.

———. "The Names of God: *Scripts for the Pageant*." In Lehman and Berger, q.v., 246–81.

———. "Recent Poetry: Five Poets." *Yale Review* 71.1 (1981): 97–121.

Young, David. "John Ashbery—At Play in the Fields of Poetry." *Washington Post Book World*, 7 June 1981, 4, 8.

Young Bear, Ray A. *The Invisible Musician*. Duluth, Minn.: Holy Cow! Press, 1990.

Zimmer, Paul. *Ancient Wars*. Pittsburgh: Slow Loris Press, 1981.

———. *Big Blue Train*. Fayetteville: University of Arkansas Press, 1993.

———. *Earthbound Zimmer*. Milton, Mass.: Chowder Chapbooks, 1983.

———. *Family Reunion: Selected and New Poems*. Pittsburgh: University of Pittsburgh Press, 1983.

———. *The Great Bird of Love*. Urbana: University of Illinois Press, 1989.

———. "The Importance of Being Zimmer." In Susina, q.v., 15–22.

———. *The Republic of Many Voices*. New York: October House, 1969.

Zimmerman, Lee. "Against Apocalypse: Politics and James Merrill's *The Changing Light at Sandover*." *Contemporary Literature* 30.3 (1989): 370–86.

Zuckerman, Solly. *Nuclear Illusion and Reality*. New York: Random House, 1982.

———. *Scientists and War: The Impact of Science on Military and Civil Affairs*. New York: Harper and Row, 1967.

INDEX
OF
POETRY
TITLES